Read what folks have to say about the best-selling Music Theory book versatile enough to be used by kids, adul ▮▮▮▮▮▮▮▮▮▮▮ !

"Fun and engaging. A real winner!"
—Terrie Lyons, PhD, P.C.

"Jonathan Harnum has taken an overly complicated subject matter and made it learnable for anyone. And I do mean anyone! Harnum de-cryptifies all that is involved with music theory for the non-musician. But this book is not just for the non-musician. I have been a student of music for more than 13 years and a teacher for 3 and I found new, interesting and humorous facts about music theory. This book can teach anyone music theory and keep a smile on their face the entire time."
—Robin Gibelhausen, music teacher, Illinois

"Basic Music Theory by Jonathan Harnum is an excellent book for people of all levels. I have played various instruments over 24 years and because of Harnum's matter of fact, conversational tone, this book has lent more to my understanding of basic music theory than all my private instructors combined."
—Solstice 1221, Anon. reader in LA

"I appreciate the clever and humorous ways that you introduce many of the concepts. The illustrations and pictures are very helpful. Can't wait to get to the bookstore to get a copy for myself."
—Dave Larsen, elementary teacher, Hawarden, IA

"The more I think about your book the more brilliant it becomes. See, the tough part is knowing how to limit the depth to keep it true to your goal of making {music theory} fun and fathomable. You excelled at it!"
—Charles Reynolds, music educator, Alaska

"Basic Music Theory is an ideal and highly recommended text for anyone of any background wanting to become proficient in the reading, composing, and performance of written and notated music."
—Midwest Book Review (5 stars, highest rating)

"This is a book that covers lots of ground without ever appearing "difficult." It is written in a breezy, conversational manner, so one "talk" naturally drifts into the next."
—KLIATT Library Review Service

"After the first read you can't help but wonder if music was invented by humans or whether it is nature's gift to help one appreciate and understand one's sense of purpose."
—Randy Mac, entrepreneur/adventurer, Baja Mexico

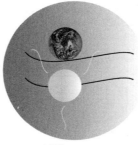

SolŪt Press

EVEN LISTENING TO MUSIC IS PROVEN TO MAKE YOU SMARTER! NO JOKE.

One important center for this research has been the University of California at Irvine, where Drs. Gordon Shaw and Fran Rauscher have found that active music making improves children's math skills. Shaw is a physicist who found that the inner working of the human brain operates in patterns that resemble musical structures, and he suspects that music may be the key to understanding intelligence.

Other research supports similar conclusions: at McGill University in Canada, researchers found that kids who take piano lessons showed improved general and spatial cognitive development, and studies at a Miami Veterans Administration hospital indicate that music making may improve the brain's natural production of regulatory hormones like melatonin. Piano students who begin studying by age 7 have a larger corpus callosum (the channel through which the two hemispheres of the brain communicate). And most amazingly, an experiment by Rauscher showed that listening to the first ten minutes of the Mozart Concerto for Two Pianos in D Major (K. 448) improved the listeners' spatial-temporal reasoning!

In the days of the New England singing-schools, people believed in teaching and learning music because it was good for the soul. We've learned a lot since then.

If music really can make a person better at math, science and engineering, and if just *listening* to music can make you smarter, why wouldn't everyone want to benefit from music?

As we begin a new century, there is proof about the power of music and music education.

And it's still good for your soul.

For more information about music and the brain visit:
www.QuestionsInk.com/brain

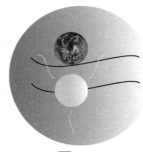

SolŪt Press

Support Music and Musicians.
www.Sol-Ut.com

BASIC MUSIC THEORY

HOW TO READ, WRITE, AND UNDERSTAND WRITTEN MUSIC

In the early fifteenth century, music was read from scrolls like the one above drawn by Giovannino di Grassi.

SolUt Press

Find Musical Support at:
www.Sol-Ut.com

Basic Music Theory: How to Read, Write, and Understand Written Music, 2nd ed.

Published by Sol Ut Press
A Music Education Business

Find musical support at:
www.Sol-Ut.com

send E-mail regarding this book to BMT@QuestionsInk.com

LCCN: 2001086279 (1st ed.)

ISBN: 0-9707512-8-1

For general information about this book or SolUt, visit our web site at www.Sol-Ut.com.

Publisher's Cataloging-in-Publication

Harnum, Jonathan.

    Basic music theory: how to read, write, and
understand written music / Jonathan Harnum. -- 2nd ed.

    p. cm.
    Includes index.
    LCCN 2005086279
    ISBN 0-9707512-8-1

    1. Music Theory. 2. Conducting. 3. Musical
notation. I. Title.

JUST AS THERE CAN BE NO MUSIC WITHOUT LEARNING, NO EDUCATION IS COMPLETE WITHOUT MUSIC.

THIS BOOK IS DEDICATED
TO ALL MY TEACHERS AND
TO MY STUDENTS, WHO ARE
ALSO MY TEACHERS.

THANK YOU.

Special thanks for help with the second edition goes out to Bruce in Australia and Reinhart Frosch in Switzerland.

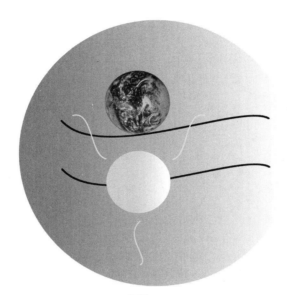

SolŪt Press

Support Music and musicians.
Find musical support.

www.Sol-Ut.com

Basic Music Theory
Table of Contents

PART TWO

PART THREE

PART FOUR

PARTFIVE

PART SIX

PART SEVEN

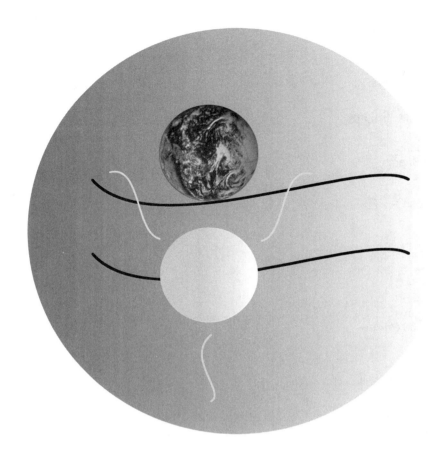

The Sol-Ut Logo

Sol, in addition to being the name for our sun, is also the name of the fifth note of the Major scale. *Ut* is another name for Do (pronounced doe), the root note (home base) of the Major scale. The interval of *Sol* to *Ut* establishes a tonal center in Western music. The curvy lines represent staff lines, upon which rest the notes *Sol* (the sun) and *Ut*, our home base, the Earth.

THE CHAPTER EVERYONE SKIPS

*A journey of one thousand miles
must begin with a single footstep.*

— Lao Tzu c531 B.C.

In This Chapter

- Welcome to *Basic Music Theory!*
- Why this book?
- Book Overview
- How to Use the Special Features
- Moving On

Welcome to *Basic Music Theory*!

If you never thought you would pick up a book on music theory, you're not alone. I never thought I'd write one. But in my experience as a student, a player, and a teacher, I have searched for and used many different methods of learning music theory. Some methods were good, most were okay, and a few were bad, but none of them satisfied me.

I've tried to take all the positive things about teaching theory, thrown in many of the tricks I've used with thousands of students, and tossed in a little humor in an effort to make learning music theory both easier and more enjoyable. These methods and suggestions have worked well with all students of all sizes. I hope they'll work for you too.

What It's All About

Basic Music Theory is your introduction to another language—the rich and often strange language of music. By the time you've completed even two lessons in this book, you'll have made big steps down the path toward understanding written music.

With this language you'll be able to reproduce sounds from nearly a thousand years ago by someone like Guillame de Machaut. And with this same language you can play music by someone like Alannis Morisette, or Limp Bizkit, or Dave Matthews, or Garth Brooks. Name your favorite artist. If it's written down, you'll be able to understand and interpret it!

But let's not get too carried away. Those musicians you look up to (some of whom have earned millions upon millions of dollars) have spent thousands of hours learning both their instrument and in many cases, their music theory. Learning theory will take some focus and some work, but that work will be clearly explained, and you'll be surprised to find how easy it can be.

Nobody likes to work on a task endlessly. For that reason, the theory lessons are broken up by Interludes every few chapters. These interludes cover things like practice, conducting, Italian terms, and a brief history of musical notation.

So, if you're interested in the music of Mozart or Metallica, Beethoven or B.B. King, Dizzie Gillespie or Vince Gill, you've finally found the right book.

Why *Basic Music Theory*?

Learning music theory doesn't have to be a long and difficult process. It does take some work, but with this book you can make that work much easier. I've suffered through some of the most boring music courses a person should be forced to suffer, and before this book was available I've had experience *inflicting* such boredom on others as well. Believe me, it's not fun on either side! Whether you're a teacher or a student, I'd like to spare you any of that frustration and difficulty.

Music theory is a language that is used by all Western instruments. Whether you play the kazoo or the krumhorn, voice or vibraphone, French horn or nose flute, pigsnout psaltery or percussion, trombone or triangle, bagpipes or bass fiddle, Sousaphone or Saxophone…you get the idea. Whatever instrument you play, reading music will be a useful tool in your studies, and this book will give you that tool.

What's Inside

Basic Music Theory is divided into seven Parts and in each Part are several chapters.

Between some of the Parts are Interludes — stand-alone sections giving information on aspects of music other than theory.

The Codicil (stuff at the back of the book) contains a musical terms glossary, a book index, the keyboard template, guitar fretboard, practice aids, and blank staff paper for photocopying.

Parts

Each Part is made up of four to seven chapters. The division isn't arbitrary. Information in each Part is related and the reviews come at a point where a review will do the most good.

Part Review

At the end of each Part is a comprehensive review in the same format as the chapter reviews. Cross-references below the questions allow you to quickly find and re-read any section that you haven't quite remembered yet.

Chapters

Each chapter is fairly short and contains detailed information on one or two topics. When an important term appears for the first time, it is in **bold and italics** so that when you do the chapter review and need to go back to the chapter, you can find the information easily.

Chapter Reviews

At the end of each chapter is a brief review covering the material in the chapter. The reviews are generally very short, the longest being around fifteen questions.

Practical Use

Also at the end of each chapter is a short list (often only one item) of written exercises to hone your music-writing/reading ability.

About the Reviews

After each chapter and Part is a section which contains questions on the information presented. The reviews are arranged as quizzes, but with one important difference. *The answers are in the margin*! That's right, the answers are right there. How is that supposed to help you? Read on…

The best way to learn is to get immediate feedback. There is no better way to get feedback than to have the answer right there with the question. Of course, this does you no good if you can see the answer before reading the question, so you have to cover up the answers while you give yourself the quiz. In the back of this book is a cut-out bookmark with a piano keyboard on it (if this is a library book, please photocopy the keyboard and leave the original for others to copy as well). Use the keyboard to cover up the answers while you test yourself.

After you answer the question, simply uncover the answer in the margin and kiss yourself on the elbow for giving the correct answer. If you didn't get the answer correct, at least you have the answer right there to remind you.

Voila. Instant feedback, and your memory of the material is sped right along.

Once you're confident you know the information, you can either go on to the next chapter or take the written quiz. You can find the free quizzes and a whole lot more in the *Basic Music Theory Teaching Packet*. For more information go to **www.QuestionsInk.com/classroom1,** (that's the number one, not the letter "l" at the end of the web address).

Basic Music Theory is meant to be used as a textbook and study guide, with written work taking place on the blank staff paper photocopied from the back of the book. That way the book may be used over and over again. Of course, if you've bought this book for your own personal use, mark it up!

The Icons

Memory Tip

This icon is placed near methods to improve your memory of terms, notes, and other fun stuff. These little memory tricks will save you a lot of brain strain.

Take Notice

This icon is placed near information that is particularly useful to know. Heed this information and you'll avoid common mistakes.

Theory Geek Alert

This icon is placed near information that isn't especially necessary, but which you might find interesting.

Chapter 0: The Chapter Everyone Skips

In addition to what you've already read, this part will give you an overview about the book as well as tips on how to study the information.

Part I: Start Me Up

Prelude, Chapter 1. This section is where the fun begins. And what better way to start than with something other than music theory! The first chapter is an ultra-ultra-brief history of written music. It'll be painless, I promise.

In Chapters 2-5 you'll learn some of the most basic terms and symbols (no, not cymbals) of written music, how they look, what they mean, and what they do. Included are note lengths and rests. You'll be reading music in only one or two lessons.

Once you're done with Part I, peruse the Comprehensive Part Review and see how much you remember.

Part II: You Got Rhythm

Chapters 6-10. The party continues. In this section you'll find more symbols used in written music including more note lengths, a counting system, time signatures, dotted notes and triplets. And of course, a Part Review.

Interlude: To Play or Not to Play

Chapter 11 and it's time for a break. This Interlude is all about practice. How to go about it, how to structure it, how to record it in a journal and on a tape recorder, equipment you'll need and how to use it, and how to do what must be done to become a better player.

Part III: Clef Notes

Chapters 12-17. For the first two chapters of this section you'll learn about the letter names for notes and how pitch is shown in written music. The other four chapters are devoted to clefs. You'll learn treble clef, bass clef, percussion clef, and a few other clefs as well.

A Comprehensive Part Review

Interlude: Musical Terms

Time for another break with Chapter 18. This Interlude is all about musical terms, most of which are in Italian. You'll learn the terms, what they mean, and what they tell you to do.

Part IV: See Sharp or Be Flat

Chapters 19-22. Once you've got the basics of reading music down, we go into more advanced concepts. This section shows you how to use the piano keyboard, covers whole steps and half steps, sharps, flats, and naturals, the chromatic scale, enharmonic notes, and key signatures. A Comprehensive Part Review when you're ready for it.

Part V: Intervals and Minor Scales

Chapters 23-26. In this section you'll learn how to measure the interval from one note to another, and using that information you'll learn how to construct a minor scale beginning on any note. From there you'll move on to modes, and finally to several other types of scales.

A Comprehensive Part Review.

Interlude: Conducting Yourself

Chapter 27 is your final Interlude. In this Interlude you'll learn the basics of conducting, conducting patterns, body and facial language, and the work it takes to become a good conductor. Also learn how to use conducting patterns to enable you to write down what you hear.

Part VI: Chords

Chapters 28-31. Here you'll learn about how chords are constructed and the many different types of chords. You'll also learn about chord extensions and the symbols they use, chord inversions, and several basic chord progressions.

A Comprehensive Part Review.

Part VII: More of the Same

Chapters 32-34. In this final short section are some concepts which go further than when they were originally introduced. Included are double dots, double sharps and double flats, faster notes, 6/8 time and odd meters.

A Comprehensive Part Review.

Codicils

Teacher Information: A quick summation of the free *Basic Music Theory Quiz-Pack*.

Glossary of Musical Terms: Here they are. A quick reference and not exhaustive by any means, but you'll find most of what you might be looking for.

Index: This is a cross-reference to all the terms and concepts presented in the book, so you can find any topic covered quickly and easily.

Blank Staff Paper: To be used for the Practical Use sections at the end of the chapter Reviews. Keep the staff paper in the book so you can photocopy it as often as you need. Give them to your friends.

Piano Keyboard: One side with the note names, one side without. Also used with the End-of-Section Reviews as mentioned later.

Guitar Fretboard: Guitar is one of the most popular instruments around, so here's a fretboard labeled with note names to help you guitarists out there.

How to Use the Special Features

The End-of-Section Reviews

What's different about all the reviews in *Basic Music Theory* is that the answers are right there with the questions. In the end-of-section reviews you will also have a reference, in case you want to go back to review the information, there's a reference (in itty bitty writing) to the page where you can look at the information again.

The answers are on the right side of the page, and the questions on the left. While reviewing the chapter, to cover up the answer, you'll use the piano keyboard in the back of the book.

The Keyboard

In the back of the book is a piano keyboard template, double-sided with the keys named on one side and blank on the other. The keyboard is used as a bookmark, as a cover for the study guide answers and—can you believe it?—also as a keyboard. If you're borrowing this book, please help keep the book useful for everyone and photocopy the keyboard instead of tearing it out.

Practical Use

After the chapter Reviews are Practical Use exercises, most of which will be done on the staff paper you've copied from the back of the book. There may be as many as four exercises, or as few as one.

Moving On

Okay, enough details. If you've read them, good job! You'll have a better handle on how to get the most out of this book and you won't be at all surprised or confused about what's next.

Part I: Start Me Up is next, and the first chapter is about how written music came to be. Hope you like it!

In an effort to use all the available space in this book, any blank pages will be
filled with staff lines for you to practice your music-writing skills.

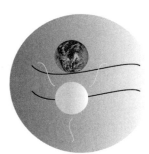

SolŪt Press

Find links for most instruments.
www.Sol-Ut.com

PART ONE

Start Me Up

In This Section You Will Learn:

- A Brief History of Notation
- The Staff
- Bar Lines
- Measures
- Note Length
- Rests

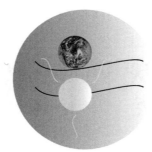

SolŪt Press

Support Music and Musicians.
www.Sol-Ut.com

CHAPTER 1

Prelude

AN ULTRA-BRIEF HISTORY OF MUSICAL NOTATION

*History doesn't repeat itself,
but it does rhyme.*

— Mark Twain

In This Chapter

- The Origin of Hearing
- The Origin of Music
- Music Performed
- The Origin of Written Music

Terms to Know

- **pinna**: fleshy part of the outer ear.
- **cochlea**: small part of the inner ear which changes sound vibration into nerve impulses which are then sent to the brain.
- **Boethius**: Roman poet/philosopher author of a treatise on music used throughout the middle ages. First to use letters (Latin) to represent sound.
- **neumes** (nooms): symbols written above the text of a song which can show note length, pitch, and movement from note to note.
- **Guido d' Arezzo**: Benedictine monk given credit for innovations in written music.
- **monophonic**: only one musical part. No harmony.
- **polyphonic**: more than one musical part. Harmony.

Hear, There, Everywhere

When you hear something you like, thank a fish. About five hundred million years ago fish began to develop the ability to sense vibrations, but not with anything we would call an ear. Amphibians improved on the fishy system with sack-like organs containing clumps of neurons devoted only to sensing vibrations, much like the ears frogs have today. Birds improved the design even further.

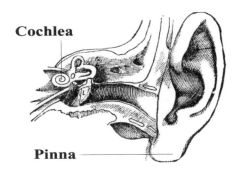

The ear reached its peak with mammals and the appearance of *pinna*, the fleshy outer ear which funnels sound to the *cochlea*, one of the many tiny pieces of the inner ear. The cochlea takes sound vibrations, converts them into nerve impulses and sends them to the brain.

It took over one hundred million generations of critters to evolve an ear capable of hearing the ecstasy of the *B Minor Mass*, the groove of the blues or the blistering Bebop of Charlie Parker.

With this wonderful ability to hear, it's no surprise that we humans began to organize sounds into patterns of rhythm and pitch. That's music. A question that will remain unanswered forever is what the first instrument was. Some say drum, some say voice, but we'll never know for sure. Maybe it was something completely different.

Music Performed

From the very beginning, music was linked with magic and shamanism, and still is. Wherever you find a shaman, you'll probably find a drum.

Music has magical powers. It can transport you into an altered state, heal sickness, purify the body and mind, and work miracles in nature. In the Old Testament David cures Saul's madness with a harp, and the walls of Jericho were brought tumbling down by horns.

Figure 1.1 Rembrandt's painting, *David and Saul*, c. 1658.

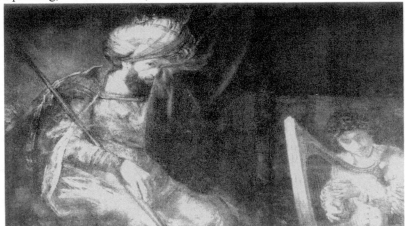

You may scoff at such primitivism, but do it softly and don't let anyone hear you. Recent discoveries are showing that such ideas are not so cracked as you might think. Don't believe me? Okay, here are some examples:

Imagine. It's night. A cavern begins to fill with creatures which normally keep distance between themselves and the others of their kind. They rarely touch. Tonight, because of sound, they will experience an altered state of being.

Soon there will be ten thousand of them. Then twenty thousand. Thirty. More. Tonight they will crush together and dance to the music. On a raised platform, anywhere from three to a dozen or more people stroke or bang on or breathe into instruments which produce complex rhythms and pitches. The sound causes us humans to behave in a way that's different from the everyday norm, especially if we really like the band.

Here's another scenario.

You've had a long hard day and you arrive home exhausted. At home loud and annoying music plays—something you really hate, like your dad's vinyl Barry Manilow, or your kid's Megadeth Live! CD—and it grates and grinds on your nerves.

Once it's turned off, you heave a deep sigh and a peacefulness settles over you. You put on some of your favorite music—say that Barry Manilow record, or maybe that rockin' Megadeth Live! CD—and the relaxation deepens.

Music therapy has shown positive results in those undergoing cardiac rehabilitation, and drug rehabilitation. Music has also helped sufferers of asthma, depression, high blood pressure, migraines and ulcers. Music can help with the production of melatonin, an important chemical in the body. The use of music therapy in healing has gained much credibility and its use is increasing.

Or how about this:

You listen to the Mozart piano sonata in D, and when it's over your spatial reasoning intelligence has jumped up several points. You're temporarily smarter! Music does affect the brain.

There's more:

Ella Fitzgerald breathes deeply, begins a note and holds it. She sings with power and confidence and clarity. The note is high and clear and like a laser beam. A tall empty champagne glass sits on a stool nearby and begins to vibrate with her voice. The voice grows louder. The glass begins to tremble. Then it explodes in a shimmering cascade of shards.

Jane Goodall, the famous chimpanzee expert, relates a story about a chimp who discovered that banging two empty gasoline cans together makes a terribly wonderful racket. In a few days of banging the chimp had become the dominant male of the group. A percussionist's dream.

There is power in sound.

These are only a few examples of the strange power of music. There are many, many more which you can learn about by reading Don Campbell's book, *The Mozart Effect* or take a gander at **www.QuestionsInk.com/Links/brain.html**.

How long has music been around? Nobody really knows, but we all suspect it's been with us from the beginning.

Figure 1.2 **LEFT**: 35,000 year old mastodon bones with markings for resonance points (places where it sounds really good to hit). This bone xylophone was found with two bone flutes. **RIGHT**: A figure from North Africa playing the talking drum, one of the oldest forms of communication.

Use your imagination to think about what the very first musical experience was. You have about as much chance being correct as anyone, and it's fun to imagine.

Sound and music have been with us from the beginning. Being the creatures that we are, it was only a matter of time until we developed a written language which could record these rhythms and pitches so that others could make them too.

Just like with language, music existed for a long, long time before it was written down, and some think music may have existed *before* spoken language. Music was taught by rote, which means copying what another has played or sung. No need to read music, just listen carefully and copy the sounds, the fingerings, or whatever. It's a method that takes a lot of time but works well and many, many people still learn this way.

But with a system of writing music, a song can be shared with an audience far away, played by a musician who can read the lines and squiggles created by someone she has never met.

Writing Down the Bones

Our western tradition of written music—what you're about to learn—has only been in existence a thousand years or so and that's not very long in the grand scheme of things.

There are older traditions of written music. Ancient Hindus and then the Greeks made use of their alphabet to write out music; the Persians used numbers and a kind of staff with nine lines between which the numbers were written; the Chinese used special signs for their pentatonic scales.

But it wasn't until around 500 AD that we see the first glimmer of written western music.

Boethius lived around this time, a Roman poet and philosopher who wrote a famous Latin treatise on music which was studied throughout the Middle Ages. In it was the first use of Latin letters to represent musical sounds.

Monks in the monasteries of the Catholic Church studied this treatise by Boethius and improved upon his ideas for their own system.

After a few hundred years, in addition to letter names for notes, a system of ***neumes*** (pronounced *nooms*, from the Greek word for *sign*) were invented. Neumes are signs written above the text of a song which show note length, pitch, and movement from one note to the next.

After a while, neumes began to be written on, above, or below a single line. The line represented a specific pitch. A neume written above the line was higher in pitch than a neume written below the line.

Around 1,000 AD many innovations in written music came to be. Though it isn't clear who invented them, **Guido di Arezzo** is given most of the credit. He was a Benedictine monk who was thrown out of his monastery for his radical innovations in music. It's believed that he didn't actually invent the staff, but increased the lines from two to four.

We're lucky he got kicked out of the monastery because it caused his ideas to be spread more widely. After he had an audience with the Pope who recognized Guido's skill, his monastery wanted him back.

Figure 1.3 **LEFT**: 9th Century manuscript with neumes written above text. **RIGHT**: 12th Century manuscript with two lines, neumes, and text.

Guido di Arezzo was definitely responsible for adding more lines to the staff, and he was also thought to have invented the **Guidonian Hand**, a system for singing together. He would point to specific places on his upraised hand which indicated a specific note. This allowed a large number of monks to sing together. The following example on the right shows the notes from low to high, starting with the thumb.

Figure 1.4 Two versions of the Guidonian Hand. Notice the staffs in the left example.

Up until this time music in the monastery was **monophonic**, which means it had only one part, usually vocal. All of the musical examples which survive from this time come from the church. There *were* popular secular (non-religious) musicians around at the time, but they weren't writing down what they played and so there is almost no record of it.

The oldest written secular music in existence is *Sumer is Icumen In*, a song celebrating the coming of summer. Listen to it at **www.QuestionsInk.com/Links/random.html**

One example of monophonic music is a type of song called a ***plain chant***. Some of the first examples of written western music are plain chants. They sound more like inflection than singing and are still used in Roman Catholic churches today. Eventually all those monks got bored with singing one-line music and began to add other parts. Music was becoming more complex.

Music with more than one part is called ***polyphonic*** music. Polyphonic music soon became popular in the monasteries, but was difficult to write out.

Because polyphonic music is more complex than monophonic music, it was necessary to add more lines to show the other voices. This is where Guido di Arezzo comes in. He expanded the staff to four lines. Soon after that a fifth line was added.

Over the next five hundred years, composers experimented with different systems of writing music. It was written in elaborate shapes and sometimes with a six-line staff. By about 1500 we arrived at a system which has remained nearly unchanged until today.

Figure 1.5 LEFT: 4-line staff. MIDDLE: Heart-shaped staff. RIGHT: 6-line staff.

The Future

The spirit of experimentation with written music still exists. Modern composers like John Cage or Stephen Reich use notation which is radically different from what you'll learn in this book.

Figure 1.6 LEFT: Part of John Cage's *Piano Concerto*. RIGHT: *Extension No. 1* by William R. Maginnis, 1964.

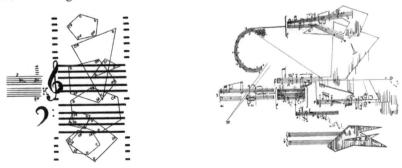

Music, like any language, evolves over time. Maybe in another thousand years we'll be reading music based on smells. Who knows? What do *you* think music will look like and sound like in another thousand years?

LINES, LINES, EVERYWHERE THERE'S LINES

All music is folk music. I ain't never heard no horse sing a song.

— Louis Armstrong

In This Chapter

- The Staff
- Lines
- Spaces
- Study Guide

Terms to Know

- **single line staff**: a single line upon which rhythms are written. Often used for percussion music.
- **staff (plural-staves)**: a system of five lines and four spaces upon which music is written.

Everything You Don't Hear

All of the things in the next two chapters are things you don't hear in written music. These are the things which create the structure upon which the sounds (the notes) can be written. Think of this stuff as something like punctuation. You don't really hear it, but it's there, and it serves a purpose.

The Staff

The first type of **staff** you'll learn is the one line staff. Music that is written for one percussion instrument like snare drum or bass drum often uses only one line. This is the type of staff we'll get the most use out of for the next several chapters as we learn how to write and play rhythms.

Using a one line staff keeps things simple. It will allow you to concentrate on the rhythms you'll soon be learning. Think of this as progressing through the history of written music. As you probably remember, in the beginning all written music used just one line.

Staff 2.1   Here's the one line staff. Not too tough, is it?

Unless you play percussion or are learning to read rhythms as you'll be doing soon, you won't often see the one line staff. What you'll see is the regular staff which has more than one line.

Instruments which have specific pitches (trumpet, flute, guitar, piano, etc.) use music which is written on a staff (plural **staves**) of five horizontal parallel lines. The five lines create four spaces between them.

Staff 2.2   Blank staff.

Lines and spaces are numbered from bottom to top.

Staff 2.3   Staff with lines and spaces numbered.

line 5
line 4   space 4
line 3   space 3
line 2   space 2
line 1   space 1

Theory Geek Alert

When you count things in music—staff lines, degrees of a scale, intervals, even the strings of a guitar (don't worry, you'll understand all these concepts soon) they're *always* counted from the bottom up.

Memory Tip

The following exercise works. It may feel a little silly, but kinesthetic learning, learning with your body, works.

Take your hand—left or right—and put it in front of your face *with the palm toward you*. Pretend your fingers are the lines of the staff. The spaces between your fingers are the spaces of the staff. Pinky is line one, ring finger line two, middle finger line three, index finger line four, and thumb line five. Between your pinky and ring finger is space one, between your ring and middle finger is space two, between the index and middle finger is space three, and between the index finger and thumb is space four. Touch each finger and say the number of the line. Do the same with the spaces.

The example below shows a right hand. The only difference between this example and *your* hand is that you might use your left hand, and your hand will probably have more skin on it.

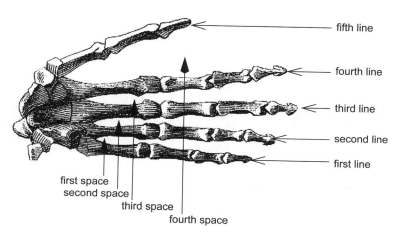

Moving On

So much for the staff. Pretty simple so far, right? Stick with it, because most of music theory is easy to understand as long as you've mastered previous chapters.

Coming up next is Chapter 3 in which you'll learn about more lines that are used in written music: bar lines and double bar lines. It's all simple stuff, but you probably guessed that.

Chapter 2 Study Guide

1. What types of instruments use the one line staff?

2. Why use a one line staff?

3. How many lines make up regular musical staff?

4. How many spaces in the regular musical staff?

5. Using a separate sheet of paper and a pencil, draw a five line musical staff.

6. What is the number of the bottom line?

7. What is the number of the top line?

8. What is the number of the bottom space?

9. What is the number of the top space?

1. *non-pitched instruments like percussion*

2. *easier to read*

3. *five*

4. *four*

5.

6. *one*

7. *five*

8. *one*

9. *four*

Practical Use

1. Hold your right hand up in front of your face. Use the other hand to count the lines (your fingertips) starting with the finger closest to the floor as "1." Count the spaces between your fingers the same way.

2. Draw three five-line staves, each one a different size. Draw in your own type of notes and be as creative as you want to be. Try to discover which size staff works best for you.

3. Photocopy the staff paper in the back of this book (make at least 20 double-sided copies), and use the magnification button on the copier to make the staves bigger or smaller as you see fit.

4. Hole-punch the copied blank staves and make a folder for yourself. You will use it to keep track of your progress. For less effort, blank manuscript and guitar tablature notebooks are available at your local music store.

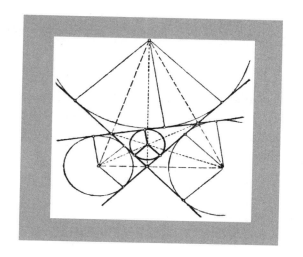

MORE LINES

Can we ever have too much of a good thing?

— Cervantes, *Don Quixote*

In This Chapter

- Bar Lines
- Double Bar Lines
- Measures

Terms to Know

- **bar line***:* vertical line used to separate written music into measures or bars. Bar lines make music easier to follow.
- **double bar line**: two bar lines close together indicating the end of a section or piece of music.
- **measure**: the area between two bar lines.

Bar Lines and Double Bar Lines

To make music easier to read, the staff is divided into sections by vertical lines called *bar lines*. There are two types of bar lines. The single bar line is a thin line perpendicular to the lines of the staff and goes from the top line to the bottom line. Bar lines simply divide up the staff into small sections which are easier to read.

The *double bar line* marks the end of a section, or the end of a song. It has a regular-sized line in addition to a thicker line close by to the right.

Measure

The area between two bar lines is called a *measure,* or a bar. To avoid confusion, from here on, I'll call them measures. The staff below is divided into four measures. Because some measures may have more notes in them than others, the space between bar lines doesn't have to be equal (notice the first measure is a bit longer).

Staff 3.1 Full staff and single line staff with bar lines, double bar, and measures marked.

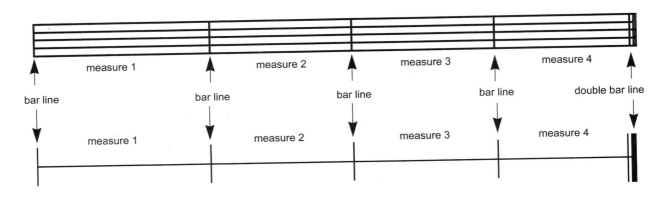

Bar lines aren't put in arbitrarily. There is a rhyme and a reason to their placement. You'll find out all about that soon. For now, just remember that bar lines divide up a staff into smaller parts.

Moving On

So, bar lines are pretty simple, right? Coming up next you'll learn some of the basic notes used in written music: whole notes, half notes, and quarter notes.

Chapter 3 Study Guide

1. What is a bar line used for?

2. Where is a double bar used?

3. On another piece of paper draw a single staff and a five line staff. Make them fairly long.

4. Divide each staff into four measures (they don't have to be equal length). The bar line should touch the upper and lower lines of the five-line staff without going over.

1. *Divides the staff into measures. Makes music easier to read.*

2. *The end of a section and/or the end of a song.*

3.

4.

Practical Use (If you're borrowing this book, make a photocopy!)

1. Divide each of the staves below into 4 equal measures and put a double-bar line at the end of the last measure.

2. You've seen written music before. Write in the measures what you think music looks like. Be creative if you have no idea at all. When you can truly read music, it'll be fun to come back and see what you did when you didn't know as much.

Basic Music Theory

WHERE'S THE BEAT?

Days full of wanting.
Let them go by without
worrying that they do.
Stay where you are inside
such a pure, hollow note.

— Rumi

In This Chapter

- The Beat
- Whole Note
- Half Note
- Quarter Note
- Note Anatomy 101
- Note Stems: Up or Down?

Terms to Know

- **whole note**: note that receives 4 beats in common time. All note names are derived from their relationship to the whole note.
- **half note**: half the length of a whole note. Receives two beats in common time.
- **quarter note**: one fourth the length of a whole note. Receives one beat in common time.
- **note head**: the part of the note that tells what pitch and how long the note will be.
- **stem**: line that stretches up or down from the note head.

The Beat Goes On

Rhythm is the essential glue that binds music together. Rhythm is so important that without it music wouldn't exist. The rhythm of a piece can be felt through the **beat**.

The beat of nearly any piece of music is easy to feel. It's what sets your toe tapping, it's what makes you dance. The beat is a regular pulse, like your heartbeat, which lasts throughout a piece of music.

Speaking of pulse, did you know that music with a fast beat makes your heart beat faster and speeds up your breathing? And music with a slow beat makes your heart and breathing slow down? It's true.

The beat is music's pulse, and like yours, it doesn't stop until the performance is over.

The Notes

There are only three different note lengths you have to know at first. You'll notice that the half notes and quarter notes have two examples. Keep reading to find out why. From longest to shortest the notes are:

whole note, 4 beats each: 𝅝

half notes, 2 beats each: 𝅗𝅥 𝅗𝅥

quarter notes, 1 beat each: 𝅘𝅥 𝅘𝅥

> All notes are named from their relationship to the *whole note*. Whole notes are hollow.
>
> A *half note* is half as long as a whole note (two half notes = 1 whole). Half notes are hollow.
>
> A *quarter note* is one fourth as long as a whole note (4 quarters = 1 whole). Quarter notes are filled in.

The Note Head

Let's dissect a note. You'll need to know the parts so that later in the book, when I say, "Make sure the note head is in the space and flip the stem," you'll know exactly what I'm talking about. No notes were harmed for this dissection.

Just like with people, the **head** is the round part where almost everything is happening. It's the position of the note head which gives us the important information about a note.

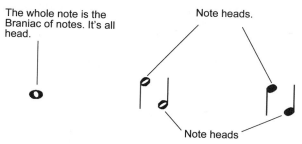

Notice how the shapes of the note heads are similar? Good. Some might have holes in the middle, and some might be filled in, but they're all the same basic shape.

Size Doesn't Matter

A whole note the size of your house and a whole note the size of a house fly would each get the same number of beats.

The Stem

Whole notes don't have stems. Half notes and quarter notes do have stems. The *stem* is the part that sticks up or down from the note head.

Notes with the stem down go on the third line and above. Notes with the stem up go on the third line and below. Right now this detail isn't too terribly important. We'll be using the one-line staff mostly, and for that the stem goes up.

Put Your Stems Up, Put Your Stems Down

The stem can go either up or down. When a note is on the third line of the staff or below, the stems grow up from the right side of the note head.

Putting the stem on the wrong side of the note head is one of the most common mistakes made. Be sure your notes look like the following:

Staff 4.1 Half notes and quarter notes, 3rd line and below, with their stems up. The last three notes use leger lines, which you'll learn about them when you get to "Learning Leger Lines" on page 93.

If the notes are on the third line or above, the stems go down on the left side.

Staff 4.2 Half notes and quarter notes, 3rd line and above, with their stems down. Notice the first three notes above the staff in this example. You'll learn about the small lines when you get to "Learning Leger Lines" on page 93.

Here's an easy way to remember what the stems look like:

A note **up** high on the staff looks like this.

A note **down** low on the staff looks like this.

Third Line Notes Are Conformists

The stem will be up for a note on the third line if it's with other notes whose stems are up.

The stem will be down for a third line note if it's with other notes whose stems are down.

On a one-line staff the note stems can be either up or down but they are nearly always shown with the stem up.

Staff 4.3 An example of third line note stems conforming to those around them.

third line stem up

third line stem down

Basic Music Theory

Moving On

This was a very important chapter because if you don't recognize and know the lengths of notes, reading music will be impossible. Stay with this chapter until you've understood it, and read it over again if you think it'll help.

Now you're ready for rests, which show silence in music. Study the review until you know all the questions, then read on!

Chapter 4 Review

1. What is the beat in music?

2. Name the notes you learned from shortest to longest.

3. Which notes have stems?

4. How many beats does a whole note get?

5. How many beats does a half note get?

6. How many beats does a quarter note get?

1. *a steady pulse; what makes your toe tap*

2. *quarter, half, whole*

3. *quarter and half notes*

4. *four*

5. *two*

6. *one*

Practical Use

1. Fill up the single- and five-line staves with quarter, half and whole notes on different spaces and lines. Be sure to check the direction of the stem (up or down) when using the five line staff.

THE SOUND OF SILENCE

The rest is silence.

— Shakespeare, *Hamlet,* Act v, sc.2

In This Chapter

- Rests in General
- Whole rest
- Half Rest
- Quarter Rest

Terms to Know

- **whole rest**: shows 4 beats of silence in common time.
- **half rest**: shows 2 beats of silence in common time.
- **quarter rest**: shows 1 beat of silence in common time.

Take a Rest

Ovid said that silence is strength. If that's true, you'll be much stronger after this chapter because it's all about silence. Silence in music is as important as sound, and of course we crafty humans have invented a way to show this silence in music; *rests*.

Rest lengths and rest names are the same as the note lengths you learned in the last chapter. The three you'll learn in this chapter are ***whole rests***, ***half rests***, and ***quarter rests***.

The Rests of the Story

Whole rests are 4 beats long, and look like this: ▬

Half rests are 2 beats long, and look like this: ▬

Quarter rests are one beat long and look like this: 𝄽

Whole or Half, Hole or Hat

Whole rests and half rests look very much the same, and can be easily confused with each other. Here's a way to remember which is which.

The whole rest looks like a *hole* in the ground, like so:

The half rest, looks like a *hat* (I know, *half* and *hat* don't sound quite the same, but work with me here):

Making a Quarter Rest

This is probably one of the trickiest symbols to make in written music, but it certainly isn't tough. Make a letter 'Z', then put a letter 'C' right below it. It won't look exactly like the quarter rest above, but anyone who reads music will know what it is (as long as you aren't too sloppy with it).

Z + C =   𝄽

Rests On The Staff

Whole rests hang from the 4th line of the staff, half rests sit on the third line, and quarter rests are plastered over the middle 3 lines. Notice the brim of the "hat" and the edges of the "hole" are gone when the half and whole rests are written on their proper line.

Staff 5.1   Whole rest, half rest, and quarter rest on the staff.

Rests on the Single Line Staff

When using the single line staff, whole rests will hang from the staff, half rests will sit on the staff, and quarter rests are centered on the staff line. Like so:

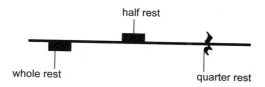

Long Rests

Rests can be stretched out over several measures and instead of writing a whole bunch of whole rests, the measures of rest are combined and the music is marked with how many measures of rest are to be counted. Like so:

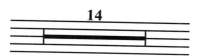

Moving On

Without silence there can be no sound; without sound there can be no silence. Now you know how to show silence in music using whole, half and quarter rests. Make sure you can answer all of the study guide questions for this chapter before you move on.

Coming up next is the Review for all of Part I. This is very important information, so be sure you've got it all before you move on. It's very common to review this information many times until it sticks. Keep at it!

Chapter 5 Review

1. What does a rest show?

2. Which three rests did you learn?

1. silence

2. whole rest, half rest, quarter rest

3. How many beats does a quarter rest get?

3. *one*

4. How many beats does a half rest get?

4. *two*

5. How many beats does a whole rest get?

5. *four*

6. Which line does the whole rest hang from?

6. *fourth line*

7. Which line does the half rest sit on?

7. *third line*

Practical Use

1. Fill up a single staff line with alternating whole and half rests. Put an *h* below the half rests and a *w* under the whole rests. Do the same thing but on a 5-line staff.

2. On a single staff line write in as many notes and rests as you can comfortably fit. Include all notes and rests you've learned. Do the same thing on a 5-line staff. Remember that though the rests must go in specific places, the notes can go in a space or have a line through them (for more information on where to place notes, see "Spaced Out and Lined Up" on page 92).

PART I REVIEW

Whew! You Made It.

These pages can be used to test your memory on what you've learned in Part I, and if some of the information hasn't stuck, you can go back and check it out on the page indicated below the question.

As with the chapter reviews, use your keyboard to cover up the answers while you test yourself.

When you think you've got it all down, either take the test in *Basic Music Theory Quiz Pack* (free online at www.Sol-Ut.com), or continue to the next Part.

The Review

1. How many lines make up the musical staff?
   page 18

   1. five

2. How many spaces in the musical staff?
   page 18

   2. four

3. Using a separate sheet of paper and a pencil, draw a musical staff like the one below.

   3.

4. What is the number of the bottom line?
   page 18

   4. one

5. What is the number of the top line?
page 18

5. *five*

6. What is the number of the bottom space?
page 18

6. *one*

7. What is the number of the top space?
page 18

7. *four*

8. What is a bar line used for?
page 22

8. *Divides the staff into measures.*

9. Where is a double bar used?
page 22

9. *The end of a section or song.*

10. On your separate piece of paper draw another staff. Make it a fairly long one.
page 18

10.

11. Divide the staff into four measures.
page 22

11.

12. What is the beat, in music?
page 26

12. *A steady pulse; what makes your toe tap.*

13. Name the notes you learned from shortest to longest.
page 26

13. *quarter note,
half note,
whole note*

14. Which notes have stems?
page 27

14. *quarter and half notes*

15. How many beats does a whole note get?
page 26

15. *four*

16. How many beats does a half note get?
page 26

16. *two*

17. How many beats does a quarter note get?
page 26

17. *one*

18. What does a rest show?
page 32

18. *silence*

19. Which five rests did you learn?
page 32, page 55, page 57

19. *whole rest, half rest, quarter rest*

20. How many beats does a quarter rest get?
page 32

20. *one*

21. How many beats does a half rest get?
page 32

21. *two*

22. How many beats does a whole rest get?
page 32

22. *four*

23. Which line does the whole rest hang from?
page 32

23. *fourth line*

24. Which line does the half rest sit on?
page 32

24. *third line*

25. On a scratch piece of staff paper, draw 2 whole rests, 2 half rests, and 2 quarter rests.

25.

Moving On

Okay. That was short and painless, I hope. Once you have this information stored in your little gray cells, take the quiz you can get for free at www.Sol-Ut.com or move on to Part II, *You Got Rhythm*.

Now that you understand note length we're almost ready to start putting them together to make (and play) rhythms. There are a few other things which help us organize and figure out written rhythms and in the next Part you'll learn what they are.

You're doing great! Feel free to take a break before you tackle the next Part. In Part II you'll learn about meter, a counting system, dotted notes, and more types of notes.

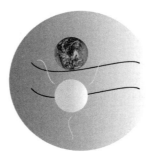

SolŪt Press

Support Music and Musicians.
www.Sol-Ut.com

PART TWO

You Got Rhythm

In This Section You Will Learn:

- Time Signatures
- Counting System
- Eighth Notes
- Sixteenth Notes
- Rests
- Dotted Notes
- Triplets

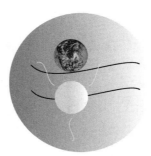

SolŪt Press

Support Music and Musicians.
www.Sol-Ut.com

METER

All times are not alike.

— Cervantes, *Don Quixote*

In This Chapter

- Meter/Time Signature
- 4/4 Time
- 2/4 Time
- 3/4 Time

Terms to Know

- **4/4 time**: the most common time signature. Four beats per measure, quarter note gets one beat.
- **C (common time)**: another way of writing or saying 4/4 time.
- **2/4 time**: two beats per measure, quarter note gets one beat.
- **3/4 time**: three beats per measure, quarter note gets one beat.

Not the Metric System

At the beginning of every piece of well-written music is the ***time signature*** or ***meter*** which gives you information about the piece of music you're about to play.

The time signature or meter tells you how many beats are in each measure. To review measures, see "Measure" on page 22. The time signature also tells you what kind of note gets one beat. To review the notes, see "The Notes" on page 26.

Staff 6.1 The most common time signatures, or meters: 4/4, 3/4, and 2/4. Notice where the numbers are written both with the single line staff and the full staff.

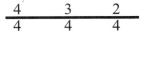

The Top Number

The top number tells you how many beats will be in each measure. So, in the examples above, in 4/4 time, there will be 4 beats in each measure; in 3/4 time there will be three beats in each measure, and in 2/4 time there will be two beats in each measure.

The top number in the meter can be almost anything, but the most common ones are 4, 3, 2, and 6, pretty much in that order.

The Bottom Number

The bottom number tells you which type of note (whole, half, quarter) gets one beat. The most common time signature has a 4 as its bottom number. Remember fractions? Another way of saying 1/4 is *one quarter*, right? And so, with a *4* in the bottom of the time signature, you know that the quarter note receives one beat.

There are several possible numbers for the bottom of the time signature because there are several types of notes (whole, half, quarter, etc. The most common numbers on the bottom of the time signature are 4 (quarter note), 2 (half note), and 8 (eighth note), with 4 being by *far* the most common. And because it's the most common (and the easiest to understand), we'll stick with 4 as the bottom number until Chapter 33, "More Meters." Then you'll learn about time signatures in which a note other than the quarter note receives one beat.

Why One Meter and Not Another?

Why have different meters? When you look at the following examples you'll see how the words and the music fall in certain patterns. The pattern might be shaped by the words or the music or both. If there is a 4-beat pattern, it'll be in 4/4 time. A 2-beat pattern is in 2/4 time, and a 3-beat pattern is in 3/4 time.

4/4 Time

This meter is much more common than all of the other meters. If you're a beginner, you'll most likely be working in this time signature for a while before moving on to others.

The examples below use nursery rhymes and folk or popular songs to show why different meters are used. The tunes are first written on the five line staff, then simplified to just the rhythm part.

Don't worry if you don't understand the up and down movement of the notes or some of the symbols on the five-line staff. We'll get to all that soon. For now focus on the rhythm only.

You can see from the examples how these songs fall easily into their metric pattern. Notice where the bar lines are drawn because you'll have to do this yourself in the Practical Use section at the end of the chapter. Notice how each measure contains 4 beats. Also take note of the fact that half notes are sustained for two beats. Whole notes would be sustained for four beats.

Staff 6.2   *Mary Had a Little Lamb* in 4/4 time. Below that is just the rhythm. Tap it out.

Top number tells you there are 4 beats per measure.

Mar - y   had   a   lit - tle   la-mb   lit - tle   la-mb   lit - tle   la-mb

A 4 in the bottom of the time signature tells you the quarter note gets one beat. All notes get their regular beats: half = 2, whole = 4, etc.

Common Time

Because 4/4 time is so common, you'll often see a letter "C" in the place of the time signature. The "C" stands for "common," and looks like this:

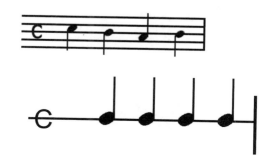

2/4 Time

This is another fairly common time signature, though not as common as 4/4. Again, notice how easily this example falls into the pattern of 2 beats per measure. Pay no attention to the up and down motion of the notes right now. Focus on the rhythm only.

Staff 6.3   A few measures of *Twinkle, Twinkle Little Star* in 2/4 time.

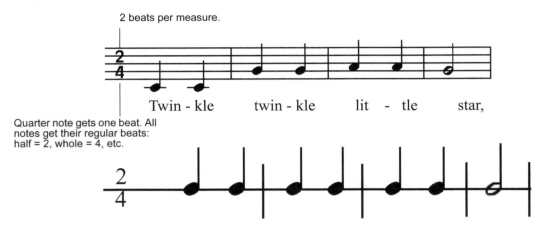

3/4 Time

Three-four is a fun meter. It has a lilting, circular feel to it, especially if you take it fast. Keep it slow at first until you get the hang of this meter.

If you've ever heard a waltz, or danced a waltz, you've heard the 3/4 pattern. It has a strong pulse on the first beat of each measure. ONE, two, three, ONE, two, three, ONE, two, three, etc. Study the use of quarter and half notes to show the rhythm below.

Staff 6.4   A few measures of *My Favorite Things* (from "The Sound of Music" by Rogers and Hammerstein) in 3/4 time. Below it is just the rhythm on the one-line staff.

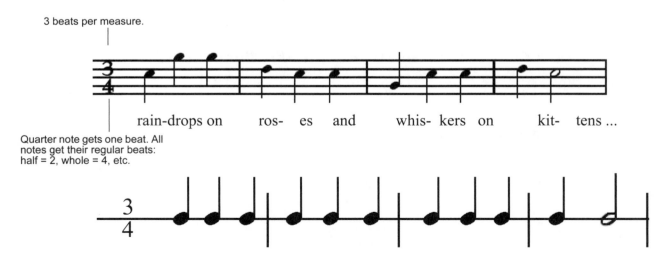

Moving On

Now that you've learned what meters and/or time signatures are, and what the numbers mean, you're ready to learn a counting system to help you hear how a written rhythm should sound. You'll get all that in the next chapter, *Down With the Count*.

But first, the chapter review.

Chapter 6 Review

1. What is another name for meter?

   1. *time signature*

2. Where does the time signature appear?

   2. *At the beginning of a piece of music.*

3. What information does the time signature give?

   3. *how many beats in each measure, and which note gets one beat*

4. Which are the three most common time signatures?

   4. *4/4, 2/4, 3/4*

5. What does the top number tell us?

   5. *how many beats in one measure*

6. What does the bottom number tell us?

   6. *what type of note gets one beat*

7. Why are different meters used?

   7. *Each song has a pattern. The meter depends on the pattern of each song.*

Practical Use

1. Are you using a pencil? Do. Most people use a pencil when writing music because it can be erased. Write each meter you have learned at the beginning of a single-line staff (4/4, 2/4, and 3/4). Do the same at the beginning of the five-line staff.

2. Fill up each line and staff with notes and rests. Place bar lines correctly based on the meter.

DOWN WITH THE COUNT

I like to see you move with the rhythm;
I like to see when you're dancin' from
within.

— Bob Marley

In This Chapter

- Tap Your Foot
- Counting Quarter Notes
- Counting Half Notes
- Counting Whole Notes
- Counting Rests

Can You Count to 4?

Now that you know the note lengths and time signatures, we can move on to the counting system.

The counting system is *very* helpful, especially for difficult rhythms. *Every* time I have a student count a difficult passage out loud, it becomes much easier. When you count, do it rhythmically, and tap your foot with a steady beat at the same time.

The rhythms we'll be using at first won't be tough, so you can get a good idea of how the system works. Gradually I'll introduce more and more difficult rhythms on which to practice this counting system.

The good news is that you only have to know how to count to 4, the length of a measure of 4/4 time. And because we don't need a specific pitch for this exercise, we'll use the one-line staff for the examples.

Tap Your Foot

It's one thing that both beginning musicians and masters have in common. It's what keeps your rhythms the right length, and it keeps you synchronized with others you may be playing with. It's the foot tap.

Over the last few days I watched Eric Clapton, B.B. King, Wynton Marsalis, Leo Kottke, then Metallica, and all of those musicians, almost the entire time they played, were tapping their feet. And if they didn't tap their foot (which was seldom), their bodies moved in some other way to keep time steady. Rhythmic movement helps your music.

If you're in a large group in which 20 or more people tapping their feet sounds like a marching army, tap your toe inside your shoe, or tap your heel softly instead. If you're playing solo guitar, maybe a blues tune, you can stomp your foot on beats 2 and 4 to add a little percussion to your song. Chris Smither does this masterfully. Either way, if you tap your foot your performance will be better for it.

If you're not used to tapping your foot when you play, it'll take a little concentration and a little coordination to get it. Just keep practicing and soon you'll be tapping your foot without thinking about it.

If you don't tap, or keep some rhythmic movement going, you're pretty much guessing where the beat is. What you're after is precision. To make this precision your own, tap your foot. Practice by tapping your foot to the beat of any music you hear.

On to the counting system.

Quarter Note Count

The count is directly related to the beat. In 4/4 time (or any meter with a *4* as the bottom number) the beat is the same as the quarter note. When you tap your foot with the music, those are eighth notes. Here's what a measure of quarter notes in 4/4 time looks like with the proper counting:

Staff 7.1

Basic Music Theory

Simple and straightforward. At the beginning of the measure, the count begins again at "1". In a meter with a different number on top (like 3/4 or 2/4) you only have as many numbers as there are beats in a measure. So a measure of quarter notes in 3/4 time is counted 1 2 3, 1 2 3, etc.

Don't forget to tap your foot. As you say the numbers out loud, say them rhythmically, so you can feel the beat. If you're doing it correctly, each number is said as the foot hits the floor.

This will come in handy later. Trust me.

Half Note Count

Half notes, because they're two beats, are treated a little differently. It's easier to show than to explain. Remember that the sound of a half note in 4/4 time is sustained for two beats each. Here you go:

Staff 7.2   Two measures of half notes with counting.

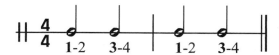

You probably guessed the count would look something like that, right? The dash shows that the sound is continuous. When you say this rhythm, say it rhythmically, and say the *1* and *3* louder than the *2* and *4*.

Each half note will have two foot taps. The foot taps go with the beat (1, 2, 3, 4), not with the note. The tap remains continuous throughout

For these two measures, you would say (rhythmically), "ONE-two, THREE-four, ONE-two, THREE-four." To show the half note sound is continuous, connect the sound of 1-2 and 3-4.

Whole Note Count

I'm sure you could figure out the whole note counts for yourself, but I'll give them to you anyway.

Staff 7.3   Two measures of whole notes with counting.

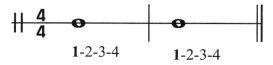

For these two measures, you'd say, "ONE-two-three-four, ONE-two-three-four."

Remember, the tap goes with the numbers, not with the note, so for a whole note, you'd tap your foot four times while holding out the sound.

When you play whole notes on your instrument, the sound is continuous, so when you count, strive to make your voice also smooth and continuous within the four beats of the whole note.

Mix 'Em Up

Any combination of notes will be counted similarly. I won't include whole notes in the example because, in 4/4 time whole notes get the entire measure to themselves.

Staff 7.4   Counting for mixed quarter and half notes.

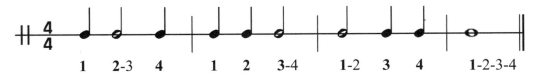

1   2-3   4   1   2   3-4   1-2   3   4   1-2-3-4

Other Meters

Other meters, like 2/4 and 3/4 would be treated the same, the only difference being there would be less counts in each measure. An added bonus is that in those meters, whole notes aren't used.

Count the Rest

Counting rests is very similar to counting notes. Because rests are silent, parentheses ( ) are used to indicate the silence. Here are three measures with whole, half, and quarter rests. And just for kicks, we'll use the 5-line staff.

An added help when you count rests out loud is to count them softly, with a whisper.

Staff 7.5   Whole, half, and quarter rests with counting.

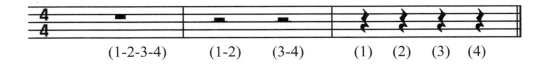

(1-2-3-4)   (1-2)   (3-4)   (1)   (2)   (3)   (4)

All Together Now

I'd rather be guilty of overkill than guilty of not being thorough, so here's an example with notes and rests of several different values. Knock yourself out.

Don't worry about the up and down motion of the notes. This will be explained in the next Part. Focus on the note and rest lengths. Count out loud rhythmically and don't forget to tap your foot.

Staff 7.6   Notes, rests, and their counts in 4/4 time.

1-2   (3)   4   1   2   (3-4)   (1)   2-3   4

Moving On

Being able to read rhythms is one of the most valuable skills you can have as a musician, and this counting system (combined with a foot tap) will help you figure out how a rhythm sounds.

Coming up next you'll learn what a tiny little dot (.) can do to the length of a note.

Chapter 7 Review

1. The count of any measure, in any time signature/meter, begins with what number?

   1. 1

2. How is a measure of quarter notes in 3/4 time counted?

   2. 1 2 3

3. How is a measure of half notes in 4/4 time counted?

   3. 1-2, 3-4

4. How is a whole note counted in 4/4 time?

   4. 1-2-3-4

5. When writing out the counting, what is used to indicate a rest?

   5. parentheses ( )

6. When counting out loud, how should you count a rest?

   6. softly

Practical Use

1. Write out 8 measures of each meter: 2/3, 3/4, and 4/4. Use notes and rests randomly. Get as many in as you can. Place bar lines correctly. Go back through and write in the counting. Say it out loud (remember the rests are whispered) while you tap your foot. See how fast you can go and still be correct.

NEW NOTES

*Indeed, what is there that does not
appear marvellous when it comes to our
knowledge for the first time?*

— Pliny the Elder

In This Chapter

- Eighth Notes, Eighth Rests
- Counting Eighth Notes and Rests
- Sixteenth Notes, Sixteenth Rests
- Counting Sixteenth Notes and Rests

Terms to Know

- **eighth note**: in common time, 1/2 of a beat. Two eighth notes per beat.
- **eighth rest**: in common time, 1/2 a beat of silence.
- **sixteenth note**: in common time, 1/4 of a beat. Four sixteenth notes per beat.
- **sixteenth rest**: in common time, 1/4 of a beat of silence.
- **downbeat**: the beats in a measure which fall on a number. When tapping your foot, it's on the floor for the downbeats.
- **upbeat**: the second half of each beat. When tapping your foot, it's in the up position.

Eighth Notes and Rests

Remember when I said all notes get their name because of their relationship to the whole note? If you don't remember, check out "The Notes" on page 4-26 for a refresher.

Eighth notes are no different. You can tell by their name that they're 1/8 as long as a whole note (which I'm sure you remember gets 4 beats). What is 1/8 of 4 beats? The answer is 1/2 of one beat.

An eighth note gets half of a beat in 4/4 time.

It might be easier to say that there are 8 eighth notes in one whole note.

Or that there are 4 eighth notes in one half note.

Or that there are 2 eighth notes in one quarter note.

Or that there are 2 eighth notes per beat.

"I get it," you say. "Just show me the notes!" Well, before I do, there's something you should know about. They're called *flags*, and we're not talking about the stars and stripes.

A flag is a doohickey which hangs from the end of the stem of an eighth note, and it has two forms. The first type can be seen dangling from the eighth notes on the left below. The second version on the right is used for two or more eighth notes. When there are two or more eighth notes, the flags are connected with a *beam* to make the notes easier to read.

Staff 8.1   **LEFT:** Single eighth notes. **RIGHT:** Eighth notes grouped by twos and fours with beams (flags connected).

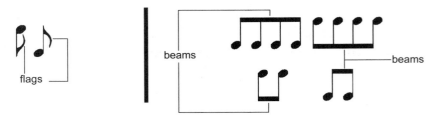

Counting Eighths

Because there are two eighth notes for every beat, the count is a little different than what you've learned already. With eighth notes, the beat is *subdivided*, which means chopped up (but evenly chopped up).

Here are two measures of eighth notes in 2/4 time. When said out loud, the "+" sign is pronounced "and."

Be sure when you count these, that your foot comes down firmly on each number. Your foot will be in the "up" position for the "+."

When a note falls on an "+," it's called an *upbeat*. Coincidence? I don't think so. A *downbeat* is a note or rest that falls on a number, or when your foot is hits the floor.

Basic Music Theory

Staff 8.2   8th note count in 4/4 time.

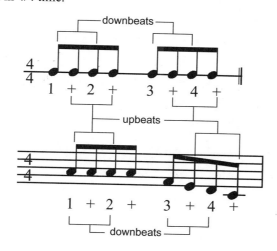

In 2/4 time the count for two measures would be "One And Two And, One And Two And (said rhythmically with your foot tapping away like a machine).

Eighth Rests

The eighth rest also gets only 1/2 of a beat, but is silent. The eighth rest looks like a seven with a strange growth at its tip and it lies in the middle of the staff, like so:

Staff 8.3   One little bitty eighth rest, all by its lonesome.

Counting Eighth Rests

The count for eighth rests is the same as the count for eighth notes, only there is a parentheses ( ) around either the number or the +. When counting the eighth rest, be sure you know which part of the beat the rest falls on, the upbeat (when your foot is up), or the downbeat (when your foot hits the floor).

Here are a few measures of eighth notes and eighth rests with the counting. Again, don't be distracted by the things you haven't learned yet. Focus on the eighth notes and the counting. Be sure to count it rhythmically, and say the rests more quietly than the notes.

Staff 8.4   A whole mess of eighth rests and eighth notes, with counting.

Sweet Sixteenth Notes

Why sweet? Because *sixteenth notes* are the last type of note you'll learn until Chapter 32. Yippee!

You've probably already figured out that, because of the name, there are 16 of these babies in each whole note. Okay, time for a little math. If you divide up 4 beats (the whole note) sixteen ways, how long is each sixteenth note?

The answer is...1/4 of a beat. *A sixteenth note gets 1/4 of one beat in 4/4 time*.

So there are 16 sixteenth notes in one whole note,

or 8 sixteenth notes in one half note,

or 4 sixteenth notes in one quarter note,

or 4 sixteenth notes in one beat of 4/4 time,

or 2 sixteenth notes in one eighth note.

So what do they look like? Sixteenth notes also have flags, with one added bonus: there are two of them.

When a flag is added to a note, it cuts the note length in half. For example, add a flag to a quarter note and you get an eighth note. Add another flag to an eighth note and you get a sixteenth note.

Staff 8.5   **LEFT:** Single sixteenth notes. **RIGHT:** Sixteenth notes in groups of 4 and 2.

Counting Sixteenths

I love counting sixteenth notes. Just like with eighth notes, the beat is subdivided, but even more so than with eighths. Each beat is split up into 4 parts, and each part has a name. Practice this count with your foot VERY SLOWLY until you've got it down enough to do it more quickly.

Staff 8.6   A measure of sixteenth notes with counting.

Again, when you're counting, make sure your foot is tapping down on each number (each beat), and up with each "+" symbol, just like with eighth notes. The "e" occurs halfway up and the "a" occurs halfway down.

Sixteenth Rests

Sixteenth rests look like eighth rests but have an extra little flag:

Staff 8.7   A single sixteenth rest, all by its lonesome.

Counting Sixteenth Rests

The same count is used (1 e + a) but as before, there are parentheses around the rests. Below are some measures with the sixteenth rest in different positions in the measure. Ignore the up and down motion of the notes and concentrate on the count.

Staff 8.8   Sixteenth rests scattered around the measures.

1 e (+) a   2 e +(a)   3 (e) + a   (4) e + a   (1)   e   (+)   (2)   (3-4)

How to Figure out a Tough Rhythm

1 Write out the counting under the notes. Triple check to make sure you've written it out correctly.

2 Practice saying it rhythmically VERY SLOWLY, and be sure to tap your foot down on each number, and up on each "+."

3 If there are rests, say them more quietly than the notes.

4 Repeat from step two, and as your brain becomes used to the rhythm, gradually increase speed. If it's frustrating or you're making mistakes, slow it down and try again.

5 Keep at it! Persistence and repetition are the parents of success.

6 If all else fails, find someone who reads music better than you and ask them for help.

Moving On

I'm sure you're discovering that the notes and counting system don't stick in your brain with just one reading. Not to worry, this is normal. It takes a while living with these new concepts before they seem familiar and easy. You may have to refer back to these chapters often, and that's okay too. Stick with it.

You've now been introduced to all the types of notes and rests that you'll probably ever need for reading music. However, there are ways to change the length of the notes you just learned.

One way to change note length is to place a small dot following a note. In the next chapter you'll learn all about these dots and what they do to the length of a note.

Chapter 8 Review

1. How long is an eighth note in 2/4 time?

                                                              1. *1/2 beat*

2. How long is an eighth rest in 3/4 time?

       2. *1/2 beat*

3. How many eighth notes in one quarter note or
   one beat of 4/4 time?

       3. *two*

4. How are eighth notes counted in 4/4 time?

       4. *1 + 2 + 3 + 4 +*

5. How are eighth rests counted in 2/4 time?

       5. *(1) (+) (2) (+)*

6. What is the count for this example?

       6. *1 + 2 (+) 3 (+) 4 (+)*

7. How long are sixteenth notes in 4/4 time?

       7. *1/4 beat*

8. How many sixteenth notes are in one quarter note or
   one beat of 4/4 time?

       8. *four*

9. How do you count sixteenth notes in 4/4 time?

       9. *1 e + a 2 e + a*
          3 e + a 4 e + a

10. What is the count for this example?

       10. *1 e (+) a*
           2 e + (a)
           3 (e) + a
           (4) e + ac

11. What is an upbeat?

       11. *The part of the beat when your*
            foot is in the "up" position; the
            "+" of a beat.

Practical Use

For these exercises, place notes all over the staff, on lines or in spaces, just like all the examples you've been reading so far.

1. On a blank staff below, write out eight single eighth notes, four with the stem up and four stem down. Write out another eight eighth notes barred in groups of two with stems up and down, and a final eight barred in fours.

2. Write in the counting under the notes you've written. Use a 4/4 time signature and place the bar lines correctly.

3. On a blank staff write out sixteen single sixteenth notes, eight stem up and eight stem down. Another eight barred in groups of two, and finally eight barred in groups of four.

4. Write the count under the sixteenth notes you've written. Use a 3/4 time signature and place the bar lines correctly.

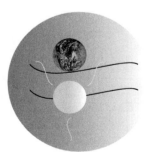

SolŪt Press

Support Music and Musicians.
www.Sol-Ut.com

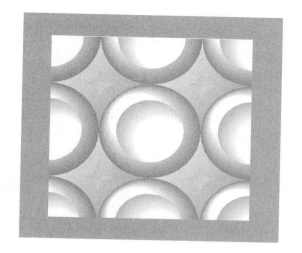

SEEING DOTS

We see things not as they are, but as we are.

— H.M. Tomlinson,
Out of Soundings

In This Chapter

- The Effect of a Dot
- Dotted Whole Note
- Dotted Half Note
- Dotted Quarter Note
- Dotted Eighth Note

Terms to Know

- **dot**: appears next to the note head and lengthens the note by 1/2 its original value.
- **dotted**: refers to a note that has a dot after it, i.e. dotted half note, dotted quarter note, etc.

You Are Not Seeing Things

Those dots you see behind some notes are supposed to be there. A dot just to the right of a note makes the note longer. How much longer? Well it depends on what note the dot follows. Let me explain.

A dot adds half the amount of the note it follows. Another, perhaps simpler, way of saying it, is that a dotted note is 1.5 times the length of the same kind of note without a dot.

Sounds weird doesn't it? An example might throw more light on this peculiar practice. Let's use a whole note as our first example.

The Dotted Whole Note

A whole note (𝅝), as you know, gets 4 beats. Half of that is two, for a total of six.

Or, 4 x 1 1/2 = 6; or 4 + 2 = 6

A dotted whole note (𝅝.) has six beats.

But wait a minute, you might be saying, there are only 4 beats in a measure. Well, for 4/4 time, you're right. But for dotted whole notes we need a new meter, 6/4 time. Remember the top number tells us there are six beats per measure; the bottom number tells us that the quarter note gets one beat. Here are a few measures of 6/4 time:

Staff 9.1   Three measures of dotted whole notes.

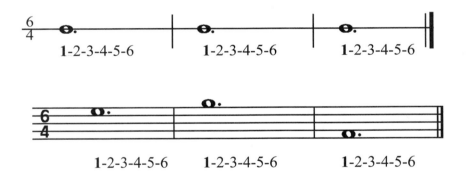

The Dotted Half Note

A more common type of dotted note is the ***dotted half note***. How long is a dotted half note? Use the formula. The half note gets two beats, and half of that is one. Two plus one is three.

Or, 2 x 1 1/2 = 3.

The dotted half note gets three beats.

Though a dotted half note could happen in any time signature with more than three beats in the measure, in the following example, I've used 3/4 time.

Staff 9.2   Three measures of dotted half notes.

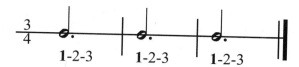

1-2-3   1-2-3   1-2-3

1-2-3   1-2-3   1-2-3

The Dotted Quarter Note

Here's where things get a little tricky, but it's still not too tough. A quarter note gets one beat. Half of that is half of a beat.

Or 1 1/2 x 1 = 1 1/2

A dotted quarter note gets 1 1/2 beats in 4/4 time.

To make the counting easier, think of the dotted quarter note in terms of how many eighth notes are in it. Because it's 1 1/2 beats, that comes out to be 3 eighth notes.

Notice that when counting dotted quarters, you use a count similar to eighth notes. This is so that you can keep track of exactly how long each dotted quarter note is. Say the bold items in a normal voice, and the rest in a softer voice, as always with a steady foot-tap.

Staff 9.3   Two measures of dotted quarter notes and eighths in 4/4 time.

1-+-2   +   3-+-4   +   1   +-2-+   3   +-4-+

1-+-2   +   3-+-4   +   1   +-2-+   3   +-4-+

Musical Example

Because this rhythm is a little trickier, below is an example which you should recognize (be sure to tap your foot):

Staff 9.4   First two measures of *My Country, 'Tis of Thee.*

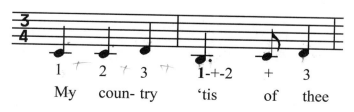

1   2   3   1-+-2   +   3

My   coun- try   'tis   of   thee

Dotted Eighth Note

This is the last type of dotted note we'll discuss. Find the length with the same process as the other dotted notes.

An eighth note is half of a beat. There are two sixteenth notes in one eighth note. So half of an eighth note is 1/4 of a beat, or 1 sixteenth note. When we add that to the eighth note, we get 3/4 of a beat, or 3 sixteenths.

Or, 1 1/2 x 1/2 = 3/4.
A dotted eighth note gets 3/4 of a beat.

You'll rarely see a dotted eighth note without a sixteenth note following it to round out the beat. In fact, it's so common, that the figure has a name. Dotted eighth-sixteenth. Go figure.

Here is a measure of dotted 8th-16ths. Notice that a sixteenth note count is used so that you can keep track of exactly how long the dotted eighth is. Be sure your foot hits the floor on the numbers.

Staff 9.5   The dotted 8th-16th figure.

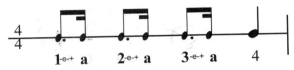

Musical Example

Here's a musical example you'll recognize which uses the dotted 8th-16th figure.

Staff 9.6   First few notes of *The Star Spangled Banner*

Dotted Rests

Dotted rests are treated exactly the same as dotted notes, the only difference being that the count will be in parentheses.

This example has dots like a sickness, and that's for the sake of illustration. You won't normally see a musical passage with this many dots.

Staff 9.7   Dotted notes and rests with counting.

1-+-2   (+)   (3-4-5)   6   (1-+-2)   +   3-e-+ a   4   (e-+-a) 5   6   (1-2-3-4-5-6)   1-2-3-4-5-6

Moving On

The concepts you're learning are becoming more complex, and you'll probably find it will take some time living with these ideas before they really stick, so come back and review as much as you want.

Now that you understand that a dot increases the length of a note by half its original value, you can decipher the length of any dotted note.

Coming up next is another treatment of the notes you already know, called *triplets*, which is a grouping of three notes. Find out what it all means in the next chapter.

Chapter 9 Review

1. What does a dot do to a note?

2. How long is a dotted half note in 4/4 time?

3. How long is a dotted quarter note in 4/4 time?

4. How long is a dotted eighth note in 4/4 time?

5. Which type of note usually follows a dotted eighth note?

6. Why?

1. *makes the note before it 1 1/2 times as long*

2. *three beats*

3. *1 1/2 beats*

4. *3/4 of a beat*

5. *sixteenth note*

6. *to round out the beat*

Practical Use

1. On the staves below, experiment with dotted notes. Include every dotted note you've learned. Use several different meters (with bar lines!) and don't forget the rests, too. When you've finished, write in the counting. Check your work with a friend.

CHAPTER

10

TRIPLETS!

People are flowers.
Music is water.
Musicians are the hose.

— Carlos Santana

In This Chapter

- General Tuplet Information
- Eighth Note Triplets
- Sixteenth Note Triplets
- Quarter Note Triplets

Terms to Know

- **tuplet**: a grouping of notes (duplet, triplet, quintuplet, etc.).
- **triplet**: a group of three notes played in the time of two notes of equal value (confusing, no? This means that an eighth note triplet takes place in one beat).

10: Triplets!

67

General Tuplet Information

The notes you're about to learn are called **triplets**, and they belong to a group of notes known as **tuplets**.

A tuplet is a group of notes that doesn't follow the normal rules of counting. Some examples would be duplets (2 notes), **triplets (three notes)**, quintuplets (5 notes), and sextuplets (6 notes). Of course there are also septuplets, octuplets and on and on, but you get the idea, right? In this chapter you'll learn triplets because they're the most common, and the easiest to understand.

The rule you'll want to remember for triplets, is that a **triplet (three notes) takes place in the amount of time it would normally take to play two of the triplet notes at their regular length**. Sound confusing? A concrete example will help explain.

Eighth Note Triplet

Eighth note triplets are the most common triplet and the easiest to count and to feel. The three notes of the triplet are beamed together, and there is a small three over the beam telling you the figure is a triplet. They look like this:

All triplets are played in the time of two notes of equal value. What this means for the eighth note triplet is that the eighth note triplet is played in the amount of time it normally takes to play two eighth notes, which is one beat.

An eighth note triplet is one beat long.

In the next example you can see how eighth note triplets are counted. Be sure to tap your foot as you count so that your foot hits the floor on all the numbers.

Staff 10.1   A few measures of eighth note triplets with counting.

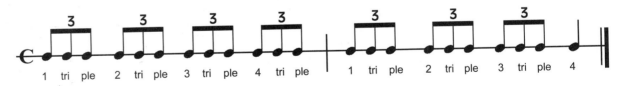

Basic Music Theory

Sixteenth Note Triplets

To find the length of a sixteenth note triplet, we use the same rule: a triplet's length is the same length as two notes of equal value. That means a sixteenth note triplet happens in the time it takes to play two sixteenth notes, which is half of a beat.

A sixteenth note triplet is a half beat long.

Sixteenth note triplets look like this:

The counting for sixteenth note triplets is a little trickier than most other rhythms, but with a couple tries and some foot coordination, you shouldn't have any trouble.

The count for two beats of sixteenth note triplets is 1 la li + la li, 2 la li + la li. The "1" and "2" occur when your foot hits the floor, the "+" is the upbeat, or the second half of the beat when the foot is in the "up" position. The "la" and "li" should fit between the number and the "+", while your foot is either going up or coming down.

Sixteenth note triplets are fast even at a slow tempo, so you have to spit out that "la-li" quickly. It'll probably take a few tries to get it right, so keep at it until you've got it.

In the example which follows, notice that in measure two and three the sixteenth note triplet is connected to an eighth note. Sixteenth note triplets are often paired with eighth notes to round out the beat.

From here on out you won't get the simplified version of the rhythm on the one line staff. Coming soon you'll be learning what all the other symbols mean and do, so consider this your time to get used to seeing the notes on the five line staff. Focus on the rhythm only for now.

Staff 10.2   Sixteenth note triplets and their count.

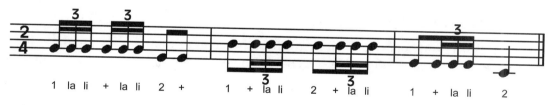

Quarter Note Triplets

Quarter note triplets are difficult to count accurately, so I've saved them for last.

Using the triplet rule for quarter note triplets means that the quarter note triplet takes place over the length of two quarter notes, or two beats.

Quarter note triplets are two beats long.

Quarter note triplets have a curvy line over them, with the three in the middle. This curvy line simply groups the notes together so you can tell which three notes are in the triplet. Here's what they look like.

The reason quarter note triplets are difficult to count is that you have to divide two beats three ways, and we don't easily think in thirds. If we divide 2 by three, we get 2/3, so ***each note of the quarter note triplet is 2/3 of a beat long***.

This makes regulating the length of a quarter note triplet with the foot tap difficult, but not impossible. Let's break it down.

The first note of the triplet is easy because it starts right on the beat, or when the foot hits the floor. The second note of the triplet happens 2/3 of a beat after the first, so your foot will have gone up and will just be coming down when the second note starts.

The third note of the triplet happens 4/3 of a beat after the first (or 1 1/3 beats), so the third note starts just after the foot taps down on the second beat of the triplet. If you notice the count below, you won't see this second beat of the triplet written. This is because you don't start a note on this second beat of the triplet.

This is a confusing concept, and I would highly suggest you get someone familiar with quarter note triplets to show you some. It will be worth your time.

When you hear quarter note triplets, they feel as though they are dragging, and that's why you see "drag it" in the count. The word *drag* is split up so that the *g* goes with the *it*.

Staff 10.3   Quarter note triplets with the count.

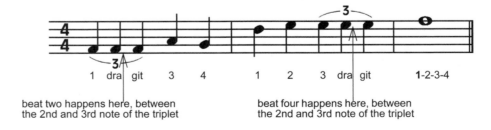

Moving On

In a week or two you may find your memory of triplets fuzzy. This is pretty normal. Just like with learning a language, learning to read music takes time and a lot of exposure. If the information about triplets is tough to remember, keep coming back to it until you've got it.

Well, it was a long section, the longest in the book, but now it's over! After the review for this chapter is the big review for the entire section.

Coming up in the next section, you'll learn about flats, sharps and naturals, the piano keyboard, the Major scale, and key signatures.

Chapter 10 Review

1. How long is an eighth note triplet in 4/4 time?

    1. One beat

2. How is a measure of eighth note triplets counted in 4/4 time?

    2. 1 tri ple 2 tri ple 3 tri ple 4 tri ple.

3. How long is a sixteenth note triplet?

    3. 1/2 beat

4. What is the count for a measure of sixteenth note triplets in 2/4 time?

    4. 1 la li + la li 2 la li + la li

5. Where is your foot positioned on the "+" part of the beat?

    5. Up

6. How long is a quarter note triplet?

    6. Two beats

7. How long is each note in the quarter note triplet?

    7. 2/3 beat

8. On which part of the foot tap does the 2nd note of the quarter note triplet fall?

    8. Just after the "+" of the first tap.

9. On which part of the foot tap does the 3rd note of the quarter note triplet fall?

    9. Just after the second tap.

10. Ask a teacher or musician to demonstrate quarter note triplets to you.

Practical Use

1. Write out three measures of 4/4 time using all the triplet figures you've learned. Don't forget the bar lines. Write in the count underneath the triplets you've written.

2. Tap or or say what you've written. If it's too difficult, simplify it until you *can* tap or say it.

3. Have someone demonstrate quarter note triplets for you. Imitate what you hear.

Basic Music Theory

PART II REVIEW

Whew! You Made It

These pages can be used to test your memory on what you've learned in Part III, and if some of the information hasn't stuck, you can go back and check it out on the page indicated below the question.

As with the chapter reviews, use your keyboard to cover up the answers while you test yourself.

When you think you've got it all down, either take the test in *Basic Music Theory Quiz Pack* (available free at www.Sol-Ut.com), or go on.

The Review

1. What is another name for meter?
   page 42

2. Where does the time signature appear?
   page 42

3. What information does the time signature give?
   page 42

4. What are the three most common time signatures?
   page 42

5. What does the top number tell you?
   page 42

6. What does the bottom number tell you?
   page 42

1. *time signature*

2. *at the beginning of a piece of music, directly after the clef*

3. *how many beats in each measure, and what type of note gets one beat*

4. *4/4, 2/4, 3/4*

5. *how many beats in one measure*

6. *what type of note gets one beat*

7. Why are different meters used?
page 42

    7. The meter depends on the rhythmic pattern of the song.

8. The count of any measure, in any time signature/meter, begins with what number?
page 48

    8. 1

9. How is a measure of quarter notes in 3/4 time counted?
page 49

    9. 1, 2, 3

10. How is a measure of half notes in 4/4 time counted?
page 49

    10. 1-2, 3-4

11. How is a whole note counted in 4/4 time?
page 49

    11. 1-2-3-4

12. When writing out the counting, what is used to indicate a rest?
page 50

    12. Parentheses ( )

13. When counting out loud, how should you count a rest?
page 50

    13. Softly

14. When counting out loud in 4/4 time, how would you say a measure of half notes?
page 49

    14. ONE-two, THREE-four

15. How long is an eighth note in common time (4/4)?
page 54

    15. 1/2 beat

16. How long is an eighth rest in 2/4 time?
page 55

    16. 1/2 beat

17. How many eighth notes in one quarter note or one beat of 3/4 time?
page 54

    17. 2

18. How are eighth notes counted in 4/4 time?
page 55

    18. 1 + 2 + 3 + 4 +

19. How is a measure of eighth rests counted in 2/4 time?
page 55

19. *(1) (+) (2) (+)*

20. How long is one sixteenth note in 4/4 time?
page 56

20. *1/4 beat*

21. How many sixteenth notes are in one quarter note or one beat of 4/4 time?
page 56

21. *4*

22. How do you count sixteenth notes in 4/4 time?
page 56

22. *1 e + a 2 e + a*
3 e + a 4 e + a

23. What does a dot do to a note?
page 62

23. *Makes it longer by half its original value*

24. How long is a dotted whole note?
page 62

24. *Six beats*

25. How long is a dotted half note?
page 62

25. *Three beats*

26. How long is a dotted quarter note?
page 63

26. *1 1/2 beats*

27. How long is a dotted eighth note?
page 64

27. *3/4 of a beat*

28. Which type of note usually follows a dotted eighth note?
page 64

28. *Sixteenth note*

29. How long is an eighth note triplet in 4/4 time?
page 68

29. *One beat*

30. How is a measure of eighth note triplets counted in 4/4 time?
page 68

30. *1 tri ple 2 tri ple 3 tri ple 4 tri ple*

31. How long is a sixteenth note triplet?
page 69

31. *1/2 beat*

32. What is the count for a measure of sixteenth note triplets in 2/4 time?
page 69

32. *1 la li + la li 2 la li + la li*

33. Where is your foot positioned on the "+" part of the beat?
page 69

33. *Up*

34. How long is a quarter note triplet?
page 70

34. *Two beats*

35. How long is each note in the quarter note triplet?
page 70

35. *2/3 beat*

36. On which part of the foot tap does the 2nd note of the quarter note triplet fall?
page 70

36. *just after the "+" of the first foot tap*

37. On which part of the foot tap does the 3rd note of the quarter note triplet fall?
page 70

37. *just after the second tap*

CHAPTER 11

INTERLUDE

DON'T SAY *PRACTICE*

I never practice; I always play.

— Wanda Landowska, 1952

In This Interlude

- Don't Say the *P* Word
- A Note on Private Teachers
- How Much to Play
- When, Where, How
- The Ideal Practice Session

Terms to Know

- **metronome**: a mechanical device used to keep perfect rhythm. Many varieties from digital to analog, electrical and mechanical. An essential tool for musicians serious about playing with rhythmic precision.
- **tuner**: a mechanical device used to check the pitch of notes you play. Used as a tool to tune stringed and wind instruments, or to help you tune pesky out-of-tune notes on your instrument.

Don't Say the P Word

Johann Sebastian Bach said, "There's nothing remarkable about it. All one has to do is hit the right keys at the right time and the instrument plays itself."

That quote was probably delivered with a heavy dose of sarcasm. If only old Bach was right and playing an instrument was that easy.

If playing an instrument well or singing well could happen only by wanting it badly enough, there would be many more great musicians in the world than there are. But that's not how it works. To learn an instrument you've got to practice. Oops, I said a bad word.

I don't like to say the p-word. When I think of the word "practice," what usually comes to mind is a boring task, one which I'm forced to do. So let's do away with that word.

I prefer a friendlier p-word. Play. Which would you prefer saying, "I've got to go practice," or "I've got to go play." I don't know about you, but I like the second much better. If you think you have to say the *p* word, try *rehearse* instead.

What does *play* mean? You play music. It's *supposed* to be fun. If it's not, something might be wrong. I say *might be wrong* because no matter what you do in this life, if you do it often enough, no matter how much you like it, there will be times when it doesn't seem so pleasant. Especially when you push yourself toward improvement. It's bound to get frustrating once in a while. Not to worry. Those feelings pass.

In order to do something well, you have to spend a lot of time doing it. This may seem obvious but you would be surprised by how many students—especially the younger ones—don't quite understand this. Whether it's sports or art or business or any old thing you care to name, to become something more than a beginner takes focused effort and time.

Now, keep in mind there are some people out there who are so naturally gifted that they need little time to master a skill. They're the type of people who can pick something up—art, sports, music, dance, mathematics, Spanish—and start doing it well almost immediately. They're the kind of people we admire and envy. They're the kind of people we secretly want to strangle.

What this section is geared towards is you and me. People with average abilities, average intelligence and average coordination. And even so, if you *are* one of those rare and gifted individuals, this section will help you too, so don't skip it.

A Note on Private Teachers

No book can teach you everything, or teach it as well as a good private teacher can. The fastest way to learn anything is one-on-one, just you and the teacher in a room. Half an hour each week is pretty standard for beginners, but an hour is better.

A good teacher can save you years of time and show you tricks that make playing much easier and more fun. A good teacher knows what songs you can handle, knows which ones are fun, and will show you things you aren't doing quite right as well as how to do them better.

A good teacher is invaluable. Find one. Study with him or her until you've soaked up all you can (usually 2-4 years), then find another and do it all over again. You'll learn the most this way, the fastest this way, and you'll never regret the money you spend. It's well worth it.

Good teachers aren't cheap though, and if you can't afford one you have several options. One good alternative, especially if you're a beginner, is to find someone who plays your instrument and is further along than you are (high school and college students work well). Another way is to find musicians that will let you hang out with them while they play. You can pick up a lot of free tips this way. All the musicians I know feel it's important to pass on knowledge of music.

How Much is Enough?

This is one of the most often-asked questions, and it's a lot like asking how much you should pay for a pair of shoes. The answer depends on many things: what do you want to spend, what *can* you spend, what do you need, what quality do you want, what style, etc., etc.

As far as playing music is concerned, you should be aware of a few things: your desire to play, your ability on the instrument, and how much time you can *make* to play (I purposefully didn't say, "how much time you can *spare*," because nobody can spare time—everyone is always busy).

The very best answer is: play as much as you feel like. That may seem like a cop-out answer, but let me explain. Playing is supposed to be enjoyable, first and foremost, never forget that. When you learn something new, there is a very high possibility of frustration. Avoid this like the plague. If you begin to feel frustrated, keep at it another couple minutes to see if the frustration goes away, and if it doesn't, stop. It's that easy. Pick it up again later in the day or tomorrow.

Come on Baby, Light my Desire

The single most valuable thing you can have is your desire. Foster it. Imagine yourself playing somewhere. Anywhere. You could be on stage in front of 10,000 screaming fans, you could be at Carnegie Hall, you could be at the local coffee shop, you could be playing a song for a loved one, or even in a room alone playing for yourself. There are many excellent players in the world who play only for personal enjoyment. Use your imagination to see yourself performing, keep with it and you'll get to experience it!

Desire will keep you motivated through exercises and repetitions and slumps in mood. The only problem with desire is that it's not like a metronome. You can't bop down to the local music store and pick some up, so you've got to foster it, be aware of it, let it grow. You can't buy it, but there are ways to increase it.

> Take a music bath once or twice a week for a few seasons, and you will find that it is to the soul what the water bath is to the body.
>
> Oliver Wendell Holmes, Jr.

Live Music is Best

The single most beneficial thing to your development as a musician is to go see music performed live. It will increase your desire to play more than any other thing. There are many places to hear live music: coffee shops, concerts, even just sitting around in a friend's living room and listening to her play. Somehow, seeing music being done right in front of you makes it more real, more within reach. Recordings are great, but live is better.

Your Stereo is Next Best

Listening to good music is important and can be very inspiring, especially if you realize the musicians you listen to were once as clueless as you may be right now. So listen as much as you can.

If you like grunge rock, get the best there is and listen to it. If you like speed metal, find the best and listen to it. If you like classical music, find the best symphony orchestras under the best conductors and listen to them. I could go on, but I'm sure you get the idea. Find the best.

And the best is simply what you *like* best. Don't give up. There is so much music out there that most of it will do nothing for you. But on the other hand, there is so much music out there, you're bound to find something you love to hear. And you'll love to play it, too. Keep your ears out and wide open.

How to Get Better

Beginnings are Delicate Times

If you're a beginner, it's essential to take things slowly. As a beginner you're trying to get the hang of a very complex task that involves many different and difficult skills, and it takes time. Stick with it. You'll get it. I have **never** run into someone who has said, "Gee, I'm sure glad I quit playing my guitar/clarinet/trumpet/piano." It's always the opposite.

Tack up encouraging notes to yourself. On my desk I have a fortune cookie message which says, "Be persistent and you will win."

As a beginner, your playing sessions might be ten to fifteen minutes, three or four times a week. The less you play, the longer it will take to get better. Remember this. It seems very common sense, but I see it all the time with new students—playing is difficult and unfamiliar at first so they don't play much or not at all and it *remains* difficult and unfamiliar and frustrating.

The less you play, the longer it will take to get better. There is no getting around this. Once a week will simply not cut it. Of course it's better than nothing, but it's too easy to forget all that information over a week's time and when you get back to your instrument, very little will have changed. This will be very frustrating. Avoid frustration by playing more often.

Play as long as you can, but don't push it too hard. Remember that the best indication of when it's time to stop is your frustration/boredom level. You have your whole life to work on this. Don't be lazy, but don't overdo it either.

Improvement

As you continue to play, you'll become better and better and the amount of time you spend on your instrument will naturally increase. This will happen for several reasons: you'll be able to play more songs, your understanding of what you need to do will increase, your skill exercises will take longer to go through, and the very best part is that it will become more and more fun!

Don't Beat Yourself Up

Remember that it usually takes a long time to sound really good, and the progress is gradual. Anyone who plays an instrument has been a beginner at one point. And let's be honest. Beginners make some really funny noises: squeaks, blats, bellows and bleats. We've all done it. It's part of the process of becoming better. Have the patience to wait out your frustrations and the funny sounds you might make. Things will get better. I promise, but only if you stick with it.

Start a New Habit

We are creatures of habit. Starting new ones is easy enough, and breaking old ones is sometimes painful. If you can make playing music an old habit, you'll never have to worry. It's a habit you'll never want to break.

One way to grow this habit is to choose a specific time every day to play. Have a routine. This will take some time to figure out and will change as you discover what works for you. Try different times of the day. Some people like early mornings and sit in a quiet house with a latté and strum their guitar, some play right after dinner or after school, some like to play just before going to bed (this option doesn't work well for brass players unless they live far from others).

Take at least one day off a week, two at most, to give yourself a rest—take a hike, read a book, take a swim, a nap, anything. Of course, if you don't *want* to take a break, that's also a good option. There are no rules.

Television

My first piece of advice is to throw the time-bandit out. No? You're unwilling to do that? Okay then, use it to your advantage. During one hour of prime time television there are over twenty minutes of advertisements. That's twenty minutes you could use to play. And besides, you don't need to buy all that stuff people are trying to sell you. Save your money and buy a nicer instrument instead. Press the mute button and play! (This technique works best when nobody else is in the house.)

When in Doubt, Leave it Out

I leave all my instruments out and ready to play. I have to be careful when I pick one up because once I do, often it's at least an hour before I can put it down again. By leaving your instrument out you can pick it up at a random moment and toss off an exercise or a song. Five minutes later you're back to what you were doing before.

Where to Do It

A Garage of One's Own

When I was a kid and had to practice trumpet (I use the *p* word on purpose—back then I didn't know the difference), my parents finally ended up sending me to the garage. It sounds cruel, but it was an excellent thing. They didn't have to hear my squawks and blats, and I didn't have to feel self-conscious about making so much noise.

When you start to play an instrument as a beginner, your self-image as a musician is very fragile. You'll feel self-conscious, maybe a little silly, and you'll be very aware of how bad you sound.

Yes, it's true. You *will* sound bad at first. That's part of it. For some it can feel embarrassing, and for others simply uncomfortable. Only a rare few don't care. If you're one of these, consider yourself lucky. If you do feel uncomfortable playing with others around, the solution is to play when you have lots of privacy, either when nobody else is home, or in a separate building. Even a closed door is better than nothing.

Repetition is the Mother of Success, and the Father of Irritation

Charles Reynolds, a master teacher and man of great enthusiasm coined the first part of that phrase, and I added the second. When you're learning to play a song, you must play it over, and over, and over, and over, often hundreds if not thousands of times. And not the whole song at once, but measure by measure until you've got the whole thing. Then you get to play the whole thing over and over and over.

It's a lot like jet skis—plenty of fun for the one doing it but not fun at all for anyone who has to listen to it. Even if you're Yo Yo Ma or Carlos Santana, the same phrase or scale or exercise played over and over and over again will drive even the most patient person bug-nuts.

Get a private place to play if you can. Those you live with will love you for it and will enjoy your music more when you're ready to perform it for them.

How to Do It

There are as many ways to play as there are people who play, but all of them share some similar characteristics. There are certain tools which can make your progress on an instrument or voice much faster.

Some of these tools are crucial, some are less so, but all of them will put you further down the road toward musical mastery if you use them correctly.

Equipment

Arturo Sandoval, a world-renown trumpet player, grew up very poor in Cuba. He wanted to play very badly. He would walk miles to the next village where someone had a copy of *Arban's Complete Conservatory Method for Trumpet*, a book that is hundreds of pages long, crammed full of thousands of exercises and songs; the trumpet player's bible. Because he couldn't afford the book, Sandoval kept returning to the distant village until he had the whole book memorized.

All you really need is your instrument and desire. The rest will come. However, here are some things which will make your experience much more pleasant and more successful in a shorter time. In order of importance they are:

- **instrument**: If you're a singer, you won't have any problems with forgetting it somewhere. Get the best instrument you can afford and treat it well.

- **metronome**: Apart from your instrument, this is the most useful tool you can own as a musician. Get one early on and use it often. I'll discuss its use later in this chapter.

- **music**: This may be method books, sheet music, or both. Not every practice session will require music. There are many things that can be done without it.

- **music stand**: There are many different types, from inexpensive fifteen dollar wire stands which fit in an instrument case to beautiful and expensive hardwood stands which aren't so portable.

- **pencil**: This will be used to mark up your music with notes to yourself and also to record your sessions if you choose to do so. Keep several in your case so you'll have one when needed.

- **practice journal**: A spiral notebook in which to keep a record of what you play, how long you play, and how you feel about your playing. You can also use this to track progress on specific exercises. This is a valuable tool to look back on. Not a requirement, but a good idea. In the index of this book you'll find photocopyable journal sheets and tracking sheets. Copy them and use them.

- **tape/CD player**: A very useful tool. Not only to provide good music to listen to, but also something you can try playing along with. Trying to figure out a favorite song is good training for your hand-ear coordination.

- **tuner**: A tuner can tell you exactly what pitch you play, and whether it's in tune or not. You're now in the world of sound and even slightly out of tune notes are audible to most listeners.

- **tape recorder**: Not essential, but very helpful. Hearing yourself recorded is much different than hearing yourself while playing, and you'll be surprised how many mistakes you hear that you weren't aware of while you recorded. The tape recorder tells no lies.

- **instrument stand**: Not essential, but useful. If you leave your instrument out you'll pick it up and play more often. My guitars, trumpet and flute are always out on their stands.

The Ideal Session

The Best Time

Directly after a lesson is the very best time to practice. When all that new information is fresh in your head, take the time to go over it again on your own. If there is something you don't understand, write down any questions or problems you may have so your teacher can explain them in your next lesson.

Warm-up

This is a short part. Use it to make sure your instrument works properly, is tuned, and you have all you need for the coming session (valve oil, music, extra strings, reeds, pencil, etc.).

Depending on your instrument, there are several things you want to keep in mind. Generally speaking, keep things in the low register of your instrument and do exercises to get you fingers, your wind, and your brain warmed up.

Exercises

If a playing session is a meal, this section is the broccoli. It may not taste very good (unless you like lots of cheese), but it's good for you. Do the exercises for your instrument religiously—it will pay off. Dessert is coming up.

This is when you do your scales, finger-stretching exercises, long tones, interval studies, chord progressions…whatever your teacher assigns you. The list is nearly endless, but your time is limited. Keep time spent on exercises down to about 1/3 of your playing session.

If you're a beginner and none of the above makes sense to you, don't worry, it will soon.

Long Tones

When I was a beginner in middle school, my mom made me practice for half an hour every day, five days a week. Some of the time I hated it, but I'm very grateful now. On the days I really didn't want to be at it, I would choose one note and play it for the entire half hour. Well, I *did* stop to breathe now and then. If I got daring and a little less stubborn, I *might* switch to another note. I didn't know it, but I had stumbled upon an essential ingredient to creating a good sound on *any* instrument.

When you play long tones, take a huge breath (if you're a wind player) and play a note that is comfortable for you. Don't let your mind wander, though. Listen closely to the sound. Make it as perfectly clear and clean as you are able. You'll be surprised at the wavering and crackles and hitches in your sound.

Experiment with different qualities of sound (bright, dark, open, pinched, soft, loud, etc.)

If you're a string player, long tones are equally important but done differently. It's a good way to improve your bowing, or to check your finger position all the way up the neck on each string.

I take the time to mention long tones because they're often neglected and are important to achieve a good sound. And they're so easy to do! Especially for beginners. Three or four minutes is long enough. Do them every day and you'll soon have a great sound on your instrument.

The Heart of the Session

Here is where you will do most of your work. This is the longest part of your playing session. This is where you work on the song you're learning to perform. Use the *tuner*, the *metronome* and the *tape recorder*.

The Metronome (or: The Torture Device)

There is a legend about Chinese Water Torture. I have no idea if it's true, but it makes for a good story. You're strapped down to a table and above you is a barrel full of water. The barrel has a small hole in it through which a tiny drop of water falls every minute or so down onto your forehead. This goes on for a long time, finally driving you mad. The metronome is kind of like that, only it's actually *good* for you.

A metronome is a mechanical foot-tap which keeps perfect time. Each metronome has a series of gradations on it, usually from around 40-200 **beats per minute (bpm)**. The higher the number, the faster the clicks. You set the metronome on the tempo you need and away you go.

Metronomes come in many different shapes and sizes. There are electronic varieties with different beeps and dings, or the simpler wind-up pendulum variety like the one pictured. Loudness of your instrument and the metronome is a consideration when buying one. Some have an earplug that will send the clicks right to your ear, a good option for loud instruments, like drums and brass.

Nobody likes being wrong. That's one of the reasons metronomes are so neglected. They keep perfect time and we humans usually do not. But if you think about it, we learn the most when we're wrong, as long as we're paying attention. So really, being wrong can turn into a good thing.

Of course *staying* wrong is *not* a good thing. You use a metronome to fix mistakes in rhythm.

How to Use the Metronome

When you're learning a song, use the metronome on only a short section at one time—several measures at the most, two notes at the least. It's important to *start slowly*. Whatever you learn is what you will play, so ***if you set it at a speed which is too difficult, you will learn mistakes***.

1 Set the metronome to a tempo that is slow enough so your playing feels comfortable and easy. Play the short section through a few times at this tempo. If you're making mistakes, the tempo is too fast. Slow it down some more until you find an easy tempo. Play 5-10 times correctly before going on.

2 Click up to the next fastest tempo. One click only. The clicks may not *sound* any faster, but when you play the passage you'll notice the difference. Play at this tempo until it's easy. Play 5-10 times perfectly.

3 Click up to the next fastest tempo. One click only. Play the section several times at the new tempo. It may take more repetitions to get the passage perfect. Keep at it. If it's too hard at the new tempo, go back one click until it's perfect again. Play 5-10 times perfectly.

4 Continue with this process until the correct tempo of the song is reached. This may take several days, weeks or months.

Remember, you're in this for the long haul. Don't bash your head against something for too long. If you become very frustrated or discouraged, go back to a slower tempo and play it a few times correctly before you quit.

The first song I learned on guitar was much too difficult for my abilities and I probably shouldn't have chosen it, but I did. At first, the song was so incredibly slow it was

---

unrecognizable. It took about three or four days (of two hours a day) to get each 4-measure passage up to a decent speed. Using the metronome as mentioned above, I learned the song, but it took me six months and probably drove my wife and dog crazy.

You may not be so foolish as to choose such a hard piece at first, but if you do, using the metronome works very, very well. Try it. Play with it. Come up with your own variations. There are no rules.

The Tape Recorder Tells No Lies

I got my first stereo when I was eleven. It had a tape deck with a microphone attachment. During my enforced *practice* sessions, I came up with a plan to get away with not practicing. I'd record something on the tape deck, then turn up the volume and play it back, sometimes twice. That way everyone in the house would think I was still playing. *Ha! That'll show them*, I must have thought. *I'm not actually practicing.*

But I was. Listening to yourself play an instrument on a recording is a lot like listening to your *voice* on a recording. It doesn't sound anything like what you thought it sounded like. Every little wobble and flub and mistake is painfully obvious. Again, we learn the most from making mistakes.

But as with the metronome, don't let those mistakes stand. Fix 'em.

Try recording yourself. You'll be surprised, and you might like doing it. You will definitely improve!

You Can Tune a Trumpet but You Can't Tuna Fish

A *tuner* is a valuable tool. If you play a fretted instrument like guitar or electric bass, you'll probably need a tuner only to tune your strings.

The rest of us benefit a lot by using a tuner. With a tuner, you can become more aware of how your instrument plays, where it's out of tune, and what you need to do with your mouth or your finger placement to correct the pitch. Every wind instrument has certain notes which are out of tune. With a tuner you can find these out-of-tune notes on your instrument.

The best type of tuner for this sort of thing is an analog tuner, one which has a little arm that swings back and forth to show how sharp or flat you are. If the little arm is straight up at "0," you're in tune.

There are many types of tuners. Visit your local music store for a demonstration and decide which will work best for you.

Other Ways to Play

You aren't limited to playing only during your daily session. There are opportunities throughout the day to hone your skills, and you don't even need your instrument.

For brass players, there's always buzzing (if you don't know what this is, ask a brass player to demonstrate for you). This can be done either with or without a mouthpiece. For other wind players there are other lip-strengthening exercises.

Using only your lips (no teeth), hold a pencil out parallel to the ground for as long as you can. This will strengthen your pucker muscles.

For fingerings, woodwind players can practice on a pencil. Valve players can get an old valve casing from an instrument at the pawn shop and carry that around instead of the whole instrument; or simply do fingerings on your thumb or palm. String players can find an old instrument, saw off a five-fret section of the fretboard and use that to practice fingering.

These are just a few suggestions. Use your noggin to think up some other options. There may be a lot of "down" time in your day which you can use to improve your playing.

Another Instrument

Don't be afraid to switch instruments. If an instrument just isn't working, give it a fair chance for two or three months. Then, if you still want to play, try something else.

I have a wonderful guitar student who began on the trombone. After a couple months, she decided the trombone wasn't for her and switched to guitar. She's playing very well and is progressing quickly. She was not good on trombone. She's becoming an excellent guitar player.

Even if you're doing well on an instrument you can always pick up another. Another of my students, a good beginning trumpet player, expressed interest in the flute. We had a flute lesson and he has decided to play that as well.

Many famous musicians started on a different instrument and continued on to learn many others. Stevie Wonder, Prince, and Beck play *all* the instruments on their early albums. Beck still does it. Those three are only a few. There are many more. Nowhere is there a rule that says you can only play one instrument. Heck, learn 'em all if you want to. A new instrument can light the fire inside you again.

And if you can read music, learning songs on a new instrument is much, much easier.

Speaking of reading music, let's get back to it!

Some Instruments

Ever wonder what all those instruments are? Ever call a trombone a trumpet, or other embarrassing *faux pas*? Now some of your problems are over. Below are many instruments and their names.

Accordion   Bass Clarinet   Bassoon   Banjo

Oboe   Tenor Flute   Piccolo   French

Horn   Flugel Horn   Trombone   Alp Horn

Baritone Horn   Baritone   Tuba   Timpani

Castanets   Sitar   Washtub Bass   English

horn   Cello   Double Bass   The saxes

For loads of information about your instrument, visit the SolUt web site: **www.sol-ut.com**

SolŪt Press

www.Sol-Ut.com

PART THREE

Clef Notes

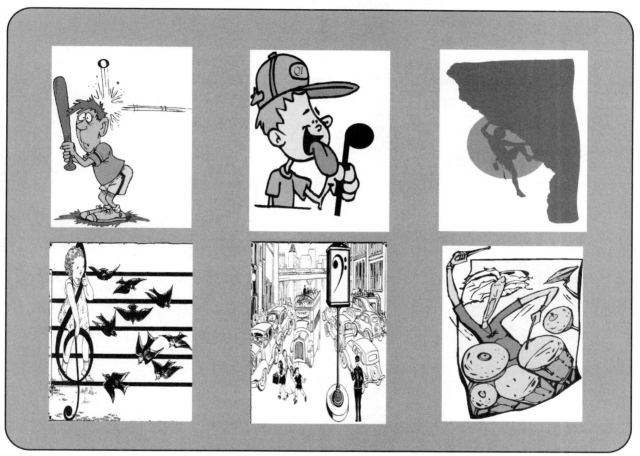

In This Section You Will Learn:

- Pitch
- Note Names
- Clefs in General
- Treble Clef
- Bass Clef
- Rhythm Clef

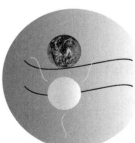

SolŪt Press

Support Music and Musicians.
www.Sol-Ut.com

THE WIND-UP AND THE PITCH

*Making music should not be left to
the professionals*

— Michelle Shocked

In This Chapter

- Space notes
- Line notes
- High and Low
- Leger Lines

Terms to Know

- **line note**: a note with a staff line through it.
- **space note**: a note in a space of the staff.
- **leger line**: a short line used to extend the range of a staff.
- **range**: the highness or lowness of a note.

Spaced Out and Lined Up

Notes on the staff will be either *space notes* or *line notes*. A space note is any note which rests within a space of the staff *without crossing over a line*. A line note is any note split through the middle by a line. Notice in the examples that I've included leger line notes.

Space Notes

A space note fits within a space on the staff (or between leger lines). At first, it might be tough to draw a note exactly in the space, but keep at it. If you go over the line, your space note may look more like a line note.

Staff 12.1   Space notes, low to high.

Line Notes

Line notes have a line going through their middle. When you draw a line note be sure the line goes through the middle of the note, otherwise it might look more like a space note, and that can be confusing.

Staff 12.2   Line notes, low to high.

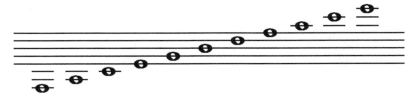

Ah, Togetherness

Line and space notes alternate one after the other. After a line note comes a space note, and after a space note comes a line note. This message brought and delivered to you by our Department of Redundancy Department. Here's what it looks like:

Staff 12.3   Line and space notes combined, low to high (there are notes both higher and lower than those shown here).

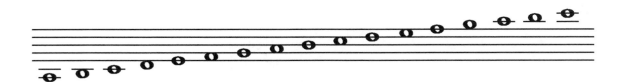

Basic Music Theory

The High and the Lowly

Pitch is not only something you find in a tree and at a baseball game. As it relates to sound, Webster's definition of pitch is: *the property of a sound and especially a musical tone that is determined by the frequency of the waves producing it.* Don't you sometimes just hate dictionaries?

What pitch means in music is the highness or lowness of a sound or note.

If the pitch of one note is higher than another, it will be written higher up on the staff. And if one note's pitch is lower than another's, it will be written lower down on the staff.

Staff 12.4   Examples of low and high.

This note is higher than .... this one.   This note is lower than .... this one.

What? *More* Lines?

Learning Leger Lines

Take a look at the staves at the beginning of the chapter on page 92. See the notes above and below the staff? Most notes are written on the staff, but some notes are higher or lower than the staff can show. When a note goes beyond the range of the staff (higher or lower), small horizontal lines are used to show where the staff would be if it had more than five lines and four spaces. These are called **leger lines** (sometimes spelled "ledger lines").

The words "leger line" appeared around 1700, though the practice of writing leger lines is older. To keep music from looking cluttered, leger lines are never used unless they're with a note. How about some examples?

The last two measures show extreme examples which you'll rarely see, but give you an idea of what's possible.

Staff 12.5   Four measures of leger line examples

Moving On

Okay. You should now have a good handle on line and space notes and how pitch is shown in written music. Is it all clear? Be sure you've got it before you move on.

Coming up in Chapter 5 you'll learn the musical alphabet and how these letter names are applied to the lines and spaces and leger lines of the staff.

Chapter 12 Study Guide

1. What is a line note?

2. What is a space note?

3. What does pitch mean in music?

4. If one note's pitch is higher than another, it will be written _____ on the staff.

5. If one note's pitch is lower than another, it will be written _____ on the staff.

6. In the examples below:

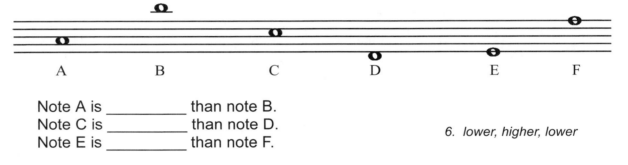

| A | B | C | D | E | F |

Note A is _____ than note B.
Note C is _____ than note D.
Note E is _____ than note F.

7. In the examples below:

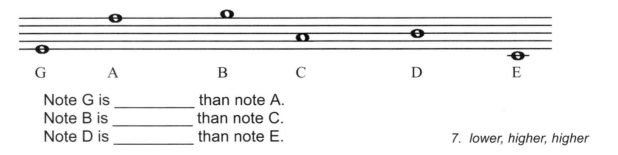

| G | A | B | C | D | E |

Note G is _____ than note A.
Note B is _____ than note C.
Note D is _____ than note E.

1. Any note with a line through it

2. Any note lying in a space

3. The highness or lowness of a note

4. Higher

5. Lower

6. lower, higher, lower

7. lower, higher, higher

8. The stems of notes above the third line go _____.

9. The stems of notes below the third line go _____.

10. Notes on the third line have stems which go _____.

11. When will a note on the 3rd line have its stem up?

12. What are leger lines?

13. What are leger lines used for?

14. Draw in some leger lines both above and below this staff. Draw some notes on your leger lines. Use any kind of note.

8. Down

9. Up

10. Either up or down

11. When it is with other notes with their stems up

12. Small lines above and below the staff

13. Used for notes that are higher or lower than the staff will show

Practical Use

1. In the first staff below, in 4/4 time, draw in several quarter, half, and/or eighth notes per measure. Vary the highness and lowness. Use leger lines. Go through your example and identify lower and higher from note to note. Write in the counting.

2. On the second blank staff below, draw in all the line and space notes from one leger line below the staff all the way up to one leger line above the staff. Use any type of note. Go further than that if you are bold and adventurous.

Basic Music Theory

Home, Home on the Ranges

Range refers to the notes an instrument is able to play, from lowest to highest. Each example below shows the range of an instrument from its lowest note to its highest note. There are some exceptions, like pedal tones (very low notes) for brass, a low B foot for a flute, you can put your foot into the bell of a baritone sax and get a half step lower, and other such tricks, but for now don't worry about those unless you want to.

Since voice *is* an instrument, I'll show vocal ranges first. I'm doing this mostly to show you that all instruments use leger lines. You didn't believe me, did you?

While you look at these examples, compare the ranges of the instruments. Notice that the highest note for a soprano is higher than the highest note for an alto; or notice the guitar is able to play lower than the violin.

Staff 12.6 Ranges for Voice: Soprano, Alto, Tenor, Bass

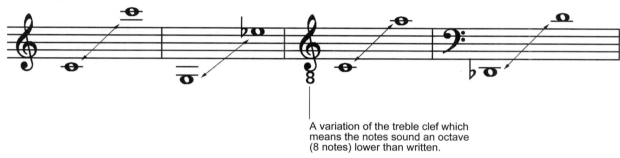

A variation of the treble clef which means the notes sound an octave (8 notes) lower than written.

Staff 12.7 Ranges for: Violin, Guitar, Bass.

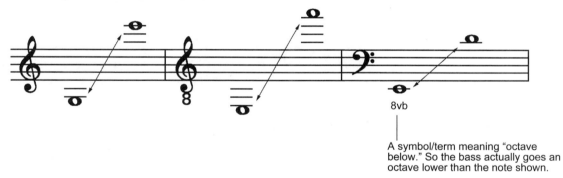

8vb

A symbol/term meaning "octave below." So the bass actually goes an octave lower than the note shown.

Staff 12.8 Ranges for: Trumpet, Alto Sax, Flute, Bb Clarinet.

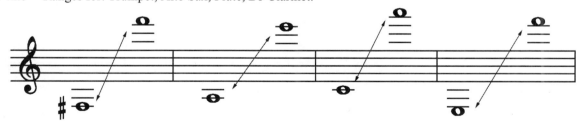

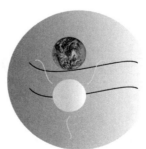

SolŪt Press

Support Music and Musicians.
www.Sol-Ut.com

A NOTE BY ANY OTHER NAME WOULD SOUND AS SWEET

Sweetest melodies
Are those that are by
distance made more sweet.

— Wordsworth, *Personal Talk.*

In This Chapter

- The Musical Alphabet
- Note Names
- Naming Leger Line Notes

Terms to Know

- **A, B, C, D, E, F, G**: letter names used to name musical notes.

What's in a Name?

You'll be happy to find you only need the first seven letters of the alphabet for music.

The music alphabet uses **A**, **B**, **C**, **D**, **E**, **F**, and **G**. You'll never find an "H" in music, or a "Q", or anything other than **A through G**. This is one of those few rules that has *no exceptions*!

Remember when we talked about line and space notes coming one after the other? If not, see "Ah, Togetherness" on page 92. The notes are named alphabetically when the notes are written one after the other (line-space-line-space, etc.).

Round and Round

But wait a minute, you're saying, I *know* there are more than seven notes in music. There are at least 88 on a piano keyboard, right? What are *their* names?

Good question. After **G**, the pattern begins again with **A**. Below is an example showing this.

Don't worry about the things you see that you don't know yet, like the funny-looking symbol at the beginning of the staff; you'll learn it in the next chapter. Focus on the letter names and how they work.

Staff 13.1   Note names in the treble clef. Notice the letter change from the 3rd note to the 4th note.

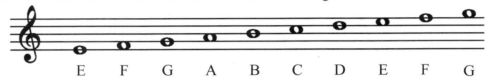

E   F   G   A   B   C   D   E   F   G

Remember Leger Lines?

Notes on leger lines or spaces are named the same way. Following is an example with leger lines below the staff. These are the first 8 notes for both guitar and clarinet. Again, don't worry about the things we haven't gone over yet. Focus on the note names only.

Staff 13.2   Leger line note names below the treble clef staff.

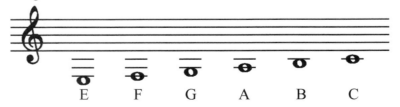

E   F   G   A   B   C

And here are some examples of leger line note names above the staff. Notice there is a different loopy symbol at the beginning of this music. Not to fear, you'll learn what that is soon. For now you can ignore it. These are notes you might find in trombone music, electric bass music, or bassoon music.

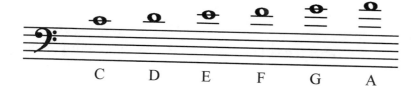

C   D   E   F   G   A

Moving On

Not much to note names, is there? Just remember that A-G repeats over and over and that's all you need. Make sure you know the information in the Chapter Review on the next page before you go on. Shouldn't be too hard.

Chapter 13 Study Guide

1. What letters are used to name notes in music?

    1. A B C D E F G

2. What letter comes after G?

    2. A

3. What kind of note comes right before or after a space note?

    3. A line note

4. What kind of note comes right before or after a line note?

    4. A space note

5. Write out five times, "After G comes A."

6. Can you think of a better system for naming notes? How about using colors? Shapes? Textures? Tastes? Smells? Numbers?

Practical Use

1. Say the letters A-G in a repeated loop as fast as you can. Do the same thing backwards. Say every other letter: A, C, E, G, B etc. Say every other letter, but start with B. Say every third letter until you've said them all. Every fourth. Every fifth.

2. Write out the letter names under the notes on the staves below. A reference pitch has been given as a starting point. In what specific way are the two systems of lettering different?

3. Write out each system of lettering the staff on the blank staves below. In addition to whole notes you may also use quarter, half, eighth or sixteenth notes.

A

C

Basic Music Theory

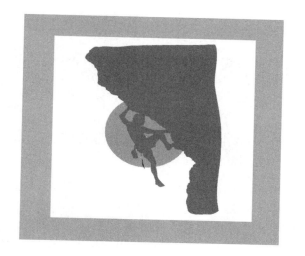

GOING OVER THE CLEF

*Sometimes it takes a long time to play
like yourself.*

— Miles Davis

In This Chapter

- What is a Clef?
- What a Clef does
- Types of Clefs

Terms to Know

- **clef**: a symbol found at the beginning of a musical staff which indicates the pitches for that staff.
- **bass clef**: the clef used for instruments of low pitch. Indicates where the note "F" is on the staff.
- **c clef**: a moveable clef which indicates the note "C" is on the staff.
- **rhythm clef**: a clef used for percussion instruments and any instrument with a non-definite pitch.
- **treble clef**: the clef used for instruments of high pitch. Indicates where the note "G" is on the staff.

What's a Clef?

A *clef* is a symbol used at the beginning of a musical staff to tell the reader which letter name goes with which line or space. The word *clef* didn't show up until around the middle 1500s. Clef is a French word that means *key*, as in, "Hey man, what *key* are we in?"

In early music, a letter was written at the beginning of the text of a plainchant (remember monophonic music on page 15?). The letter told the singer which note to start on.

Around 1000 AD some bright soul thought to draw a line from the letter all the way across the page. Then Guido di Arezzo added more lines and we had our staff. Over time, composers made that beginning letter more and more fancy until it no longer looked like a letter at all. That was probably when somebody in France in the middle of the 1500s decided to call them clefs.

There are several different kinds of clefs: **C clefs**, **treble clef**, **bass clef**, and **rhythm clef** (also called the **neutral** or **percussion clef**). We'll only be learning the three most common ones: treble clef, bass clef, and the rhythm clef.

Staff 14.1   The Clefs.

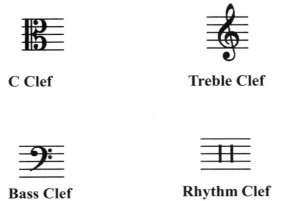

C Clef   Treble Clef

Bass Clef   Rhythm Clef

Each clef has something which shows the letter name of one line. Because you now know how letter names are used in music ("A" through "G", right?), you can figure out what all the other letters are for that staff once you know the name of one line. I'll show you how when we look at each clef in its own chapter.

For now, just remember a clef points to and names one line of the staff. I'll show you all the gory details when we go over each clef in its own chapter.

Some clefs are used more frequently than others. We'll get the odd ones out of the way first so you can forget them more quickly. You'll rarely (if ever) need them, unless you're a viola player or a trombone player with a good high range.

C Clefs

The **C clef** isn't used much any more, except by viola players and occasionally trombone and bassoon players.

It's pretty easy to imagine the symbol looks like the letter *C*, which is what it used to be. It's also obvious which line is being indicated. That big arrow pointer in the middle is what tells you which line or space is *C*.

The C clef can be confusing at first because it's a ***moveable clef***. Depending on which line the clef indicates, the name of the clef is different. Confused? Don't worry about it. You don't really need to know much about these clefs, but you should be able to generally identify them and know what they do. In case you already forgot, they're C clefs.

Actually, *all* clefs are moveable, but over time only the C clef has retained its mobility.

I couldn't resist, so here are the names of the different C clefs. Feel free to forget them immediately. Except maybe you should remember that the alto clef is used by viola players.

Staff 14.2   The four types of C Clef.

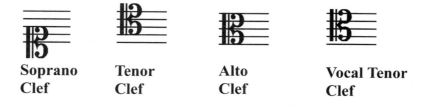

Soprano Clef   **Tenor Clef**   **Alto Clef**   **Vocal Tenor Clef**

Treble Clef

This is the most common clef. Remember up above when I said each clef has something about it which tells the letter name of a line? Well, with treble clef, it's the inner loop which circles the second line and gives it a name.

What name, you ask? What letter does the treble clef look like? Take a guess now and see if you're right. You'll find out all these niggling details in the next chapter.

The treble clef used to be a moveable clef like the c clef, but has taken up permanent residence on that second line.

Staff 14.3   The treble clef. Notice how the inner loop circles the second line.

Treble clef is used for instruments with a high pitch. Some of them are: piccolo, flute, clarinet, oboe, guitar, violin, French horn, saxophone, trumpet, and piano.

Bass Clef

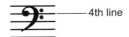 The second most common clef. The bass clef uses both the head (that bulbous part) and those two dots to indicate which line it names.

The bass clef was also once a letter. Which one do you think it was? We'll go over the details in Chapter 9. The only thing to remember at the moment is that both the head of the bass clef and the dots indicate the fourth line.

Staff 14.4 The Bass Clef. The bass clef indicates the fourth line.

Bass clef is used for instruments with a low sound. Some of them are: tuba, cello, double bass, trombone, bassoon, electric bass, and piano.

Because of their large range between high and low, keyboard instruments like piano, organ, and synthesizer use *both* the treble and bass clefs.

Rhythm Clef

 This is a clef which shows rhythms, not pitches like the other clefs.

The real name for this clef is the **neutral clef**. It's also called the **percussion clef** because it's used by percussionists and drummers and other instruments that produce a sound that isn't a clear pitch. These types of instruments are called non-pitched instruments.

For clarity's sake, from here on I'll call it a rhythm clef.

Staff 14.5 The Rhythm Clef. Notice how this clef carefully avoids indicating any one line?

The rhythm clef was never a letter and doesn't indicate any specific line. For this reason, letter names aren't used with this clef. Because the instruments that use this clef have no clear pitch, there's no need for letter names. Sound simple? Well, it is and it isn't. We'll go over the details of this clef in Chapter 10.

Some instruments that use rhythm clef are: drum set, small percussion (tambourine, maracas, claves, triangle, vibra-slap, guiro, etc.—the list is nearly endless), snare drum, bass drum, and anything you can hit to make a sound. A percussionist's instruments are everywhere!

Moving On

Okay, once you've got the general details of clefs down, you'll be ready to chew more deeply into the juicy specifics of each clef. We'll start with treble clef in Chapter 15.

Chapter 14 Study Guide

1. What did clefs used to be?

2. About when and where was the word *clef* first used?

3. What does a clef do?

4. What are the three most common clefs?

5. Which line does the treble clef name?

6. Which line does the bass clef name?

7. Which instruments use the rhythm clef?

8. Which line does the rhythm clef name?

9. On any scrap of paper, draw five treble clefs.

10. On the same piece of paper, draw five bass clefs.

11. On the same piece of paper, draw five rhythm clefs.

12. Name two instruments which use treble clef.

13. Name two instruments which use bass clef.

14. Go make yourself a snack.

1. A letter at the beginning of a piece of music indicating a specific note.

2. Mid-1500s, France

3. Names a line of the staff which also names the rest of the staff.

4. Treble clef, bass clef, rhythm clef.

5. 2nd

6. 4th

7. Drums and other non-pitched instruments.

8. None.

12. Some possibilities: flute, piano, guitar, trumpet, sax, piccolo, violin, F horn, oboe, clarinet, accordion

13. Some possibilities: trombone, tuba, piano, bass guitar, acoustic bass, electric bass, bassoon, baritone, euphonium, timpani/kettle drum, double tenor steel drum...

Practical Use

1. Below (if this is your book) or on your copied staff paper draw a line of treble clefs, a line of bass clefs and a line of rhythm clefs. Experiment. See how fast you can make each one and still have it look like a clef.

2. On a blank staff, draw a bass clef. Since the 4th line is F, place a letter name on all the other lines and spaces.

3. On a blank staff, draw a treble clef. Since the 2nd line is G, place a letter name on all the other lines and spaces.

4. Invent your own clef.

NO TROUBLE WITH TREBLE

The flute is not an instrument which has a good moral effect; it is too exciting.

— Aristotle, *Politics*

In This Chapter

- The Treble Clef
- The Letter *G*
- Notes on the Treble Clef Staff
- Mnemonic Devices for Lines and Spaces

Terms to Know

- **G clef**: another name for the treble clef as it places G on the staff.
- **mnemonic device**: a method used to speed and improve memorization.

Golly G

Okay, I'm sure you're dying of suspense. The **treble clef** used to be the letter **G**

You can kind of see its "g-ness" if you squint your eyes and use some imagination. The treble clef is also called the **G clef** because it shows where the note G is on the staff.

The inner loop of the treble clef circles the second line and thus names it *G*.

Staff 15.1   The treble clef, languidly looping line two.

Once you know where "G" is, use the musical alphabet (A-G) to fill in the rest of the notes. Remember that when naming notes in order, the notes go: line, space, line, space, line, space, etc. Like so:

Staff 15.2   The treble clef note names, alphabetically from the bottom line to the top of the staff.

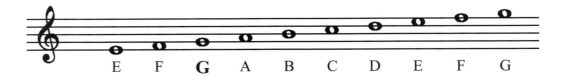

What? You Want it Easier? Okay.

Instead of memorizing that long string of letters above, you can memorize two short strings of letters. Five letters for the lines, and four letters for the spaces.

A **mnemonic device** will make it even easier.

A *What* Device?

Mnemonic (the first m is silent) came from a Greek word meaning *to remember*. A mnemonic device is a trick you can use to remember a long series of things—grocery lists, test answers or, in this case, note names.

Use a mnemonic device to learn the names of the lines and spaces. Usually the sillier, crazier or weirder the sentence you make up, the easier it is to remember.

Mnemonics for Treble Clef Lines

Staff 15.3   The treble clef line-names.

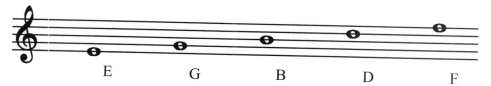

E   G   B   D   F

Empty	**E**lephants	**E**very
Garbage	**G**o	**G**ood
Before	**B**ackwards	**B**oy
Dad	**D**own	**D**eserves
Flips	**F**reeways	**F**udge

Mnemonics for Treble Clef Spaces

Staff 15.4   The treble clef spaces.

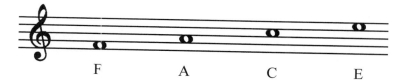

F   A   C   E

Fat	**F**arting	**F**requent
Alligators	**A**lways	**A**sking
Chew	**C**auses	**C**an
Elephants	**E**nemies	**E**nlighten

Take a couple minutes to come up with your own mnemonic device. If you make up your own, you're more likely to remember it. But, if nothing comes to you, memorize one from above that you like, or just use the word *face*.

If you come up with some good ones, send them to me: **BMT@QuestionsInk.com** and I'll put the best ones in the next edition of *Basic Music Theory* and give you credit for your ideas.

Moving On

Because so many instruments use treble clef, it's important to learn this clef even if you're instrument uses another type of clef. Once you understand this clef and how it names the second line you'll be ready for Chapter 16, which shows you all the fascinating details of the bass clef.

Chapter 15 Study Guide

1. What letter did the treble clef used to be?

2. The inner loop of the treble
     clef circles which line?

3. What is a mnemonic device?

4. What letter name does the treble clef give to the
     2nd line?

5. On a piece of blank staff paper, draw a dozen
     treble clefs. Try them in different sizes. Try to
     loop the second line of the staff.

6. What is another name for the treble clef?

7. What are the names of the treble clef lines?

8. What are the names of the treble clef spaces?

9. What is your mnemonic device for remembering
     the lines of the treble clef staff?

10. What is your mnemonic device for remembering
     the spaces of the treble clef staff?

1. G

3. 2nd

4. A trick to improve memory

5. G

6. G clef

7. E G B D F

8. F A C E

Practical Use

1. Put your *right* hand up in front of your face, palm facing you (you're using your right hand because that's the treble clef hand when you play piano). Use your left hand to point to the fingertips and "valleys" of the right hand fingers. Say each line/space name as you touch it. Look at the illustration below if you need a little help. Be sure to say the names out loud and to touch your hand. It'll help you remember.

2. On the staff below write in the line and space numbers. Draw a treble clef and then write the correct letter names in the lines and spaces. Also name two leger lines above the staff, and two leger lines below the staff (don't forget the spaces between leger lines).

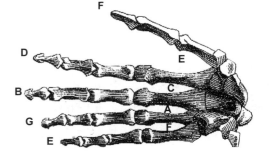

Basic Music Theory

THE BASS OF THE CLEF

Never look at the trombones. You'll only encourage them.

— Richard Strauss

In This Chapter

- The Bass Clef
- The Letter *F*
- Names of Bass Clef Lines and Spaces
- Nmore Mnemonics for the Lines and Spaces

Terms to Know

- **F clef**: another name for the bass clef as it places F on the staff.

This Clef is Not a Fish!

Remember clefs used to be letters way back when? Well, **bass clef** is no exception (by the way, this bass is not a fish. This kind of bass is pronounced *base*).

The bass clef used to be the letter *F* until those nutty artistic-type composers kept messing with it, making it fancier and fancier until we got what we have today, something that looks nothing like an *F*. And even though it looks nothing like an *F*, it's called the **F clef** because it shows us where the note *F* is on the staff.

Staff 16.1   The bass clef in all its bulbousness.

The bass clef tells us that the fourth line is an *F* in two ways. The first way is the head of the clef, the round part at the top left of the clef. It's smack-dab on the fourth line. In case that isn't enough, there are also two little dots which straddle the fourth line as if they're saying, "Hey! Hey You! This is an F!"

Staff 16.2   The bass clef as it sits on the staff. Notice the 4th line?

Okay, you know the drill. Now that you know the name of that one line, you can apply the musical alphabet to all the spaces above and below it.

Staff 16.3   Note names on the bass clef staff.

Nmore Mnemonics

Here are some more memory tricks to remember the bass clef line and space names.

Mnemonics for Bass Clef Lines

Staff 16.4   The bass clef lines.

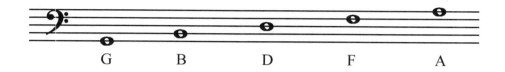

G   B   D   F   A

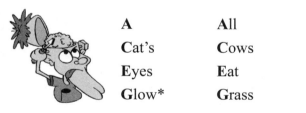

Good	**G**reat	**G**oofy
Bubbles	**B**ig	**B**abies
Do	**D**ogs	**D**o
Fizz	**F**ight	**F**unny
Always	**A**lligators*	**A**cts

*Created by Preston Epley of Wasilla, Alaska.

Mnemonics for Bass Clef Spaces

Staff 16.5   The **bass clef** space names.

A   C   E   G

A	**A**ll	**A**ll
Cat's	**C**ows	**C**ars
Eyes	**E**at	**E**at
Glow*	**G**rass	**G**as

*Created by Erin Downey of Big Lake, Alaska.

Make Up Your Own

Take a couple minutes to make up your own mnemonic device for the bass clef lines and spaces. If you make your own, and make it wacky, it'll be easier to remember.

Moving On

Even if you're instrument uses a different clef, it's still good to know bass clef. Once you've got it memorized, you're ready for Chapter 9 in which you'll learn about the rhythm clef.

Chapter 16 Study Guide

1. What letter did the bass clef used to be?

   1. F

2. Which staff line goes between the two dots of the bass clef?

   2. 4th

3. Which line is the bass clef head on?

   3. 4th

4. What letter name does the bass clef give to the fourth line?

   4. F

5. On a scratch piece of paper, draw a dozen bass clefs. Don't forget the dots!

6. What are the names of the bass clef lines?

   6. G B D F A

7. What are the names of the bass clef spaces?

   7. A C E G

8. What is another name for the bass clef?

   8. F clef

9. What is your mnemonic device for remembering the bass clef lines?

10. What is your mnemonic device for remembering the bass clef spaces?

Practical Use

1. Again with the hand. Left hand this time, palm facing you (you're using the left hand because that's the bass hand when you play piano). Pretend your hand is the bass clef staff. Name the fingers and "valleys" between your fingers using the bass clef scheme.

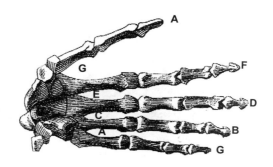

2. On the staves below draw some bass clefs. Write in the letter names for the lines and spaces. Name two high leger lines, and two low ones (don't forget to name the spaces between the leger lines.

Meet Harry Pitts, champion Armpit Player. Says Harry, "Shoot, it ain't no problem learnin' bass clef. I been readin' it for years." Harry is currently at work writing out Gershwin show tunes in bass clef for his instrument.

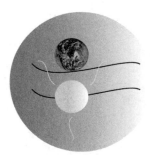

SolŪt Press

Support Music and Musicians.
www.Sol-Ut.com

To Fathom the Rhythm Clef

Music is nothing else but wild sounds civilized into time and tune.

— Thomas Fuller, *History of the Worthies of England.*

In This Chapter

- The Rhythm Clef
- The Single Line Rhythm Clef
- The 5-Line Rhythm Clef
- The Drum Set
- Mno mnemonics!

No Letters With this Staff

Unlike the other clefs, the ***rhythm clef*** doesn't show pitch (the high and low of notes), so there is no need for letter names. The rhythm clef shows rhythms. Go figure.

This clef didn't start out as another letter, because no letters are used with the rhythm clef. Doesn't this sound like this should be easier than treble or bass clef? Well, guess again....

Staff 17.1   The **rhythm clef** in all its neutral-ness.

Why No Note Names?

Remember that note names show what pitch a note is? If not, take a look at "The High and the Lowly" on page 12-93 for information about pitch, and look at example 5.1 on page 100.

Percussion instruments, most of them, don't have definite pitches like other instruments do. Compare the sound of a flute to the sound of a drum. Flute is an instrument with high notes and low notes and everything in between. A drum has only one pitch.

The One-Line Staff with Rhythm Clef

If only one pitch, why not only one line? Great question. Some single-instrument percussion music *is* written on one line. The line looks something like this:

Staff 17.2   Single staff line with rhythm clef.

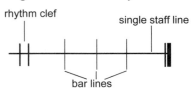

Instruments, not Pitches

You might be wondering, "Why not *always* use just one line?"

Beginners often use one line when playing snare drum, or bass drum or a small percussion instrument because it's easier to read. But soon one line isn't enough. Percussionists have dozens of instruments to learn, and there are usually many more than two instruments used in a song, and they all need a place on the staff.

Some Percussion Instruments

These are just a few percussion instruments which use the rhythm clef:

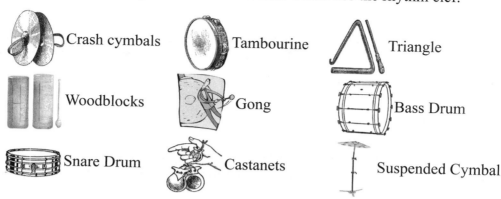

Crash cymbals · Tambourine · Triangle

Woodblocks · Gong · Bass Drum

Snare Drum · Castanets · Suspended Cymbal

The 5-Line Staff with Rhythm Clef

The drum set has at least three instruments, and usually many more. We'll use the drum set as a focus to learn the 5-line staff with rhythm clef. The drum set is also called the "trap set", or simply "traps." In the first half of the 1900s the drum set was created and was called a "contraption" which was then shortened to "traps." I'll use "drum set" from here on out.

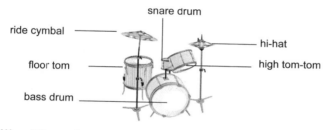

Though many people play with less, the typical drum set has 8 or 9 instruments: snare drum, bass drum, hi-hat, suspended/crash cymbal(s), ride cymbal, high tom-tom, middle tom-tom, and low tom-tom. Most people know what a drum set looks like. If not, here you go (extra points if you can name the parts that are missing in the drum set below...).

In order to read music for the drum set, the drummer has to know where each instrument is written on the rhythm staff. One of the strange things about the use of the five line staff with drum set is that there is no standard version. The snare drum (or any part of the drum set) may be written on a different line or space from one piece of music to another. At the beginning of the music will be a key to clue you in. Below is just one version of the drum set on the five line staff.

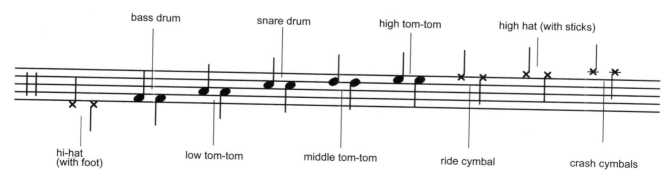

X Marks the Cymbal Spot, Maybe

The *x* notes in a rhythm clef usually show the cymbal part, but they can also be used to show the triangle part, or the cowbell part, or any other small percussion instrument.

Instruments and where they are on the staff are usually defined at the beginning of a piece of music, and what shows a triangle in one piece may be used for cowbell in a different song. It's always best to check the beginning directions to be sure.

Moving On

We won't be seeing much of the rhythm clef in this book, but it's important to know, especially if you're interested in drums and percussion instruments.

That's the end of this Part. It was a short one, but the information is essential to everything which follows, so if there's something you don't understand, go back and review until you've got it.

After the review for this chapter is the big fat review for the entire Part.

We'll take a break (sort of) from reading music with the next Interlude, called "Coming to Terms" which is all about the terms used in written music.

Chapter 17 Review

1. What does the rhythm clef show?

2. Why doesn't the rhythm clef show pitch?

3. Why use a one-line rhythm clef?

4. If the 5-line rhythm clef staff doesn't show pitches, why is it used?

5. If a note-head is an *x*, what instrument is used?

6. If you're reading say, a bass drum part, and it's on the first space, will it ever change to another line or space within that piece?

1. *Rhythm only. No pitches*

2. *Drums/percussion are non-pitched instruments*

3. *One line is all that's needed for a single percussion instrument.*

4. *The 5-line clef can show rhythm for several instruments at once.*

5. *Options: cymbals, cowbell, triangle, guiro, any small percussion instrument*

6. *NO!*

Practical Use

1. In your staff-paper notebook or on a blank staff elsewhere in this book, write a percussion clef. Write out the correct name of the instrument in the appropriate line/space of your staff. If necessary, look at page 121 to get it right.

2. Get on the "throne" of a drum set. Play each instrument of the set while looking at the appropriate space in your music from example 1. Try two instruments/drums at once. Then three. Then all four.

PART III REVIEW

Whew! You Made It.

These pages can be used to test your memory about what you've learned in Part II, and if some of the information hasn't stuck, you can go back and check it out on the page indicated below the question.

As with the chapter study guides, use your keyboard to cover up the answers while you test yourself.

When you think you've got it all down, either take the test in *Basic Music Theory Quiz Pack*, available for free at www.Sol-Ut.com, or go on.

The Review

1. What did clefs used to be?
   page 104

2. About when and where was the word *clef* first used?
   page 104

3. What does a clef do?
   page 104

4. What are the three most common clefs?
   page 104

5. What does the rhythm clef show?
   page 106

1. A letter at the beginning of a piece of music

2. Mid-1500s, France

3. Shows the letter name of a staff line

4. Treble clef, bass clef, rhythm clef

5. Rhythm only. No pitches

6. Why doesn't the rhythm clef show pitch?
page 106

7. Why use a one-line rhythm clef?
page 120

8. If the 5-line rhythm clef staff doesn't show pitch, why is it used?
page 120

9. If a note-head is an *x*, what instrument is used?
page 122

10. If you're reading a bass drum part and it's on the first space, will it ever change to another line or space within that piece?
page 121

11. Which line does the treble clef name?
page 105, page 110

12. Which line does the bass clef name?
page 106, page 114

13. What letter did the bass clef used to be?
page 114

14. What instruments use the rhythm clef?
page 106 page 121

15. Which line is "A" in the rhythm clef name?
page 120

16. On a scratch piece of paper, draw five treble clefs.
page 110

17. On the same piece of paper, draw five bass clefs.
page 106

18. On the same piece of paper, draw five rhythm clefs.
page 120

6. Drums/percussion are non-pitched instruments

7. One line is all that's needed for a single percussion instrument.

8. To show the rhythm for several instruments at once

9. Options: cymbals, cowbell, triangle, guiro, any small percussion instrument

10. No

11. 2nd

12. 4th

13. F

14. Drums and other non-pitched instruments

15. perc. clef doesn't show letter names. It shows instrumentation

16.

17.

18.

18. What letter did the treble clef used to be?
page 110

18. G

19. The inner loop of the treble clef circles which line?
page 110

19. 2nd

20. What is a mnemonic device?
page 110

20. A trick to improve memory

21. What letter name does the treble clef give to the second line?
page 110

21. G

22. What is another name for the treble clef?
page 110

22. G clef

23. What are the names of the treble clef lines?
page 111

23. E G B D F

24. What are the names of the treble clef spaces?
page 111

24. F A C E

25. What is your mnemonic device for remembering the lines of the treble clef staff?
page 111

26. What is your mnemonic device for remembering the spaces of the treble clef staff?
page 111

27. Name two instruments that use treble clef.
page 105

27. Possibilities: flute, piano, guitar, trumpet, sax, piccolo, violin, F horn, oboe, clarinet, accordion...

28. Which staff line goes between the two dots of the bass clef?
page 106 page 114

28. 4th

29. Which line is the head of the bass clef on?
page 106 page 114

29. 4th

30. What letter name does the bass clef give to the fourth line?
page 114

30. F

31. What are the names of the bass clef lines?
page 115

31. G B D F A

32. What are the names of the bass clef spaces?
page 115

32. A C E G

33. What is another name for the bass clef?
page 114

33. F clef

34. What is your mnemonic device for remembering the bass clef lines?
page 115

35. What is your mnemonic device for remembering the bass clef spaces?
page 115

36. Name two instruments that use bass clef.
page 106

36. Possibilities:
trombone, tuba, piano, acoustic bass
electric bass, bassoon, baritone,
euphonium, timpani/kettle drum, ...

37. What is a leger line?
page 23

37. A small line above or below the staff

38. What are ledger lines used for?
page 23

38. Notes that are higher or lower than the staff shows

39. What is a line note?
page 92

39. Any note with a line through it

40. What is a space note?
page 92

40. Any note in a space

41. In the example below:
    Note A is _____ than note B.
    Note C is _____ than note D.
    Note E is _____ than note F.
    page 93

41. lower, higher, lower

A   B   C   D   E   F

42. What letters are used to name notes in music?
    page 100

42. A B C D E F G

43. In the musical alphabet, what letter comes after G?
    page 100

43. A

44. In the example below:
    Note G is _____ than note A.
    Note B is _____ than note C.
    Note D is _____ than note E.
    page 93

44. lower, higher, higher

G   A   B   C   D   E

45. What kind of note comes right before or after a space note?
page 92

45. A line note

46. What kind of note comes right before or after a line note?
page 92

46. A space note

47. The stems of notes above the third line go _____.
page 27

47. Down

48. The stems of notes below the third line go _____.
page 27

48. Up

49. Notes on the third line have stems which go _____.
page 27

49. Either up or down

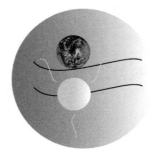

SolŪt Press

Support Music and Musicians.
www.Sol-Ut.com

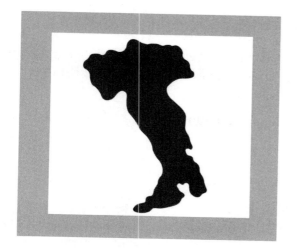

CHAPTER 18

Interlude

MUSICAL TERMS

*The mind is a musical instrument
with a certain range of tones, beyond
which in both directions we have an
infinite silence.*

— John Tyndall (1820 - 1893)

In This Interlude

- Musical Terms
- Tempo Markings
- Dynamic Markings
- Articulation Markings
- Repeat Schemes

Terms to Know

- **articulation**: the degree to which notes are separated or connected.
- **dynamics**: the level of loudness or softness. The symbols to show this.
- **tempo**: Means "time." The speed of the music.
- **tie**: curved line connecting notes of the same pitch.
- **slur**: curved line connecting notes with different pitches.

Musical Terms are Directions

Music can be loud or soft, notes can be played short and choppy or smooth and flowing, a musical phrase can be played sweetly or crassly, and music can be played at many different speeds from sleepily slow to furiously fast.

The performer needs to know this information, and in most music the information is written in Italian.

Why Italian?

Way back when, beginning in the late 1500's, there was a lot of music-making going on in Italy, and at the time, some bright soul thought to write these detailed instructions on the music. Because the composers were Italian, the instructions were written in, you guessed it, Italian.

You'll occasionally see some terms in German and French and even English (especially if you play a piece by Percy Grainger), but the vast majority of musical terms are in Italian.

Following are many Italian terms that are applied to music. They're grouped by category: *tempos* (how fast to go), *dynamics* (how loud or soft to play, *articulations* (how short or long a note is), general terms, and terms for special types of *repeats*.

Tempo

Tempo is an Italian word which comes from the Latin *tempus* which means *time*.

In order to understand these tempos (some people say *tempi* for the plural), we'll refer to the metronome and how many beats per minute each tempo is. To review the metronome, see "The Metronome (or: The Torture Device)" on page 85. Most metronomes have these markings listed somewhere on them.

Here are the most common tempos, from slowest to fastest:

TEMPO NAME	BEATS PER MINUTE
Largo	40-60
Larghetto	60-66
Adagio	66-76
Andante	76-108
Moderato	108-120
Allegro	120-168
Presto	168-200
Prestissimo	200-208

Tempo-related Terms

There are other terms that affect the tempo of a piece. They are:

accelerando (accel.) = speed up gradually.

allargando (allarg.) = slow down and grow louder.

ritardando (rit.) = slow down gradually.

rallentando (rall.) = slow down gradually.

ritenuto (riten.) = hold back the tempo.

a tempo = retvert to the previous tempo.

tempo primo = revert to the tempo used at the beginning of the piece.

Dynamics

Dynamics is another word for how loud or soft to play. The base words to remember for dynamics are *piano* (quiet) and *forte* (loud). All of the dynamic markings are variations of these two words. You'll see what I mean. Often in music, you'll see an abbreviation of the dynamic, shown in parentheses.

DYNAMIC MARKING	MEANING
pianissimo (pp)	very quiet
piano (p)	quiet
mezzo piano (mp)	medium quiet
mezzo forte (mf)	medium loud
forte (f)	loud
fortissimo (ff)	very loud

Grow Gradually

In the Romantic era—around 1800—composers began writing music which contained sections that would grow gradually louder or softer. Up until this time, dynamic changes were usually abrupt. This new technique needed a name. What did they do? They used Italian of course.

To grow gradually louder is to *crescendo* (kra-SHEN-doe), and to grow gradually softer is to *decrescendo* (DEE-kra-SHEN-doe). Below are the symbols used to show this:

You may also see the abbreviations *cresc.* or *decresc.*

crescendo   *decrescendo*

Another term for becoming gradually quieter is *diminuendo (dim.)*.

Articulations

Articulation is a fancy way to say *note length*. Depending on your instrument, there are many ways to change the length of a note. For example, with wind instruments the breath and the tongue are used; for bowed instruments like violin, viola, cello and double bass, the bow is used; for piano (the instrument, not the dynamic) articulation is controlled by how long the keys are held down and use of the sustain pedal.

Articulations are indicated with a symbol which appears either above or below the note head. Articulations can also be shown by simply writing out the whole word under the notes to be affected.

Articulations may also be combined. For example, an accent with a staccato would be a very short accent.

ARTICULATIONS (SYMBOL)	MEANING
accent (>)	note given more emphasis
marcato (∧)	note given even more emphasis
forzando (*fz*)	sudden accent
sforzanto (*sf*)	forced
sforzando (*sfz*)	even more forced
legato (—)	play the note full value
staccato (.)	short

Staff 18.1 Notes with various articulations.

Of Ties and Slurs

Two more types of articulations seen quite frequently are ***ties*** and ***slurs***. Ties and slurs are very similar but have one very important difference.

A tie is a curved line connecting two or more notes of the same pitch.

A slur is a curved line connecting two or more notes of different pitches.

The Tie

Just like tying one piece of string to another gives you a longer piece of string, so tying two notes together makes a longer note. There is no break between tied notes. Ties are often used to join notes over the bar line.

Staff 18.2   Some tied notes.

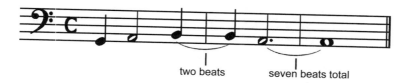

two beats   seven beats total

The Slur

Notes of different pitches with the curvy line over or under them are articulated as smoothly as possible. For wind players, this means no tonguing; for piano players it means you hold the keys down for each note down as long as possible; for guitar players it means hammer-ons and pull-offs; for bowed instruments, the notes happen in the same bow stroke. Whatever your instrument, the idea is to make a slur as smooth as possible.

Staff 18.3   Some slurred notes.

General Musical Terms

The terms you've been introduced to in the last few pages are often paired with other Italian words, giving you more specific directions. Below are the most common ones.

TERM	MEANING
al	to the
con	with
fine (pronounced FEE-nay)	the end
molto	very, much
poco	little
sempre	always

For example, molto ritardando means slow down a lot; sempre staccatto means notes are always short.

If you find a term you don't know, you can look it up in the glossary of terms at the back of this book. It's a good idea to have a pocket dictionary of terms in your instrument case. Hal Leonard Publishing makes a good small one.

Pete and Repeat

Almost all music has repetition. A single measure may be repeated, a small section, or a large section. There are several ways to indicate these repeats in a piece of music.

Repeat a Single Measure

The following sign, called a **bis**, is used to show that a specific measure is to be repeated: ✗. If there is a number with this sign, say a "2", then the previous two measures are to be repeated, as shown below.

Staff 18.4   A two-measure repeat.

Section Repeat

A section repeat is shown with two sets of dots at the beginning and end of the sequence of measures to be repeated. The second set of dots tell you to go back to the previous two dots. If there are no previous dots, the repeat goes back to the beginning of the piece.

Staff 18.5   A section repeat.

First and Second Endings

Sometimes a section is repeated, but has a different ending the second time around. The first time through the section, play to the repeat sign and return to the previous repeat sign (or the beginning, as in the example below). The second time through, skip the first ending which begins under the bracket with the number "1", and play the second ending.

Staff 18.6   First and second endings. In this example the first ending repeat returns to the beginning.

More Complex Repeats

The following terms and symbols show more complicated types of repeats.

Term	Meaning
Da Capo al Fine **(D.C. al Fine)**	Go back to the beginning and play to the *fine*.
Del Segno al Fine **(D.S. al Fine)**	Return to the sign (𝄋) and play to the *fine*.
Coda (⊕)	A closing section of a piece of music.
Da Capo al Coda **(D.C. al Coda)**	Go back to the beginning and jump to the coda section at the coda sign (⊕).
Del Segno al Coda **(D.S. al Coda)**	Return to the sign(𝄋) and jump to the coda section at the coda sign ⊕ .

Moving On

As you can tell, there are many, many terms to know. If you look in the glossary in the back of this book, you'll find even more. While I was researching terms for the glossary I learned some new terms, and I've been playing music for over twenty years.

Unless you have a photographic memory, it's a good idea to keep a pocket dictionary around in case you come across terms like, *grave, con moto, leggerio, senza sordino,* or other strange utterances.

SolŪt Press

Support Music and Musicians.
www.Sol-Ut.com

PART FOUR

See Sharp or Be Flat

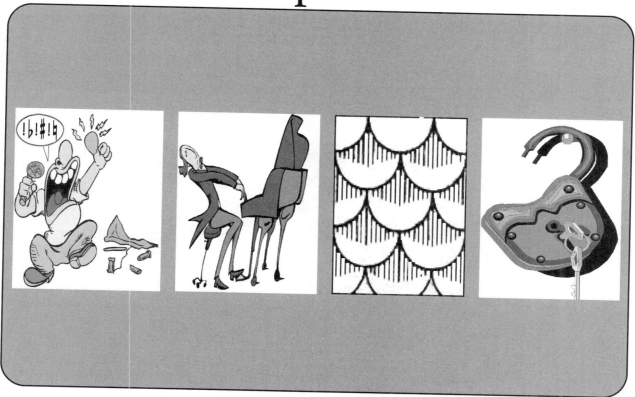

In This Section You Will Learn:

- Sharps, Flats, and Naturals
- The Piano Keyboard
- Whole Steps and Half Steps
- Major Scales
- Key Signatures

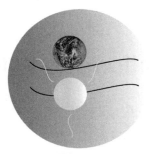

SolŪt Press

Support Music and Musicians.
www.Sol-Ut.com

ACCIDENTALS ON PURPOSE

Roaming through the jungle of "oohs" and "ahs,"
searching for a more agreeable noise, I live a life
of primitivity with the mind of a child and an
unquenchable thirst for sharps and flats.

— Duke Ellington (1899 - 1974)

In This Chapter

- General Accidental Information
- Flats
- Sharps
- Naturals
- More Accidental Rules

Terms to Know

- **accidental**: in music, a sharp, flat or natural. Symbols which alter the pitch of a note by a half step.
- **flat**: the accidental which lowers a note's pitch by a half step.
- **sharp**: the accidental which raises a note's pitch by a half step.
- **natural**: the accidental which cancels the effect of a sharp or flat.

Accidentals Are No Accident

The pitch of a note can be altered in two ways—slightly lowered, or slightly raised. This is shown by symbols which appear in front of the note on the staff, and they're called **accidentals**. Though I know the use of the word *accidental* began around 1651, I'm not really sure why, because these changes are made on purpose. They should be called *onpurposes*. But we're stuck with accidentals, so that's what I'll call them.

There are three types of accidentals: **flats**, **sharps**, and **naturals**. Each has its own sign, shown below.

Staff 19.1　　The Accidentals.

| Flat | Sharp | Natural |

General Accidental Information

Accidentals appear in front of the note they alter. This is so that when you're reading music, you see the accidental *before* you get to the note. If the accidental was placed after the note, it would be too late. Putting the accidental after the note is a very common mistake that a lot of people make who are unfamiliar with writing music.

However, there is a good reason for this mistake. When written, the accidental comes before the note, but when spoken, the accidental comes *after* the letter name of the note. For example, even though you say *B flat,* the actual note in the treble clef is on the third line with a flat sign in *front* of the note, like so:

Another common mistake is to write the accidental just anywhere in front of the note it is supposed to alter, but actually, ***the accidental should be written on the same line or space as the note it alters***. Each accidental has an open spot in the center which is placed on the line or space. You'll see what I mean in the examples to follow.

Remember that when notes are above or below the range of the staff they need leger lines. Accidentals don't need a leger line; they simply hang in front of the note which uses the leger line.

Flats

A flat **lowers** the pitch of a note by a small amount (a half step, a term you'll learn in the next chapter). One way to remember a flat lowers a note's pitch is that when something is flattened, it's lower than it was before it was flattened.

Flats look a little like a squashed letter *b* (or maybe I should say flattened letter *b*), and the open part in the center of the flat is the part which will be on the line or the space. Although I've only shown you six notes below, a flat can be used with *any* note.

Staff 19.2   From left to right: B flat, D flat, E flat, A flat, B flat, D flat, and A flat.

Sharps

A sharp **raises** the pitch of a note by a small amount (also a half step) and looks like a number symbol. The center of that little grid is where the sharp should be centered on the line or space. Just like with flats, a sharp can go in front of *any* note.

Staff 19.3   From left to right: D sharp, G sharp, C sharp, F sharp, A sharp, C sharp, F sharp.

Naturals

Naturals are a little different from sharps and flats. ***A natural sign cancels the effect of a sharp or flat***, and is used for this purpose only. Any note which isn't affected by an accidental is already a natural note. In fact, *all* the notes you've seen before this chapter have been natural notes. When there aren't any sharped or flatted notes to be changed, the natural sign isn't used.

So ***a natural can either raise or lower*** the pitch of a note. If a natural cancels a flat, it raises the pitch of a note by a half step. If a natural cancels a sharp, it lowers the pitch of the note by a half step. And you've already guessed that a natural can be used with *any* note.

Staff 19.4   From left to right: B natural, D natural, E natural, D natural, A natural, C natural.

More Accidental Rules

When an accidental is used at the beginning of a measure, *it's effect lasts for the entire measure*. For example, if at the beginning of a measure we have a B flat, and then at the end of the measure there is another B, it is *also* a B flat unless there is a natural sign in front of it.

An accidental can't have an effect over a bar line.

Staff 19.5   The effect of an accidental lasts for the entire measure and is canceled by the bar line.

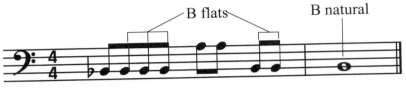

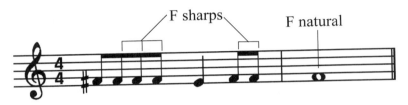

Moving On

That's it for accidentals: sharps raise, flats lower, and naturals cancel. Once you're able to answer the review questions about accidentals, you can move on to the concepts of whole steps and half steps.

But before we do that you'll get a quick lesson on the piano keyboard in the next chapter. Knowing the keyboard will make whole and half steps much easier to understand.

Chapter 19 Review

1. What does an accidental do?

2. What are the names of the accidentals?

3. Where are accidentals written?

4. What does a flat do to a note?

5. Draw six flats.

6. Draw six sharps.

7. What does a sharp do to a note?

8. Draw six naturals.

1. *Slightly alters the pitch of a note*

2. *Flat, sharp, natural*

3. *In front of the note and on the same line or space as the note*

4. *Lowers the pitch by one half step*

5. ♭ ♭ ♭ ♭ ♭ ♭

6. ♯ ♯ ♯ ♯ ♯ ♯

7. *Raises the pitch by one half step*

8. ♮ ♮ ♮ ♮ ♮

9. What does a natural do?

10. How many notes can accidentals be used with?

11. How long does the effect of an accidental last?

12. Can an accidental have an effect across a bar line?

9. Cancels a sharp or a flat

10. All of them

11. For an entire measure

12. No

Practical Use

1. Write out the following whole notes in either bass or treble clef: B-flat, E-flat, A-flat, B-flat. Find these notes on your instrument and play them. Sing them. Now write out these notes: D-flat, G-flat, C-flat, and D-flat. Find them on your instrument and play them. Sing them.

2. Do the same thing as you did in number one with these notes: F-sharp, A-sharp, C-sharp, F-sharp. Find them on your instrument and play them. Sing them. Now write out C-sharp, E-sharp, G-sharp, C-sharp. Find and play these notes. Sing them.

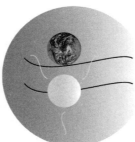

SolŪt Press

Support Music and Musicians.
www.Sol-Ut.com

THE PIANO KEYBOARD

Music is perpetual, and only the hearing is intermittent.

— Henry David Thoreau (1817 - 1862)

In This Chapter

- Note Names on the Piano Keyboard
- Flats and Sharps on the Keyboard
- Half Steps
- Enharmonic Notes
- Natural Half Steps
- Whole Steps
- Chromatic Scale

Terms to Know

- **enharmonic notes**: notes which are spelled differently but have the same pitch (like G sharp and A flat).
- **half step**: one twelfth of an octave. The smallest space between notes in Western music. Two adjacent keys on the piano.
- **natural half steps**: notes which are a half step apart without the use of accidentals. The two natural half steps occur from E—F, and B—C.
- **chromatic scale**: a scale using all 12 notes in succession. For example, from C to C on a piano using all the notes in between.

Why Learn the Keyboard?

Notes are laid out on the keyboard in a very simple way which is easy to comprehend, and the visual aid is a great help when trying to understand nearly all of the concepts you'll find in this and other sections.

In fact, one of the definitions of a half step is two adjacent keys on the piano, so there you go.

If you've been using your keyboard template on the Reviews, you've already become familiar with the keyboard, and maybe even some notes on it. When you use it, be sure to orient your keyboard like the ones shown below, with the black keys toward the top.

I don't want to insult your intelligence, but I've got to say it. Lower notes are toward the left of the keyboard and higher notes are to the right.

Note Names on the Keyboard

All of the white keys are natural notes, (A-G). All of the black keys are notes with accidentals (sharps or flats). Notice in the keyboard below how the black keys are grouped: two black, then three black, then two black, etcetera, etcetera, all the way up and down the keyboard.

Any white key to the left of a group of *two* black keys is the note C. Any white key directly to the left of *three* black keys is F. If you'd rather find the A because it's the beginning of the alphabet, it's between the second and third black keys.

Staff 20.1   A short chunk of the piano keyboard.

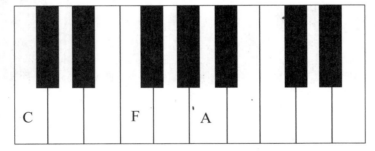

From there it's easy to fill in the rest of the note names, like so:

Staff 20.2   Piano keyboard with natural notes named.

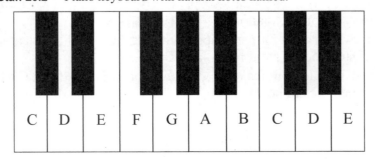

Sometimes you may see a number with a letter name, like C_1, or D_6.

This is a way of telling you where on the keyboard to find a specific note. For example, C_1 is the very first C on the left of the piano keyboard. D_6 is the sixth D from the left.

Flat Notes on the Keyboard

Any black key directly to the left of a white key is a flat note (remember to the left is lower). The note's name is derived from the natural note. So the black key just to the left of the A, is A flat. The black key directly to the left of the D is D flat. And so on.

Due to the limited space, I'll use the symbol for flat (b) next to the letter name instead of the word *flat*.

Staff 20.3   Piano keyboard with natural notes and flat notes.

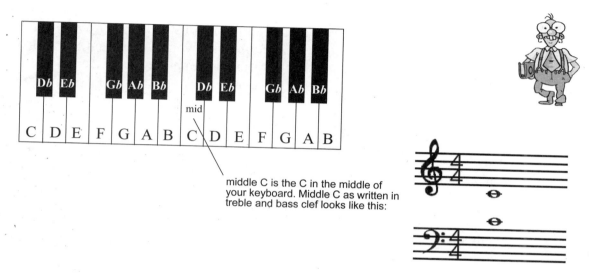

middle C is the C in the middle of your keyboard. Middle C as written in treble and bass clef looks like this:

Sharp Notes on the Keyboard

A sharp note is any black key to the right of a white key (remember to the right is higher). The sharp note names are also derived from the natural note. For example, the black key directly to the right of the C is C sharp. The black key directly to the right of the F is F sharp.

Staff 20.4   Piano Keyboard with natural notes and sharp notes.

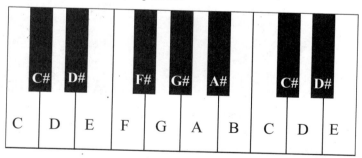

Enharmonic Notes

You probably noticed that each black key has both a sharp name and a flat name. When notes have the same pitch but different names, they're called ***enharmonic notes***.

Enharmonic notes are a lot like homonyms, words that sound alike but mean different things, like the words to, too, and two. Enharmonic notes are the same pitch but have different meanings.

A common question is, "Why bother? Doesn't that make things confusing?" Well, yes, it does make things a bit confusing but there are several good reasons for enharmonic notes. The first I'll show you later in this chapter; others will have to wait until we get to scales and chords in Parts V and VI.

Half Steps and Whole Steps

A **half step**, as it's defined by Webster's, is *one twelfth of an octave*, but that definition doesn't help us much. A better definition for a half step is **the difference in pitch between any two adjacent keys on a piano**. Or, if you're more familiar with the guitar or electric bass, a half step would be the difference in pitch between any two adjacent frets on the same string.

Natural Half Steps

This is a *really* important concept and will cause you no end of confusion if you don't understand it, so put your thinking cap on.

Most half steps involve some kind of accidental, like B to Bb, or F# to G, or C# to C natural. But if you look at the keyboard, you can see that there are two places where there is no black key between two white keys. Go ahead. Look right now and see if you can name them. I'll wait.

Remember our definition of a half step? Any two adjacent keys on the piano, right? So those notes—E to F, and B to C—are also half steps, but without the need of any accidentals. These are called **natural half steps** and if you memorize them now, you won't have to memorize them later.

Whole Steps

Two half steps make a whole step. Some easy whole steps are C to D, A to B, and F to G. Two whole steps which use the natural half step are E to F# and B*b* to C. Find others.

The Chromatic Scale

We haven't talked about scales yet, so I guess first we have to define what a scale is in music. According to Webster's it's *a graduated series of musical tones ascending or descending in order of pitch according to a specific scheme of their intervals*. And actually, that's a pretty good definition, so we'll use it.

The **chromatic scale** is the first reason for the existence of enharmonic notes. The scheme of intervals in the chromatic scale is half steps.

If you were to play a chromatic scale from C to C, you would begin at C and play every single note going up until you got to the next C, and then you'd come back down doing the same thing. Here's where the enharmonic notes come in:

As you go up the scale, sharps are used. As you come down, flats are used. An example is worth a hundred words. For this example, follow along with your keyboard.

Notice the example is two lines of music. When a song is long, the staves below the first do not need the time signature, only the clef.

Staff 20.5 Chromatic scale from C to shining C in 12/4 time. Ascending and descending. Notice the natural half steps between E-F and B-C.

Moving On

The piano keyboard will be a valuable tool in the chapters which follow, so be sure you've understood it before going on. Not only will it help you in the next chapters, it will also be valuable in your life as a musician.

Coming up next is the major scale, the basis for nearly everything in Western music. A small and simple scale, but very important.

Chapter 20 Review

1. What is the definition of a half step?

2. What is an enharmonic note? Give a couple examples.

3. What is a whole step?

4. Where are the two natural half steps?

5. Which accidentals are used when going up a chromatic scale?

6. Which accidentals are used when coming down a chromatic scale?

1. *The difference in pitch between two adjacent keys on a piano keyboard*

2. *A pitch with two different names, like C# and Db, or F# and Gb*

3. *Two half steps*

4. *Between B-C, and E-F*

5. *Sharps*

6. *Flats*

Practical Use

1. Write out the chromatic scale from A to A in both clefs ascending and descending. Refer to example 20.5 if you must.

2. Identify the notes on the keyboard.

3. From the note C, count up three half steps. What note did you get? It should be E*b*. Start on F# and count down two whole steps. What note did you get? Should be a D.

4. Get in front of a real piano/keyboard. Find all of the E-sharps on the piano. Find all of the C-flats on the keyboard. Find the F-flats. The B-sharps (hint: enharmonic notes).

5. Mess around with the piano and find sounds you like. Write out the sounds you most like. To get you oriented, the C in the middle of the piano is called *Middle C*, and it's written as a line note, one leger line *below* the treble clef staff. Middle C in bass clef is written as a line note one leger line *above* the bass clef staff.

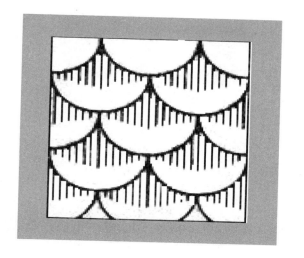

MAJOR SCALES

Without music, life would be a mistake.

— Nietzche

In This Chapter:

- The Major Scale
- C Major Scale
- The Octave
- The F Major Scale
- The G Major Scale
- The Db Major Scale
- The F# Major Scale

Terms to Know

- **major scale**: the basis for nearly all Western music. A scale of 8 notes with a specific pattern of whole (W) and half (H) steps which is WWHWWWH.
- **degree**: a note of the scale. For example, the third note of a scale would be the third *degree* of the scale.
- **octave**: the interval between the first and eighth notes of a diatonic scale. Twelve half steps.

The Major Scale

I read on the Internet that if Western music were genetic material, the **major scale** would be its DNA. A more perfect analogy I have never heard.

The major scale is the basis for nearly all music you're familiar with, from country to hip-hop, classical to jazz, grunge to punk.

Other scales are described based on their relationships to the major scale. Intervals—the measurement of distance between two notes—are based on the major scale. Chord symbols are derived from the major scale.

Remember our definition of a scale. It's kind of wordy, and you don't need to memorize it, so here it is again: *a graduated series of musical tones ascending or descending in order of pitch according to a specific scheme of their intervals.*

With the chromatic scale, the scheme of intervals was half steps. With the major scale, the scheme of intervals is a series of whole and half steps. Remember that a whole step consists of two half steps.

Every scale has a letter name and a descriptive name. The letter is the bottom note of the scale and also the top note of the scale. The descriptive name tells you what kind of scale it is, like major, minor, blues, pentatonic, etc. For example, the D Major scale would start on D and end on D and have the necessary whole and half steps which make up a major scale.

Enough words. An example will show you the pattern of whole and half steps for a major scale. The scale we'll use will be the C Major scale, because it has no sharps or flats in it.

If you have your keyboard out and use it to follow along, you'll understand these concepts more quickly and more thoroughly.

The C Major Scale

Before I show you the scale, I've got to define a couple images which are used to show half and whole steps. They're simple, and a good visual reference.

half step: ╱╲   whole step: ⊓

If you have access to an actual keyboard, play the scale below. It will be all white notes from C to C. You'll probably recognize the way it sounds.

Staff 21.1   The C Major Scale. Ascending whole and half steps shown.

Basic Music Theory

Whole and Half Steps for the Major Scale

Remember the natural half steps between E-F and B-C? In the C Major scale, these natural half steps give us the pattern of whole and half steps without the bother of accidentals.

As you can see above, the pattern for the C major scale: ***whole, whole, half, whole, whole, whole, half (wwhwwwh)***. You'll need to memorize this, because this pattern of whole and half steps is the same for *every* major scale.

Octave

This is as good a place as any to introduce you to the ***octave***, a type of interval which contains a certain amount of notes. Like octopus and octagon, the octave also has an 8 in it.

Look at the scale above, and count the notes from C to C. There are 8 of them. That's an octave. From one letter name to the next, either up or down, is an octave.

So, to be more specific, the above scale is the C Major scale, one octave, ascending.

Scales with Accidentals

Now we can take that pattern of whole and half steps and apply it to another scale. Let's start on F this time.

F Major Scale

Staff 21.2   The F major scale, ascending, with whole and half steps shown.

In order for our series of whole and half steps to be correct (wwhwwwh), we have to alter a note. Look at your keyboard while you examine the whole and half steps in the F major scale to see where those half and whole steps fall. That Bb is necessary to get the half step between the third and fourth ***degrees*** of the scale. The Bb also gives us the whole step between the fourth and fifth degrees of the scale.

A degree is a name for a scale tone, and is usually associated with a number. For example the 4th degree of a scale is the fourth note from the bottom.

In the above scale, because E to F is a natural half step, we don't need to alter either of those degrees of the scale to have the half step between the seventh and eighth degrees of the scale.

G Major Scale

Staff 21.3   The G major scale, ascending, with whole and half steps shown.

Follow along with your keyboard and you can see where the whole and half steps should be for the Major scale starting on G.

Between the third and fourth degree of the scale we have the natural half step from B-C, and between the seventh and eighth degree of the scale, in order to have a half step, we need an F#. And it just so happens that between the sixth and seventh degree of this scale we need a whole step; E to F# is a whole step.

Major Scales with Many Accidentals

This same technique can be applied to a scale with any starting note. Just for kicks, we'll do one with lots of flats and one with lots of sharps. You'll need to follow along with your keyboard for this one, so have it ready.

A Major Scale with Lots of Flats

Staff 21.4   The Db major scale, ascending, whole and half steps shown.

A Major Scale with Lots of Sharps

Staff 21.5   The F# major scale, ascending, whole and half steps shown.

More Enharmonics

Use your keyboard to understand the following concept.

Take a look at the seventh degree of the F# major scale above. An E#, right? The enharmonic note that is the same pitch as E# is F. It's that natural half step between E and F that causes this. Similarly, B# is the same pitch as C.

And going the other way, Fb is the same pitch as E, and Cb is the same pitch as B.

Moving On

If you understand the major scale, you've got a powerful tool to unlock the intricacies of much of music theory. Be sure you know the ins and outs of this scale before you move on. If you haven't already, start memorizing all 12 major scales on your instrument. You'll find them all in the Codicil at the back of the book.

Coming up in the next chapter are key signatures, devices at the beginning of a piece of music that tell you which notes are sharp or flat for the entire piece.

Chapter 21 Review

1. What is an octave?

2. What is the series of whole and half steps for the major scale?

3. What is the symbol for a half step?

4. What is the symbol for a whole step?

5. Between which degrees of the major scale do the half steps occur?

1. The distance from one note to the next note with the same letter name. Twelve half steps or 6 whole steps.

2. wwhwwwh

3.

4.

5. 3-4, 7-8

Practical Use

1. On a blank staff using the clef of your instrument, write in an E-flat low on the staff. Use your keyboard to figure out the E-flat major scale. Write it down, then play it on your instrument. Does is sound right? Sing it.

2. Do the same thing, starting on A this time. Be sure to play and sing the scale until it's memorized.

3. Write out all 12 Major scales. Learn them on your instrument. They are of immense value in your progress as a musician!

UNLOCK THE SECRET OF KEY SIGNATURES

*Servant and master am I: servant of those
dead, and master of those living. Through
my spirit immortals speak the message that
makes the world weep and laugh, and wonder, and love, and worship.
I am Music.*

— Anonymous

In This Chapter

- What is a Key Signature?
- The key of C
- Mnemonics Revisited
- Flat Keys
- Sharp Keys
- The Circle of Fifths (aka: Cycle of Fifths, Circle of Fourths, Cycle of Fourths)

Terms to Know

- **key signature**: a device found at the beginning of a piece of music which tells the performer which notes are sharp or flat in the piece.
- **BEADGCF**: the order of flats in a key signature.
- **FCGDAEB**: the order of sharps in a key signature. The reverse of the order of flats.

Key Signatures

Any piece of music has a certain feel which comes from several things, like the meter, the types of notes used, and the ***key signature***. The key signature is a device which contains sharps and flats and tells the performer type of scales the piece is based on, the most likely starting and ending notes, and most importantly, which notes in the piece are affected by accidentals. If there is improvising in the song (spontaneously making the melody), the key signature will tell the performer which notes can be used. If a song is too high for a singer, the whole song can be lowered, and this will give you a different key signature.

Just like time signatures, key signatures come at the beginning of a piece of music. The ***key signature fits between the clef and the time signature***. I have included a time signature in all of the examples so you can see where the key signature should be placed. Most of the time signatures will be familiar, but some are odd, so don't let that throw you.

A key signature is a device that tells you which notes have flats or sharps for an entire piece of music. This saves the composer from having to write in *all* the accidentals for an entire piece. The good news is that a key signature will *never* have mixed sharps and flats. It will be either all sharps, all flats, or no accidentals at all.

Another piece of good news is that the order of the flats and the order of the sharps will *always* be the same. That is, if you have only one sharp in a key signature, as long as you've memorized the order of sharps, you'll know what that sharp is. If you have seven flats in a key signature, as long as you've memorized the order of flats you'll know exactly which seven flats to use and what order to put them in.

More good news. The order of the sharps is the reverse order of the flats, or vice versa, so you only have to memorize them one way.

Why Key Signatures?

When you constructed major scales in the last chapter, you had to alter some of the notes with sharps or flats to make the whole and half step pattern correct. Each key signature is also the name of the major scale of the same name. For example, the key signature of G will give you the correct accidentals for the G Major scale. A key signature at the beginning of a song affects all the notes throughout the song, so the composer doesn't have to write out all the accidentals for every single note in the song. They key signature takes care of it.

Flat Key Signatures

There are only seven flats, and they'll *always* be in the same order in a key signature. This is one of the few rules that has no exceptions.

More Mnemonics

The order of flats is ***B-E-A-D-G-C-F***. An easy way to remember this is the word BEAD followed by **G**reatest **C**ommon **F**actor. Or you can make up your own saying which uses all the letters in the proper order. Something like, "Being Ethereal After Death, Ghosts Can Fly."

As with other mnemonic devices, if you make up your own and make it silly or funny or weird, you'll be more likely to remember it.

Here is a key signature with all of the flats in it. Notice the order (from left to right) and where the flats are placed on the staff.

Staff 22.1   A key signature in both treble and bass clef with all seven flats.

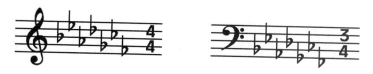

Find the Name of a Flat Key

If you're faced with a piece of music with a bunch of flats in the key signature, there is an easy way to find out what key it's in. The name of the key is the same name as the second-to-last flat in the key signature.

An example will show this better than words can:

Staff 22.2   The keys of Bb and Eb.

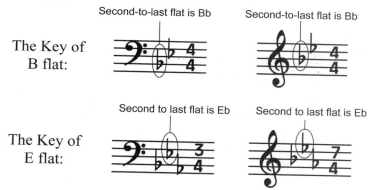

Construct a Flat Key

To create a flat key, there are three easy steps:

1 Find the name of the key you want in the order of flats. For example, if we're looking for the key signature for A flat, we'd find where the letter A is in the order of flats: B E **A** D G C F.

2 Add one more flat beyond the key signature name, and use all of the flats up to that point for the key signature. In our example, one flat beyond Ab would be Db, for a total of 4 flats.

3 Construct the key signature, putting the flats in the correct order, and on the right line or space.

And that's all there is to it.

The Key of F

There is one flat key which is a little different than the others, and that's the key with only one flat in it. Because there's only one flat, there can't be a second-to-the-last flat.

You can sort of use the same procedure above to find the name of the key with one flat. If you look at the order of flats, B is the first one. Before the B is the one at the other end of the line—F, which is the name of the 1-flat key.

Here's a more visual representation of what I'm talking about.

Here's the B flat in the key signature
|
B E A D G C F
|
And here's the name of
the key with one flat: F.

Or you could just memorize that one flat is the key of F. Whatever works best.

Sharp Key Signatures

Hopefully you've already got the toughest part learned, which is the order of sharps. It's the order of flats backwards, or: F C G D A E B. If you want, make a mnemonic device for the order of sharps, or simply reverse the order of flats.

In the following key signature, which uses all the sharps, notice the order and the placement of the sharps.

Staff 22.3   Key signatures in bass and treble clef with all seven sharps.

Find the Name of a Sharp Key

Finding the name of a key with sharps in it is much less involved than finding a flat key.

That very last sharp in a sharp key signature is the one responsible for making the half step from the seventh to the eighth degree of the major scale. Simply go up half a step from that last sharp and you have the name of the key.

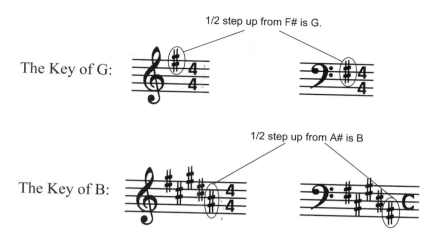

The Key of G:

1/2 step up from F# is G.

The Key of B:

1/2 step up from A# is B

Construct a Sharp Key

If you reverse the process, you can construct a sharp key. Again, three easy steps.

1 Take the name of the key you want and go to the sharp note a half step below the key note. For example, if you want to find the key of D, go down a half step to C#.

2 Find out where that note is in the order of sharps. In our example, C# is the second sharp (F **C** G D A E B), so there are two sharps in the key of D.

3 Put the sharps in the correct order on the right line or space and you've got it.

The Key of C

This is the only key signature you have to memorize. Because there are no sharps or flats with this key, there is no quick way to figure out what the key signature is. But if you know the C major scale, you know that there are no sharps or flats in the scale. You can see the key of C on the next page

The Major Keys to the Kingdom

The Key of C:

Flat Keys

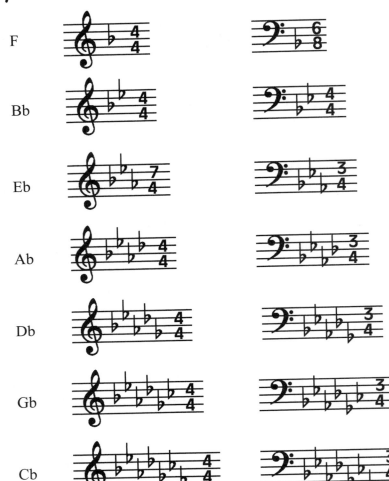

F

Bb

Eb

Ab

Db

Gb

Cb

Basic Music Theory

Sharp Keys

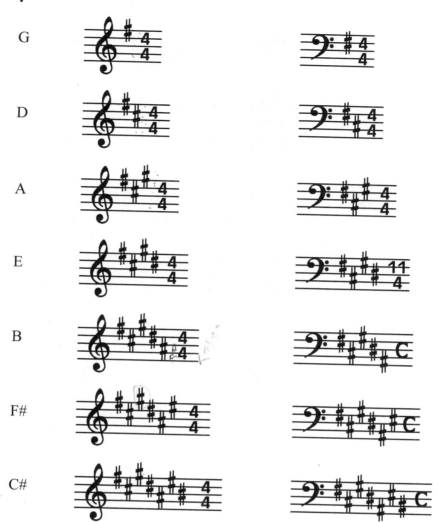

The Circle of Fifths

This device is known by a few different names. You may see "cycle" or "circle" and it may be called Cycle/Circle of Fourths, or Cycle/Circle of Fifths. Read on to find out why.

This is a device to help you remember key signatures and how they're used, especially in jazz. If you look at the diagram, you'll notice that going clockwise around the circle, each key has one more sharp than the key before it and the notes are a fifth apart (hence the name Circle of Fifths). And going counter-clockwise, each key has one more flat than the key before it and the notes are a fourth apart (hence the name Circle of Fourths).

Classical musicians often learn the cycle clockwise, while jazz musicians use the cycle counter-clockwise. The reason jazz musicians use the Circle of Fifths counter-clockwise is that it follows a very common progression called the ii-V-I progression. For example, a ii-V-I progression in C would be D-, G7, C, which follows the progression counter-clockwise on the circle below (for more on chord progressions, see "What is a Chord Progression?" on page 238).

When you practice your scales, practice them in order around the Circle of Fourths counter-clockwise. This imitates the movement you'll find in real life.

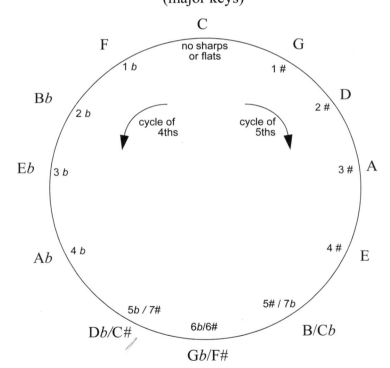

Circle of Fourths/Fifths
(major keys)

Moving On

The concept of key signatures can be difficult to understand, but I hope you've got it. If not, spend some more time with this chapter until you do. Key signatures are important.

After the review for this chapter is the review for the entire section. This has been an important section, and most of what follows builds on what you've learned in this section, so be sure you understand all of it before moving on.

After the section review, you get to take a break from music theory with another Interlude. In this one you get to learn a little bit about conducting.

Chapter 22 Review

1. How are key signatures and the major scale related?

2. What is the order of flats?

3. How do you find the name of a flat key?

4. Which key has only one flat in it?

5. What is the name of that lonely flat in the key of F?

6. Which major key signature has four flats?

7. How many flats in the key of Eb Major, and what are they?

8. How many flats are in the key of C Major?

9. Which major key signature has seven flats?

10. What is the order of sharps?

11. How do you find the name of a sharp key?

12. How many sharps are in the key of D and what are they?

---

1. *A key signature gives the correct whole and half steps for a major scale of the same name.*

2. *BEADGCF*

3. *The second -to-the-last flat in the key signature is the name of the key.*

4. *F*

5. *Bb*

6. *Ab Major*

7. *Three: Bb,Eb,Ab*

8. *None*

9. *Cb Major*

10. *FCGDAEB*

11. *Go up 1/2 step from the last sharp in the key signature*

12. *Two: F#, C#*

13. What is the name of the key signature with 4 sharps in it?

13. E

14. How many sharps in the key of C?

14. None

15. Where do you find key signatures (be specific)?

15. At the beginning of a piece of music, between the clef and the time signature.

Practical Use

1. On a low line/space of a blank bass or treble clef staff, write an F. Now put a note on each line and space above the F until you reach the F an octave above (you should end up with 8 notes). Now, just after the clef, put in the key signature for F# Major. Look at the sharp key examples for help with this if you must. Play and sing the F# Major scale you just made (have a fingering chart for your instrument handy).

2. Create a 4-measure melody in the key of Ab. Choose your own clef and meter. Play and sing what you've written. Change it if you don't like it. Do the same in two more keys of your choice.

3. Write out each of the major key signatures with their major scale.

4. From now on, whenever you see a piece of music, look at it and identify its key signature.

THE GUITAR FRETBOARD

Information is not knowledge. Knowledge is not wisdom. Wisdom is not truth. Truth is not beauty. Beauty is not love. Love is not music. Music is the best.

— Frank Zappa

In This Chapter

- Strings of the Guitar
- Guitar Fretboard
- Guitar Chords

Terms to Know

- **fretboard**: The surface of the neck of the guitar. Where you put your fingers to change the pitch of the instrument.
- **fret**: small strips of metal which stretch across the fretboard of the guitar. Also, to fret a note is to play it on the fretboard.
- **nut**: a piece on the neck of the guitar just before the tuning pegs that holds the strings off the fretboard.
- **bridge**: a piece of the guitar on the body that holds the strings off the fretboard and transfers the vibration of the string to the body of the guitar.
- **open string**: a string ringing freely for its entire length, not fretted.

Basic Guitar Details

This chapter is *not* intended to teach you how to play guitar. There are many great books and teachers out there for that. What you will get from this chapter is information about how the guitar works, how its notes and chords are written out, and a few other details.

Guitar is one of the most popular instruments in the world and that's why this chapter has been included in the 2nd edition of *Basic Music Theory*. With all those guitars out there, it's more likely that you'll own a guitar than a keyboard. They're so much more portable.

Guitar is not as easily understood as the piano keyboard, so be sure to spend some time on the concepts in this chapter if you have a guitar and want to understand it. Don't hesitate to read this chapter several times over the next year or so. Really. First we'll get to the easy stuff, like the parts of a guitar.

The strings of the guitar are strung between the ***nut*** and the ***bridge***. The nut is the piece of plastic (perhaps originally it was made out of nut) closest to the tuning pegs. The nut holds the strings off the neck of the guitar. The bridge is the piece on the body of the guitar, just past the sound hole on an acoustic guitar. The bridge holds the strings up off the body and is also partly responsible for the intonation of the guitar.

Parts of the Guitar

There are a bunch of parts of the guitar we won't cover in detail, like the sound holes, the bridge, the body, tuners and more. What you'll be learning is the fretboard, the frets and the notes on guitar as they're written down. But just for kicks, and to give you a visual of a great hollow-body electric guitar made by Gretsch, here are the parts of a guitar which you'll find on *any* guitar whether it's acoustic, electric or a comination of the two, like this one.

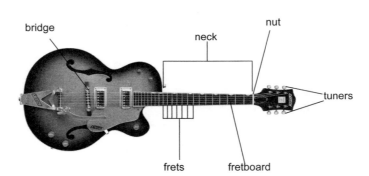

The ***fretboard*** is where half of your work will take place. It's where you change the pitch of the instrument with the fingers of your left hand (or your right if you're playing a left-handed guitar). The other half of your work takes place with the right hand which either strums or picks the strings.

Perpendicular to the fretboard are the ***frets*** of the guitar, thin strips of metal you'll use when you change notes or play chords. In order to get a good sound, your finger tips should press the string down just behind the frets. Behind the fret means closer to the tuners than the bridge.

Guitar is a unique instrument and despite the fact it's more challenging to comprehend than piano, there are compensations for this. If you were to learn all 12 major scales on a wind instrument or piano, you'd have to memorize 12 separate patterns. That's a lot of memorizing. With guitar, to memorize those same 12 scales, all you need is one pattern. This pattern started on a different fret of the guitar neck will give you a different scale. More on this wonderful attribute in a little bit.

The Strings of the Guitar

Guitar has six strings. The thickest and lowest in pitch is the sixth string. The thinnest and highest in pitch is the 1st string. I'm sure you can figure out the ones in between. In addition to a number, each string also has a letter name which corresponds to the note the string is tuned to. From lowest to highest, the letter names are E, A, D, G, B, E. Here's a graphic to show you the string names.

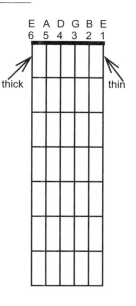

With one exception, the guitar is tuned in fourths. Remember your intervals? All but one of the intervals between the strings of the guitar are fourths. Can you spot which one is *not* a fourth? You're looking for an interval of a third. Let's go through the strings.

From the sixth string to the fifth string, E to A, is a fourth. From the fifth string to the fourth string, A to D, is a fourth. From the fourth string to the third string, D to G, is a fourth. From the third string to the second string, G to B, is a *third*. From the second string to the first string, B to E, is a fourth. So there you have it.

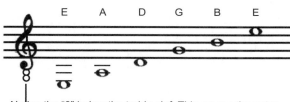

Notice the "8" below the treble clef. This means the notes you see actually sound an octave lower than written.

Here are the guitar's **open** strings as written. An open string means the string isn't fretted with a finger and is vibrating along its entire length, from nut to bridge.

Play each open string on a guitar and memorize where it's written and how it sounds.

Half Steps and the Guitar

Remember half steps, the smallest interval we have in Western music? Two adjacent keys on the piano, right? Well on guitar, the half step can be heard on adjacent frets on the same string. As you shorten the string, the notes go higher. For example, on the first string, a note on the 5th fret is a half step lower than the note on the 6th fret . If you own a guitar, play each fret all the way up each string. This is the sound of consecutive half steps.

If you've memorized the order of notes (notes are sharp ascending and flat descending), and especially the natural half steps (E to F, and B to C), you'll have no trouble finding note names on guitar.

All Notes on Guitar

To the right are all the notes on each string of the guitar up to the 12th fret. Do you remember that there are twelve half steps in an octave? There are. That's why the note at the 12th fret of each string is the same letter name as the open string. Twelve half steps is an octave.

Notice the dots to the left of the fretboard. Two dots at the octave on the 12th fret. Most guitars have these dots marked both on the surface of the fretboard, and also along the outside edge of the fretboard where you can see them from above. These dots are a visual aid to help you see the notes on the guitar and whole step patterns. Memorize the names of the fret at each of the dots on all strings, especially the fourth fifth and sixth strings.

What is the note at the 5th fret on the low E string? You should've come up with "A," which also happens to be the pitch of the open fifth string. What is the note at the 5th fret on the A string? It's D, right? Same note as the fourth string. And the 5th fret on the D string is what? Did you get G, the same note as the third string? Remember the interval from the G string to the B string is a third, so we have to move from the 5th fret. On the G string, push the string down behind the 4th fret and you'll get G, the same pitch as the second string. And finally, back to the 5th fret of the B string will give you an E, the same pitch as the 1st string. I hope you understood all that. Throwing all those numbers around can be confusing. Sit with your guitar and play all that I just wrote. It will become much more clear if you hear what I'm talking about.

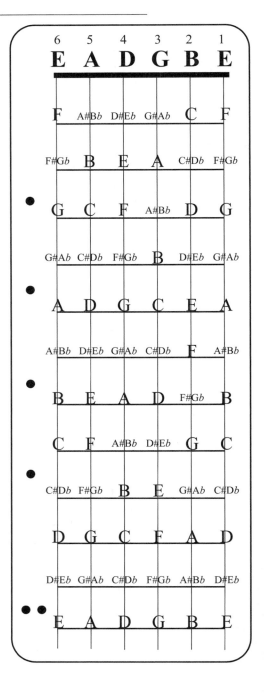

You can use this sequence of notes to tune the guitar to itself. Play the fretted note and match the pitch of the open string to the fretted note by tightening the string with the tuner to raise the pitch or loosening the string to lower the pitch.

Scales on Guitar

Once you know the notes on guitar, scales will be relatively easy to figure out. Of course, you have to remember the pattern of whole and half steps for the scale you want, but you memorized that long ago, right? We're going to use the major scale, so if you need a review, see "The Major Scale" on page 152.

At first you'll do the entire scale on one string. This will be a little awkward but it will be easier to see where the half and whole steps fall. We'll take the E major scale and play it on the sixth string. You could also play the same scale on the 1st string, which is also E, but stick with the sixth string for now because we'll soon be using the fifth and fourth strings also.

The pattern for the major scale is WWHWWWH (W=whole, H=half). So, starting on E, our scale has these notes: E, F#, G#, A, B, C#, D#, E. Play all these notes on the sixth string. Once you've done that, we'll play the scale without moving your hand so far up the neck.Go play your scale on the 6th string before you continue.

Take a look at the notes of the scale and find out which note of the scale is the first that you can play on the fifth string. It's A, right? So, after you play E, F#, and G# on the sixth string, then you'd play the next note of the scale, the A, as an open fifth string. Stay on the fifth string and play the B and C#. The next note, the D#, can be played on the fourth string, 1st fret, and the E at the top of the scale can also be played on the fourth string, 2nd fret. Viola, your scale is done and you haven't moved out of first position.

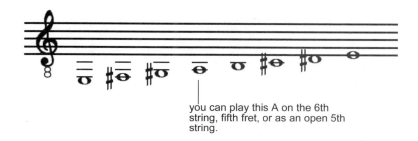

you can play this A on the 6th string, fifth fret, or as an open 5th string.

We won't go into all the scales here, that's best left up to you and your guitar teacher. Let's move on to chords.

Chords on Guitar

It's possible to play six-note chords on guitar and there are many chords which do use all six strings. Remember a chord is three or more notes, so you could use only half the guitar's strings and still get a chord.

The voicing of chords on guitar is often different than the voicings on piano. Because of the way the guitar is tuned, playing a chord in close position (no gaps between chord tones) is troublesome. I'll show you a few chords on guitar and you'll see what I mean when they're written out.

We'll start with the e minor chord, which is easy to finger and sounds cool because it uses all six strings. To the right is a chord diagram which represents the guitar fretboard. Dots indicate where your fingers are placed. Index finger is 1, middle finger 2, ring finger 3, and pinky is 4.

e minor

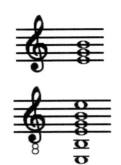

To the left you'll see two versions of the e minor chord. The first is the simplest version possible in treble clef, with only three notes, all stacked neatly together as closely as possible. Below that is the e minor chord as written for the guitar chord shown in the diagram on the previous page. There are six notes and you can see they are *not* as close as possible. As a little test, find the notes in the guitar chord that are doubled (or tripled).

If you want to learn more chords, there are many chord charts out there and you can probably find a whole bunch of them online, too. Happy searching.

Moving On

Okay, next up is a review for Part IV. Once you've got that information stored in your little gray cells, we'll move on to concepts like intervals (measuring the distance between notes), minor scales, modes (another type of scale), and the blues.

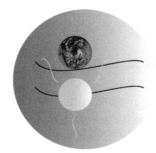

SolŪt Press

Support Music and Musicians.
www.Sol-Ut.com

Basic Music Theory

PART IV REVIEW

Whew! You Made It.

These pages can be used to test your memory on what you've learned in Part IV, and if some of the information hasn't stuck, you can go back and check it out on the page indicated below the question.

As with the chapter reviews, use your keyboard to cover up the answers while you test yourself.

When you think you've got it all down, either take the test in *Basic Music Theory Quiz Pack* (available for free at www.Sol-Ut.com), or go on.

The Review

1. What does an accidental do?
   page 140

   1. Slightly alters the pitch of a note by a half step.

2. What are the names of the accidentals?
   page 140

   2. Flat, sharp, natural

3. Where are accidentals written?
   page 140

   3. In front of the note and on the same line or space as the note

4. What does a flat do to a note?
   page 140

   4. Lowers the pitch by one half step

5. Draw five flats.
   page 140

   5.

6. Draw five sharps.
   page 141

   6.

7. What does a sharp do to a note?
   page 141

   7. Raises the pitch by one half step

8. Draw five naturals.
   page 141

   8.

9. What does a natural do?
   page 141

   9. Cancels a sharp or a flat

10. How many notes are accidentals be used with?
    page 140, page 141, page 141

    10. All of them

11. How long does the effect of an accidental last?
    page 142

    11. For an entire measure

12. Can an accidental have an effect across a bar line?
    page 142

    12. No

13. What is the definition of a half step?
    page 148

    13. The difference in pitch between two adjacent keys on a piano keyboard

14. What is an enharmonic note? Give a couple examples.
    page 147

    14. A pitch with two different names, like C# and Db, or F# and Gb

15. What is a whole step?
    page 148

    15. Two half steps

16. Between which notes do the natural half steps occur?
    page 148

    16. B-C, E-F

17. Which accidentals are used when going up a chromatic scale?
    page 148

    17. Sharps

18. Which accidentals are used when coming down a chromatic scale?
    page 148

    18. Flats

19. What is an octave?
    page 153

    19. The distance from one letter name to the next letter of the same name. 12 half steps, or 6 whole steps

Basic Music Theory

20. What is the series of whole and half steps for the major scale?
page 152

20. wwhwwwh

21. What is the symbol for a half step?
page 152

21.

22. What is the symbol for a whole step?
page 152

22.

23. Between which degrees of the major scale do the half steps occur?
page 152

23. *3-4, 7-8*

24. *3-4, 7-8*

24. Use your keyboard to figure out the following scales: A Major, Ab Major, D Major, and Db Major.
page 154

25.

25. How are key signatures and the major scale related?
page 158

25. *A key signature gives the correct whole and half steps for a major scale of the same name.*

26. What is the order of flats?
page 158

26. *BEADGCF*

27. How do you find the name of a flat key?
page 158

27. *The second -to-the-last flat in the key signature is the name of the key.*

28. Which key has only one flat in it?
page 160

28. *F*

29. Which flat is in that key signature?
page 160

29. *Bb*

30. Which key has four flats?
page 159

30. *Ab*

31. How many flats in the key of Eb, and what are they?
page 159

31. *Three: Bb,Eb,Ab*

32. How many flats are in the key of C?
page 158

32. *None*

33. Which key has seven flats?
   page 159

33. Cb

34. What is the order of sharps?
   page 160

34. FCGDAEB

35. How do you find the name of a sharp key?
   page 160

35. Go up 1/2 step from the last sharp in the key signature.

36. How many sharps are in the key of D and what are they?
   page 161

36. Two: F#, C#

37. What is the name of the key signature with 4 sharps in it?
   page 160

37. E

38. In a piece of music, where will you find the key signature (be specific)?
   page 158

38. At the beginning of a piece of music, between the clef and the time signature

39. What are the letter names of the guitar strings?
   page 169

39. EADGBE

40. What is the letter name of string number 4? Number 2? Number 5?
   page 169

40. D. B. A.

41. To get a good tone from a guitar, where do you place your fingers on the fretboard?
   page 168

41. Right behind the fret

42. What are the note names at the dots on the 6th string? (start at the third fret)
   page 170

42. 1st dot, 3rd fret: G
    2nd dot, 5th fret: A
    3rd dot, 7th fret: B
    4th dot, 9th fret: C#
    5th dot, 12th fret: E

PART FIVE

Interval Training

In This Section You Will Learn:

- General Interval Information
- Major and Minor Intervals
- Diminished and Augmented Intervals
- Natural, Harmonic and Melodic Minor Scales
- Modes

SolŪt Press

Support Music and Musicians.
www.Sol-Ut.com

24

INTERVALS

*My idea is that there is music in the air,
music all around us; the world is full of
it, and you simply take as much as you
require.*

— Sir Edward Elgar

In This Chapter

- Basic Intervals
- Major and Perfect Intervals
- Minor Intervals
- Diminished Intervals
- Augmented Intervals

Terms to Know

- **interval**: the distance between two pitches.
- **harmonic interval**: the distance between two pitches sounded at the same time.
- **melodic interval**: the distance between two pitches sounded one after the other.
- **minor**: means lesser. A minor interval is one half step below the major interval of the same number (i.e.- minor 6th is a half step lower than a major 6th).
- **perfect**: the intervals of unison, 4th, 5th, and octave.
- **augmented**: means raised, or enlarged. An augmented interval is one half step above the major or perfect interval of the same name (i.e.- augmented 6th is a half step higher than a major 6th).
- **diminished**: means lowered. A diminished interval is a minor or perfect interval lowered a half step.

24: Intervals

179

Intervals by the Number

An *interval* is the distance between two pitches. An interval is expressed as a number from 1 to 13. It *is* possible to have a number greater than 13, but it's so rare that we'll forget about it.

There are two types of basic intervals, harmonic and melodic.

A *harmonic interval* is when two notes are sounded simultaneously.

A *melodic interval* is when two notes are sounded one after the other.

Harmonic Interval

Melodic Interval

When measuring the interval between two notes (both harmonic and melodic), the interval is always measured from the lower note to the higher.

A Simple Way to Find an Interval

To find the number of an interval, simply count every line and space from the bottom note to the top note. *Be sure to count the line/space of the bottom note as 1.* This is the most common mistake when figuring out an interval. If you don't count the bottom note as 1, you'll end up with the wrong interval.

Staff 24.1 The melodic interval of a fifth and a sixth. Notice in the second example that the count starts with the *lower note* even though it comes after the higher one.

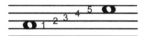
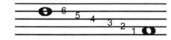

Staff 24.2 The harmonic intervals of a third and a seventh.

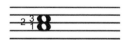

Interval Quality

In addition to having a number, each interval will also have a quality of *perfect, major, minor, diminished,* or *augmented*.

In order to understand these qualities, we've got to take a look at the major scale again. We'll use the key of C Major because it's the least complicated, but these principles can be applied to any key signature.

Basic Music Theory

Perfect Intervals

The **Perfect** intervals are: **Unison** (the same note, also called **prime**), **4ths**, **5ths**, and **octaves** (8ths). They're called perfect because the ratios of their frequencies are simple whole numbers. These sound qualities were first observed and praised in China and were first explored in the West by Pythagoras. For more information on this subject, get *Hearing and Written Music* by Ron Gorow.

The symbol for a perfect interval is "P". So the intervals, when written look like so:

PU/PP	perfect unison/perfect prime
P4	perfect fourth
P5	perfect fifth
P8	perfect octave

See example 23.3 below for the perfect intervals in the C major scale.

Major Intervals

All other intervals in a major scale are called major intervals. That leaves us with seconds, thirds, sixths, and sevenths. The letter used for a major interval is a **capital "M"**. These intervals would be written like so:

M2	major second
M3	major third
M6	major sixth
M7	major seventh

See example 23.3 below for Major intervals in the key of C major.

It takes two notes to have an interval, so in the example that follows I've put a *C* below each note, which gives us harmonic intervals up the major scale. Any of these intervals spread out one after the other would be a melodic interval.

Staff 24.3   Intervals in the key of C Major.

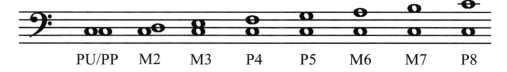

Altering Perfect Intervals

A perfect interval can be raised or lowered, and this changes the quality of the interval.

A perfect interval lowered a half step becomes a diminished interval.

A perfect interval raised a half step becomes an augmented interval.

Here's a little diagram to help remember this. The *aug* is above the P because an augmented interval is higher than a Perfect interval. The *dim* is below the P because a diminished interval is lower than a Perfect interval.

aug
P
dim

Staff 24.4   Altered Perfect intervals from C.

Altering Major Intervals

Major intervals can also be altered by raising or lowering them.

A Major interval lowered a half step becomes a minor interval.

A Major interval raised a half step becomes an augmented interval.

Here's another little diagram. Just like before, the *aug* is above because it's higher than the Major, and the *min* is below because it's a lower than the Major:

aug
M
min

Staff 24.5   Altered Major intervals from C.

And just to mess with your mind a little, a minor interval lowered a half step becomes a diminished interval. If you're wondering how a note which already has a flat can be lowered still further, see "Double Flats" on page 258.

Finding an Interval

In a few easy steps you can find an interval. It's easiest with the key of C so we'll stick with that for examples, but you should be able to find an interval from any note to any other note.

1   Count the lines and spaces up from the lower of the two notes. **Be sure to count the lowest note as 1**.

2   Determine if the number of the interval is Major or Perfect. (M = 2, 3, 6, 7; P = U, 4, 5, 8).

3   Determine if the interval is lowered or raised from what it would be in the Major scale. Use the Major scale which starts on the lower of the two notes.

For example, lets take a C and a Bb, with C being the lower of the two notes. For the first step, we count the lines and spaces to get the number of the interval.

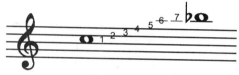

For step 2, we need to know if a 7th is a Perfect or Major interval. It's a Major interval if unaltered. But this one is altered, so....

For step 3 we determine that the 7th has been lowered a half step, which would make it a minor 7th.

Intervals Greater than an Octave

So far we've only used intervals up to the number 8 (an octave). Intervals can be greater than an octave and are called *compound intervals*. The process of finding them is the same. Simply count up from the lower of the two notes. There will be more information and study of compound intervals in Chapter 29. Here's an example showing the interval of a ninth:

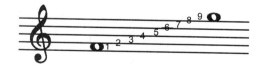

Finding Intervals in Keys Other than C

The best way to find intervals in other keys is to have all the Major scales memorized. There are only 12 of them, so it shouldn't take too long. Because I'm originally a trumpet player, I still figure out intervals by running up the major scales with trumpet fingerings. It's sort of like counting on your fingers. Very handy.

Another way is to memorize how many whole and half steps are in each interval. This takes a lot of brain space, but it's possible. Here's a little table with the number of whole and half steps for each interval.

INTERVAL	NUMBER OF 1/2 STEPS		INTERVAL	NUMBER OF 1/2 STEPS
dimU	-1		P5	7
PU	0		a5	8
augU	1		min6	8
min2	1		M6	9
M2	2		a6	10
a2	3		min7	10
min3	3		M7	11
M3	4		a7	12
a3	5		dim8	11
dim4	4		P8	12
P4	5		a8	13
a4	6			
dim5	6			

A Brief Note on Ear Training

Knowing these intervals intellectually is valuable, but knowing them by hearing them is priceless. If you've ever struggled with learning a song by ear, you'll appreciate knowing intervals by the way they sound.

The trick is to sing or play each interval over and over and over until you can sing any interval from any note. There are many ways to do this. One way is to pick an interval a week and sing/play that interval from every note you can sing/play until you've memorized the difference in pitch.

Do this everywhere you won't be looked at strangely (or if you don't mind looking strange, do it everywhere): in the car, in the shower, hum them under your breath at a boring lecture or meeting, use your imagination. Knowing these intervals by ear is a valuable skill for any musician of any level. If you can hear an interval correctly, writing it out is a cinch.

Moving On

It may take some time living with these intervals before they really stick in your head. Keep at it until you've got them. Knowing your intervals will be necessary when we get to building chords, which is coming up in a few chapters.

Coming up in the next chapter are minor scales.

Chapter 24 Review

1. What is the definition of an interval?

2. What is a harmonic interval?

3. What is a melodic interval?

4. How do you find the number of an interval?

5. What will always be the number of the lower note?

6. What are the qualities of intervals?

7. What does a Perfect interval become when lowered a half step?

8. What does a Perfect interval become when raised a half step?

9. What does a Major interval become when raised a half step?

10. What does a Major interval become when lowered a half step?

11. What is this interval?

12. What is this interval?

1. The distance between two pitches

2. The distance between two pitches sounded at the same time

3. The distance between two pitches sounded one after the other

4. Count each line and space up from the lower of the two notes

5. 1

6. Perfect, Major, minor, diminished, augmented

7. diminished (dim)

8. augmented (aug)

9. augmented (aug)

10. minor

11. min 6

12. aug 4

Practical Use

1. Draw a whole note C on the treble clef (any octave is fine). Draw another note a fifth above the C. What is name of the note a fifth above C? Sing or play the interval of a fifth until you can do it from any pitch (this m take some time...keep at it).

2. On the first three lines and two spaces of the treble staff, draw whole notes on E, F, G, and A. Next you'll make a harmonic interval (one note directly over another) above each note you've already written. Write in the note an octave above the E, F, G, and the A. What are the names of these notes an octave above? Now, in between the note and the octave, write in a fifth. Play and sing these intervals.

3. On a piece of music you are currently studying, identify at least two intervals. Sing and play the interval out the context of the piece. When you play the piece from now on, try to be aware of the sound of the intervals you've chosen. When you can identify them by their sound, pick a couple more and repeat the process.

MINOR SCALES

A painter paints pictures on canvas, but
a musician paints pictures on silence.

— Leopold Stokowski

In This Chapter

- General Minor Scale Information
- Natural Minor Scales
- Parallel and Relative Minor
- Harmonic Minor Scales
- Melodic Minor Scales

Terms to Know

- **natural minor scale**: minor scale in which the 3rd, 6th, and 7th degrees of the major scale are lowered 1/2 step.
- **harmonic minor scale**: minor scale in which the 3rd and 6th degrees of the major scale are lowered 1/2 step.
- **melodic minor scale**: minor scale in which the 3rd degree of the major scale is lowered ascending, and the 7th, 6th and 3rd are lowered descending.

General Minor Scale Info

If you hear music which evokes a feeling of sadness or melancholy, you can bet it's in a minor key.

This change in emotion is brought about by lowering a few degrees of the major scale by a half step.

There are three types of minor scale: ***natural minor, harmonic minor, and melodic minor***. Just like the Major scale, each minor scale has a different scheme of whole and half steps.

The good news is that you don't have to memorize those schemes, we'll just alter the Major scale to get the minor scales.

The Natural Minor Scale

It's easy to get a key signature for a ***natural minor scale: simply add three flats to the key signature of a Major scale***.

Which three flats? Well, it depends on the major scale. You add the next three flats in the key signature. For example, the key of F Major has one flat, a Bb. If we wanted to get f minor, we'd add the next three flats in the order of flats, which are Eb, Ab, and Db.

Staff 25.1 The key signatures of F Major and f minor.

F Major   f minor

I'm sure you're saying, "But wait a minute, that's also the key of Ab Major, isn't it?" Yes it is. I'll address the similarity of the key signatures in a couple pages. What's different is the starting note of the scale.

In this case, we'll be starting on F, so the key signature of f minor will give us a specific series of whole and half steps from F to F. In example 24.2 you'll see that adding the next three flats in the key signature will lower the 3rd, 6th, and 7th degrees of the major scale by a half step. Though the key signature takes care of the flat notes, I've put the flats in parentheses in front of the notes to illustrate which have been lowered.

Staff 25.2 The f minor scale with whole and half steps shown.

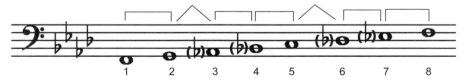

With this example, you can see ***the series of whole and half steps for any natural minor scale is: whole, half, whole, whole, half, whole, whole (whwwhww)***. Memorize this if you want, but it's easier to simply add three flats to the major key of the starting note.

What About Sharp Keys?

The process for making a minor key is the same for sharp keys. Add three flats. What's different is that the flats will cancel out the sharps. When you take the sharps away from the key signature, take them off the end of the key signature (from right to left).

For example, if we take the key of E with 4 sharps and add 3 flats, those three flats cancel out the last three sharps in the key signature, leaving us with one sharp, which is the key of e minor.

Staff 25.3   The keys of E Major and e minor.

E Major   e minor

You'll notice that the key of e minor is the same as the key of G, but what is different is the starting note, which will of course be E. I'm not going to write it out but I guarantee that if you checked the whole and half step pattern from e to e with one sharp, it'll also be whwwhww.

If you have a sharp key with only one or two sharps (keys of G and D Major), adding three flats will cancel out the sharps and you'll be left with two or one flat, respectively (keys of g and d minor).

Staff 25.4   The keys of G Major and g minor, D Major and d minor.

G Major   g minor   D Major   d minor

How Do You Tell the Difference?

You may be wondering that a key signature can be either Major or minor (as in the example above: e minor, or G Major). There is an easy way to tell. Your first signal should be the beginning and ending note, especially the ending one. It is almost always the tonic, or the note which gives the key its name. For example, in a song with one sharp, if it's in G Major, the last note (and likely the first note, too) will be G. If the piece is in e minor, the last note (and likely the first note, too) will be e. If you actually hear the song, you can tell by the way it sounds: sad is minor, happy is Major.

Parallel and Relative Minor Scales

You may hear the above terms. They aren't different types of minor scales but are different ways of finding out which notes to play in the minor scale.

Parallel Minor

The way you have just learned—adding 3 flats to the key—is how to find the **parallel minor** scale. It's called parallel because it begins on the same note as the Major scale equivalent.

Relative Minor

I pointed out above that a minor key signature can also be a major key signature, but what makes it minor is the starting note.

Take a look at example 24.3 above, the key signatures for E Major and e minor. The key of e minor has only one sharp, right? This is also the key signature for G Major. These two keys are related (hence the term "relative minor"). The key signatures are exactly the same, but the difference is the starting note.

Find the 6th note of the G Major scale and don't forget to count G as "one." I'll wait while you figure it out ....

It's E, isn't it? Play or sing a scale with the key of G (one sharp), but play it from E to E and you've got the E natural minor scale.

If you take any major scale and play from the sixth note up an octave to the next sixth note, you'll have played the relative minor scale of the major key.

So e minor is the relative minor of G Major; A minor is the relative minor of C Major; G minor is the relative minor of Bb Major; B minor is the relative minor of D Major; and so on.

The cool thing about this is that when learning natural minor scales, you don't really have to memorize a whole new set of scales, simply start on the sixth degree of the Major scale, play the notes of that major scale from the 6th degree to the 6th an octave higher, and you've got a natural minor scale.

The Harmonic Minor Scale

The harmonic minor scale is a slightly altered natural minor scale. ***The seventh degree of the natural minor scale is raised one half step to get the harmonic minor scale***.

The harmonic minor scale gets its name from how it's used. The harmonic minor scale is used in order to get the harmony correct when using chords.

When constructing chords (which are harmony—two or more notes at once), in order for the chord progressions to sound right to our ears, we need a half step between the 7th and 8th degree of the scale, and that's what the harmonic minor scale does.

This seventh degree, when it's a half step away from the tonic, is called a **leading tone**. It's called a leading tone because it leads our ear to the tonic. Try this: play a major scale and stop on the seventh degree. It feels unresolved, unfinished, and leaves us slightly unsettled.

If you remember, in the natural minor scale, there is a whole step between the 7th and 8th degrees of the scale. To change this to a half step, you must raise the 7th degree a half step.

You find the key signature of a harmonic minor scale exactly the same way as a natural minor scale: add three flats to the Major key signature of the starting note, then simply raise the seventh degree one half step.

In the example below, I took the C Major key signature (no sharps or flats), added three flats (Bb, Eb, Ab), then wrote out the scale and raised the seventh degree (Bb) a half step with a natural sign.

Staff 25.5   The C harmonic minor scale.

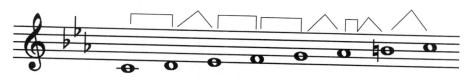

There is no key signature for the harmonic minor scale, so you have to alter the 7th degree in order to get the scale. If you tried to alter the key signature to do this, you'd have to take out the first flat, the Bb. You can't take it out without also taking out the others because the order of flats must always remain the same. It isn't just a good idea, it's the law.

Notice that between the 6th and 7th degree of this scale we have 1 1/2 steps. This is part of what gives the harmonic minor scale its distinctive sound.

Play the scale in example 24.4 above. Many people think it sounds "Arabian" or "exotic". It's a cool sound.

The Melodic Minor Scale

This is an exotic sounding scale and is often used in jazz.

The melodic minor scale is also based on the natural minor key signature with some alterations to the notes in the scale, but not to the key signature itself.

One weird thing about this scale is that it's different going up than it is coming down. Many jazz players however, only use the scale ascending. This isn't to say they only use the scale going up, but that they use the same pattern ascending as descending.

Again, use the major scale as your starting point. On the way up, the third degree of the major scale is lowered a half step. On the way down, the 7th, 6th and 3rd degrees of the major scale are lowered (this is the same as the natural minor scale descending).

In the example on the next page, I took the A Major scale (3 sharps) and lowered the 3rd degree (C# lowered to C natural) on the way up the scale. Then, coming down the scale, I also lowered the 6th and 7th degrees (G# to G, and F# to F).

To save you a little confusion, when you learn this scale, simply use the first half of it as most jazz players do.

Staff 25.6   **TOP:** The technically correct version of the a melodic minor scale **BOTTOM:** the practical version of the melodic minor scale (remember that an accidental lasts until a bar line, so the G's and F's in the lower example are all sharp)..

Circle of Fourths/Fifths Revisited

The Circle of Fourths (aka: Circle of Fifths) can also be used for the minor keys. Below is the Circle in the minor keys. Movement around the circle is similar to that explained on page 164.

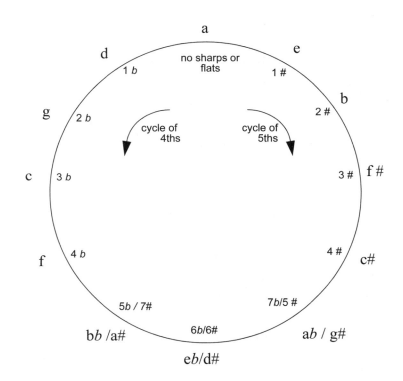

Moving On

The information in this chapter can be confusing, and many students find it a little challenging to wrap their brain around these concepts, so don't be surprised if you have to go back through it several times before it makes sense. Keep at it.

Coming up in the next chapter are modes, two of which you already know: the Major and minor scale.

Basic Music Theory

1. What are the three types of minor scale?

2. How do you make a natural minor scale?

3. Which degrees of the major scale are lowered to make the natural minor scale?

4. The key of D Major has 2 sharps (F# and C#). What is the key of d minor?

5. How do you make a harmonic minor scale?

6. What is a leading tone?

7. Do Major scales have leading tones?

8. Which minor scale does not have a leading tone?

9. How is a melodic minor scale different from the natural minor scale?

10. Which part of the melodic minor scale is generally used by jazz players?

11. What's the difference between a parallel minor scale and a relative minor scale?

1. Natural, harmonic, melodic

2. Add 3 flats to the key signature of a Major scale and use the same starting note. Or start on the 6th degree of a Major scale.

3. 3rd, 6th, 7th

4. One flat (Bb)

5. Raise the 7th degree of the natural minor scale a half step

6. One half step between the 7th and 8th degree of a scale

7. Yes

8. natural minor

9. 6th and 7th degrees are raised a half step going up; lowered again going down

10. the ascending scale

11. Parallel minor scales start on the same note as the major but the key signature has 3 extra flats. Relative minor scales begin on the 6th note of a Major scale and have the same key signature.

Practical Use

1. Write out harmonic minor scale starting on the following notes: C, B-flat, D, and F. Play them and sing them until memorized. Learn all 12 harmonic minor scales (keep at it no matter how long it takes!).

2. Write out all the key signatures and identify the major and minor for at least three of them. Example: 1 sharp is G Major, and e minor.

3. Persistence is the mother of success. Repetition is the father of success. Keep at it!

SCALES A LA MODE

Musical innovation is full of danger to the State, for when modes of music change, the laws of the State always change with them.

— Plato, *The Republic*

In This Chapter

- What is a Mode?
- Ionian Mode
- Dorian Mode
- Phrygian Mode
- Lydian Mode
- Mixolydian Mode
- Aeolian Mode
- Locrian Mode

Terms to Know

- **mode**: a type of scale using the intervals of the major or minor scale, but starting on a different degree of the scale.
- **Dorian**: mode starting on the second degree of the major scale.
- **Phrygian**: mode starting on the third degree of the major scale.
- **Lydian**: mode starting on the fourth degree of the major scale.
- **Mixolydian**: mode starting on the fifth degree of the major scale.
- **Aeolian**: mode starting on the sixth degree of the major scale.
- **Locrian**: mode starting on the seventh degree of the major scale.

What is a Mode?

A mode is a type of scale. Modes are used in certain types of music, like salsa, jazz, country, rock, fusion, speed metal, and more. To find out the details, read on.

The reason the Chapter image is of three guys jamming is that modes are very important to understanding (and using) jazz theory, and crucial to understanding how to improvise. Certain modes go with certain chords. For more information about modes and their specific uses in jazz, read James Levine's excellent book, *Jazz Theory*.

These are also called "church modes" because they were first used in the Catholic Church back in Medieval times (remember good old Guido d' Arezzo?). The names of the modes were taken from the Greek modes, but other than the names, they have no relation to the Greek modes.

The two modes which have been used the most, and the only two most people know, are now called the Major and natural minor scales. Their original names were the ***Ionian mode*** (Major), and the ***Aeolian mode*** (natural minor). The other modes are: ***dorian, phrygian, lydian, mixolydian,*** and ***locrian.***

Modes are easy to understand. We'll map out each mode's series of whole and half steps and use the key of C so there aren't any sharps or flats to bother with.

The Modes

Ionian

As you already know, the Ionian mode is the same as the C Major scale. All the white keys on the piano from C to C. And I'm sure you remember the whole-half step pattern of WWHWWWH

Ionian is used in nearly all Western music, from Classical to Zydeco.

Staff 26.1   The Ionian mode, also known as the Major scale.

Dorian

The Dorian mode begins on the second degree of the Major scale and in the key of C goes from D to D on the white keys of the piano. The pattern of whole and half steps is WHWWWHW.

There are 12 Dorian scales, corresponding to the 12 key signatures. The Dorian mode is a minor-sounding scale used in rock, jazz, blues, and fusion.

Staff 26.2   Dorian mode ascending.

Phrygian

You've probably caught on to the pattern by now. Phrygian begins on the third degree of the Major scale and in the key of C is E to E on the white keys of the piano. The whole-half step pattern is HWWWHWW.

This mode has a Spanish flavor and is used in jazz, flamenco music, fusion, and speed metal. Twelve of these, too. In fact, there are 12 of each type of mode because there are 12 different key signatures.

Staff 26.3   Phrygian mode ascending.

Lydian

Lydian begins on the 4th degree of the Major scale and in the key of C is from F to F on the white keys of the piano. Whole-half step pattern is WWWHWWH.

You might see this mode in jazz, fusion, rock, or country music. It's like a major scale with a raised 4th which gives this scale an odd sound.

Staff 26.4   Lydian mode ascending.

Mixolydian

Mixolydian begins on the fifth degree of the Major scale, and in the key of C is G to G on the white keys. Whole-half step pattern is WWHWWHW.

This mode shows up in jazz, rockabilly, country, blues, and rock.

Staff 26.5   Mixolydian mode ascending.

Aeolian

Also known as the natural minor scale, the Aeolian mode begins on the sixth degree of the Major scale. In the key of C it's from A to A on the white keys. WHWWHWW.

This mode appears in all kinds of music: jazz, pop, country, Rock, blues, heavy metal, classical, and on and on.

Staff 26.6   Aeolian mode ascending.

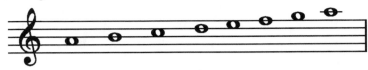

Locrian

The Locrian mode has a very exotic and other-worldly sound. All because of the placement of those half steps. You'll find Locrian in fusion and in jazz.

The Locrian mode begins on the seventh degree of the Major scale, and is B to B in the key of C.

Staff 26.7   Locrian mode ascending.

Finding Modes in Other Keys

There are two ways to find a mode in another key. You can find a mode within a certain key signature, or find a mode starting on a specific note.

To find a mode in a certain key is easiest. Just a couple steps.

1 Play the Major scale in the key you'll be using. For an example, let's say you wanted to find the Dorian mode which uses the key of Ab. First step is to play the Ab Major scale.

2 Depending on what mode you want, start on the appropriate note in the Major scale, and play an octave in the key of the Major scale. For our example, you want the Dorian mode, which begins on the second degree of the Major scale. So you'd play from Bb to Bb using the key of Ab.

To find a mode beginning on a specific note, the process is a little different but still pretty simple.

1 Depending on the mode you want, find out which major scale has that note in the appropriate place. Let's stick with Dorian for an example. You want to find the Dorian mode which begins on F. So you'd find out which Major scale has F as its second note. The answer is Eb.

2 Then use the key signature you found in step 1 for the Dorian mode. In our example, you'd play F to F using the key of Eb.

Modes Using Other Scales

Modes are also built from other scales, like the ascending melodic minor scale. This produces some interesting and exotic sounding scales. And the names are pretty wild, too. Like the Lydian augmented mode, the Lydian dominant mode, the half-diminished (also called Locrian #2), and the diminished whole tone mode.

These modes deal with more advanced harmonic practices, and I've included them to show you that there is more to learn once you've mastered the modes of the major scale. There is always something more to practice, something more to learn! How lucky we are!

Staff 26.8 Melodic minor scale (ascending) and two of its modes. The modes are named after the function of their pattern of whole and half steps, not which scale degree they are built on.

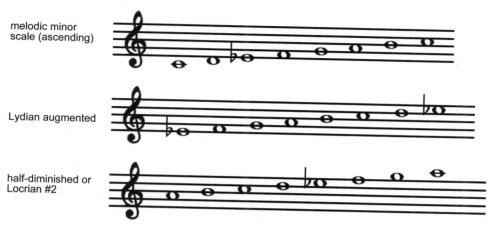

Moving On

Again, modes aren't particularly necessary to understand music theory in general, but they're crucial to gain a deeper understanding of jazz theory and especially improvisation.

Next we move on to the blues scales, which are fun and sound cool.

Chapter 26 Review

1. What are the names of the modes?

2. Which mode is the same as the major scale?

3. Which mode is the same as the natural minor scale?

4. What is the starting note for the Dorian mode which uses the key of D Major?

5. What key signature would be used for the Dorian mode beginning on an A?

6. What key signature would be used for the Mixolydian mode beginning on F?

1. *Ionian, Dorian, Phrygian, Lydian, Mixolydian, Aeolian, Locrian*

2. *Ionian*

3. *Aeolian*

4. *E*

5. *Key of G. One sharp*

6. *Key of Bb, two flats*

Practical Use

1. Write out all of the modes in the key of F. Learn them on your instrument/voice. Know where the half steps are in each. Then learn all of the modes in the key of G, then B♭, then D, etc. Another option is to learn only one mode at a time in every key, for example, the D Ionian, D Dorian, D Phrygian, etc.

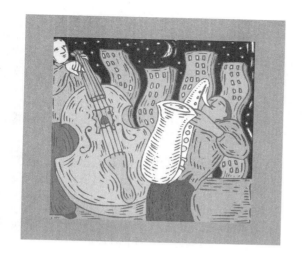

BLUES TO BEBOP
AND BEYOND

Jazz isn't dead, it just smells funny.

— Frank Zappa

In This Chapter

- General Blues Scale Information
- The Blues Scale
- 12 Bar Blues
- Other Crazy Scales

Terms to Know

- **gapped scale**: a scale that is not diatonic but has some intervals larger than a second.
- **whole tone scale**: a diatonic scale in which there is a whole step between all 8 notes of the scale.

General Blues Scale Info

Most people like blues scales. They sound cool, are fun to play and easy to learn. They also come in handy if you're improvising in blues, rock and roll, country, jazz, and many other styles of music.

Just like all the other scales, the blues scale can be made by altering notes of the major scale.

These altered notes are called *blue* notes, and their use originated with Africans who were brought to this country as slaves. A blue note was originally a bending of the pitch with the voice.

It's thought that the use of "the blues" as a term for feeling down came from a Native American tribe in the south who would cover their bodies with a blue dye when they were in mourning. Slaves in the area saw the practice and invented the term "feeling blue." Maybe it's just legend, but it's a story I like.

The Blues Scale

Standard Blues Scale

The **standard blues scale** is also called the minor blues scale.

As usual, we'll start with the key of C to avoid the confusion of lots of accidentals.

The 3rd, 5th and 7th degrees are lowered a half step, but the P5th is also needed so we'll have to slap a natural on the G to get that one in.

Staff 27.1   C blues scale.

Recipe for Any Standard Blues Scale

1 Take one Major scale of your choice

2 Use the tonic of the Major scale as the first note of the blues scale.

3 Lower the third degree of the Major scale a half step to get the second degree of the blues scale.

4 Use the P4 of the Major scale as the 3rd note of the blues scale.

5 Lower the P5 by a half step to get the 4th note of the blues scale.

6 Put the needed accidental in front of the 5th to get a P5 for the 5th note of the blues scale.

7 Take the seventh degree of the Major scale and lower it a half step for the 6th degree of the blues scale.

8 Use the P8 for the seventh note of the blues scale.

9 Turn lightly over and over in your brain and under your fingers until memorized.

10 Repeat from step one with a new scale until all 12 are memorized.

The Major Blues Scale

The Major blues scale is a slight alteration of the standard blues scale. See if you can spot the difference. There is a M2, a M3, and a M6, but no P4, and no m7.

Staff 27.2 The C Major blues scale.

If you were talking to a "jazzer", and asked her what the Major blues scale was, she'd say, "Tonic, two, flat three, three, five, six, eight," or something similar. This a shorthand version of describing each degree of the Major blues scale as it relates to the Major scale.

Other Crazy Scales

In this little section I'll show you: bebop scales, pentatonic scales, whole tone scales, and the super-locrian scale.

I'll only give you the version of each scale starting on C, and from there you can figure out the rest. If you're really gung-ho, you can take a look at **www.QuestionsInk.com/Links/student**, where you'll find a link for "Scales Galore". Go there and be amazed.

Pentatonic Scales

This is a type of *gapped scale*, which means there are intervals of more than a second in the scale. Do you see the gaps in the pentatonic scales below? In the major pentatonic, the gap is between the 3rd and 4th note, and between the 5th and 6th note. In the minor pentatonic there is a gap between the 1st and 2nd notes, and the 4th and 5th notes. See if you can identify what kind of interval in each case.

The pentatonic scale is another scale used a lot in jazz improvisation. As the name implies, there are only 5 notes in this scale. Though you see six, the bottom and top notes (tonic) count as one because they have the same name.

Staff 27.3 C Major pentatonic scale.

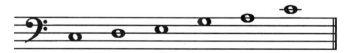

Staff 27.4 C minor pentatonic scale.

Bebop Scales

Bebop is a form of jazz begun by Dizzy Gillespie and Charlie Parker. It features blinding speed and virtuosic improvisational solos and altered harmonies. Some great bebop performers include Dizzy and Bird (Charlie Parker), Miles Davis, John Coltrane, Clifford Brown, Charles Mingus, Bud Powell, Stan Getz, Sonny Rollins, Sonny Stitt, Lee Morgan, and that's only a few.

There are three types of bebop scales: Major bebop, minor bebop, and dominant bebop.

Staff 27.5   C Major bebop scale.

Staff 27.6   C minor bebop scale.

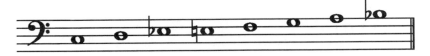

Staff 27.7   C dominant bebop scale.

Whole Tone Scale and the Super Locrian

Here are a couple of the strangest sounding scales you'll ever hear. The whole tone scale consists entirely of whole tones (whole steps), no half steps allowed.

The second scale has several names: diminished whole tone, altered, and my personal favorite, the super Locrian. The super Locrian is actually a mode derived from the ascending melodic minor scale. Can you figure out which scale degree of the melodic minor scale you'd start on to get that pattern? Hint: Locrian in this case is similar to the Locrian of the major scale in its starting note.

Staff 27.8   C whole tone scale.

Staff 27.9   The Super Locrian scale (aka: diminished whole tone; altered). This one begins on the 7th degree of the ascending D♭ melodic minor scale

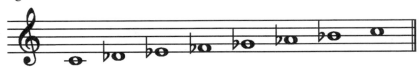

Moving On

Now that you've gotten a taste of several other scales that are out there, you can never say, "But there's nothing to practice." These scales can all be practiced in a gazillion different patterns. Get started now and you'll have that many more under your fingers next year at this time.

Coming up is the chapter review, then the hefty Section review. After that it's on to the next Part, which is all about chords: what they are, how to build them, chord extensions, and basic chord progressions.

Chapter 27 Review

1. What is a blue note?

2. As compared to the major scale, what are the notes of a standard blues scale?

3. What is a gapped scale?

4. Name at least three other types of scales.

5. Have you practiced your scales today?

1. *An altered note (usu. lowered) of the major scale*

2. *Tonic, flat 3, 4, flat 5, natural 5, flat 7, 8.*

3. *A scale with intervals of more than a second between some notes of the scale*

4. *Super Locrian, Major pentatonic, minor pentatonic, Major bebop, minor bebop, dominant bebop, whole tone*

Practical Use

1. Write out the C, F, and G blues scales. Memorize them on your instrument. Sing them. Improvise melodies and sounds with these three scales.

2. Write out, then memorize your pentatonic scales in every key.

How to Sing the Blues (Not Really)

1. Most blues begin with "woke up this mornin."
2. "I got a good woman" is a bad way to begin the blues unless you stick something nasty in the next line: "I got a good woman, with the meanest dog in town..."
3. Blues are simple. After you've got the first line, repeat it. Then find something that sort of rhymes:

    Got a good woman with the meanest dog in town,
    Got a good woman with the meanest dog in town,
    He gots teeth like Mick Jagger
    And he weigh 500 pounds.

4. The blues aren't about limitless choice.
5. Blues cars are Chevys and Cadillacs. Other acceptable blues transportation: a Greyhound bus or a southbound train. Not acceptable: BMW, hot air balloons, an R.V.
6. Walkin' always plays a major part in the blues, as does fixin' to die.
7. The best places to get the blues are Chicago, St. Louis, and Kansas City.
8. The following colors don't belong in the blues: beige, mauve, violet, periwinkle.
9. You can't have the blues in an office or mall. The lighting is wrong.
10. Good places for the blues: the highway (crossroads are best), the jail house, an empty bed.
11. Bad places for the blues: an ashram, gallery openings, wine tastings.
12. Do you have a right to sing the blues?

    Yes if:
    your first name is a state, like Georgia, or Tennessee;
    you're blind;
    you shot a man in Memphis;
    you can't be satisfied;
    "the man" doesn't like you.

    No if:
    you were once blind but now can see;
    you ski in Tahoe each year
    you have an IRA.

13. If you ask for water and yo' baby gives you gasoline, it's the blues.
14. Other blues liquids:

    wine from a bottle in a sack;
    Irish whiskey from a dirty glass;
    muddy water (usually not for drinking).

15. Not blues beverages:

    any mixed drink, or drink with an umbrella in it;
    any kosher wine;
    Yoo Hoo (all flavors).

16. If it occurs in a fleabag motel or in a shotgun shack, it's a blues death. Other blues deaths: being stabbed in the back by a jealous lover, being pushed down an old mine shaft, crying yourself to death. You cannot die a blues death during a tennis match or during a liposuction treatment.
17. Some blues names for women:

    Sadie
    Big Mama
    Bessie
    Billie

18. Some blues names for men:

    Joe (including "Big", "Old", or "Blind" in any combination, but not Little
    Willie (Little Willie could work)
    Lightnin'
    Almost anything with Howlin' in front of it
    Other possibilities include physical infirmities: Blind, Cripple, Wheezin'
    Fruit names: lemon, lime, (not pomegranate)
    Presidents: Jefferson, Johnson, Fillmore, (not Bush)

19. Persons with names like Barbie, Sequoia, or Chauncey will not be permitted to sing the blues no matter how many men they kill in Memphis.

PART V REVIEW

Whew! You Made It.

These pages can be used to test your memory about what you've learned in Part V, and if some of the information hasn't stuck, you can go back and check it out on the page indicated below the question.

As with the chapter reviews, use your keyboard to cover up the answers while you test yourself. When you think you've got it all down, either take the test in *Basic Music Theory Quiz Pack* (available for free at www.Sol-Ut.com), or go on.

The Review

1. What is the definition of an interval?
   page 180

2. What is a harmonic interval?
   page 180

3. What is a melodic interval?
   page 180

4. How do you find the number of an interval?
   page 180

5. When figuring an interval, what will always be the number of the lower note?
   page 180

6. What are the qualities of intervals?
   page 180

7. What does a Perfect interval become when lowered a half step?
   page 181

---

1. *The distance between two pitches*

2. *The distance between two pitches sounded simultaneously*

3. *The distance between two pitches sounded consecutively*

4. *Count each line and space up from the lower of the two notes*

5. *1*

6. *Perfect, Major, minor, diminished, augmented*

7. *diminished (dim)*

8. What does a Perfect interval become when raised a half step?

page 181

9. What does a Major interval become when raised a half step?

page 182

10. What does a Major interval become when lowered a half step?

page 182

11. What is this interval?

page 181

12. What is this interval?

page 182

13. What are the three types of minor scale?

page 188

14. How do you make a natural minor scale?

page 188

15. Which notes of the major scale are lowered to make the natural minor scale?

page 188

16. What is the key of B minor?

page 189

17. What is the key of Ab minor?

page 189

18. How do you make a harmonic minor scale?

page 190

19. What is a leading tone?

page 190

20. Do Major scales have leading tones?

page 190

8. augmented (aug)

9. augmented (aug)

10. minor

11. min 6

12. aug 4

13. natural, harmonic, melodic

14. Add 3 flats to the key signature of a Major scale and use the same starting note

15. 3rd, 6th, 7th

16. Two sharps (F#, C#)

17. Seven flats (Bb, Eb, Ab, Db, Gb, Cb, Fb)

18. Raise the 7th degree of the natural minor scale a half step.

19. One half step between the 7th and 8th degree of a scale.

20. Yes

Basic Music Theory

21. Which minor scale does not have leading tones?
page 190

21. *natural minor scale*

22. How is a melodic minor scale different from the natural minor scale?
page 191

22. *6th and 7th degrees are raised a half step going up; lowered again going down*

23. What's the difference between a parallel minor scale and a relative minor scale?
page 189

23. *Parallel minor scales start on the same note as the major but the key signature has 3 extra flats. Relative minor scales begin on the 6th note of a Major scale and have the same key signature.*

24. What are the names of the modes?
page 196

24. *Ionian, Dorian, Phrygian, Lydian, Mixolydian, Aeolian, Locrian*

25. Which mode became known as the major scale?
page 196

25. *Ionian*

26. Which mode became known as the natural minor scale?
page 197

26. *Aeolian*

27. What is the starting note for the Dorian mode which uses the key of D Major?
page 198

27. *E*

28. What key signature would be used for the Dorian mode beginning on an A?
page 198

28. *Key of G. One sharp*

29. What is a blue note?
page 202

29. *An altered note (usu. lowered) of the major scale*

30. Using the major scale as a reference, what are the notes of a standard blues scale?
page 202

30. *Tonic, flat 3, 4, flat 5, natural 5, flat 7, 8*

31. Name at least three other types of scale.
page 203

31. *Super Locrian, Major pentatonic, minor pentatonic, Major bebop, minor bebop, dominant bebop whole tone*

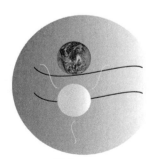

SolŪt Press

Support Music and Musicians.
www.Sol-Ut.com

CHAPTER 28

Interlude

HOW TO CONDUCT YOURSELF

*Conductors must give unmistakable
and suggestive signals to the
orchestra, not choreography to the
audience.*

— George Szell

In This Interlude

- General Conducting Info
- Conducting Patterns
- Body Language

General Conducting Information

A conductor is a musician whose instrument is a large group of singers or instrumentalists. These musicians are guided either with a baton (also called a stick) or by the conductor's hands alone.

An audience only sees a very small part of what a conductor does, because all they see is the conductor's back. The audience doesn't get to see the frowns and grimaces, the stern looks and the kind, the oh-so-rare smiles, and all the subtle nuances of body language and facial gesture. The audience sees only the wilder gesticulations of the arms and part of the body language.

Most of a conductor's work in shaping a piece of music comes during rehearsals, though a good conductor with a good group of musicians can shape a piece of music spontaneously during a performance.

A conductor's arm moves in a specific pattern which depends upon the time signature of the piece being played. It's usually the right hand and arm which beat out this pattern while the left hand controls dynamics and phrases and expressiveness. This is only a general rule.

The roles of a conductor change depending upon the level of musician in the group. Let's compare conductors at the two ends of the spectrum: the professional symphony conductor and the elementary school music teacher.

An elementary school musician needs a very clear pattern that shows explicitly where all the beats are. The job of an elementary director is primarily to help the students get through the piece and so the elementary conductor's gestures will be very clear and concise to help the student. Expressiveness is certainly important, too, but a clear beat is more important.

A professional orchestra conductor's focus is more on his or her aural vision of the piece, on the subtle nuances of the music. He or she is not concerned with teaching the clarinets an alternate fingering for low F, and such a conductor's gestures will be more expressive, sometimes to the point of being unclear rhythmically. A professional conductor might be interested with a certain passage being more marcato, a little quieter, and with less trombone. A professional conductor may however, fire the clarinetist who doesn't know the alternate fingering for low F.

Whatever the level, a conductor is responsible for many more things than the individual musician. First of all, the music a conductor reads is much more complex than the music of any player in the group. This is because the conductor reads from a *score*, which is a large, multi-paged piece of music with *all* the parts in it, from the piccolo to the percussion, from the violin to the bass voice parts.

Conductors are also musical scholars, and should know about performance practices (how a certain piece should be performed), about chord structure and chord progressions, about the intonation tendencies of every instrument, about movement and how musicians react to it, about rehearsal technique and how to get what is needed from musicians, about music history and theory, and on and on. A good conductor is always learning.

Stance

How a conductor stands will change based upon the music, and we'll get to some specifics later in the chapter, but generally, a conductor should have good posture, feet about shoulder width apart, and a relaxed stance.

At first, the left arm will simply hang relaxed at your side—you'll use it later, but for now you won't need it. The right arm will be extended, slightly bent, and will move around in an area a foot or two in front of you, from the top of your head to the middle of your chest, and from shoulder to shoulder.

If you're using a baton (a pencil will work), grip it with the thumb and index finger and wrap the other fingers lightly around it without grasping.

Eye Contact

Probably one of the most important aspects of conducting is eye contact. If a conductor's face is buried in the music, he or she won't be able to look a section of altos or a section of trumpets right in the face to be sure they understand what is being asked for.

Eye contact is a double-edged sword. It won't matter *how* fiercely the conductor looks at the musicians, or how flamboyantly his or her arms wave if the musicians don't look up from their music. Ever wonder why choirs memorize their music?

Conducting Patterns

The right arm gives each beat in each measure. Each meter has a different pattern for the right arm. The first one you'll learn is the most common pattern, the one for 4/4 time.

Each diagram that you see is given from the conductor's point of view. You'll get the right movement if you simply trace the pattern in the air.

With *all* patterns, beat one is always given straight down. Your arm is out in front of you and travels from the level of your head down to the level of your chest.

Be sure to make each beat obvious. Do this by giving a small sharp bounce with the hand on each beat.

It takes a little practice to make each pattern look natural, so keep at it. You can learn a lot by watching other conductors, and you might notice that the more accomplished the conductor, the more difficult it will be to determine exactly which pattern he or she is using. Call it creative license.

Staff 28.1   The conducting pattern for 4/4 time.

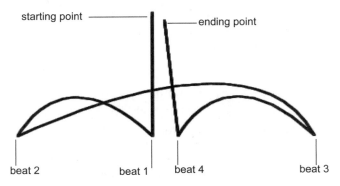

starting point ———   ——— ending point

beat 2   beat 1   beat 4   beat 3

Staff 28.2   The conducting pattern for 3/4 time.

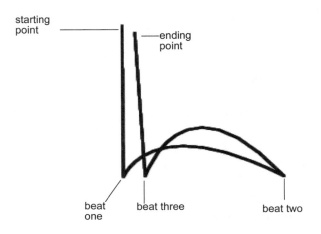

starting point ———   —ending point

beat one   beat three   beat two

Staff 28.3   Two conducting patterns for 2/4 time.

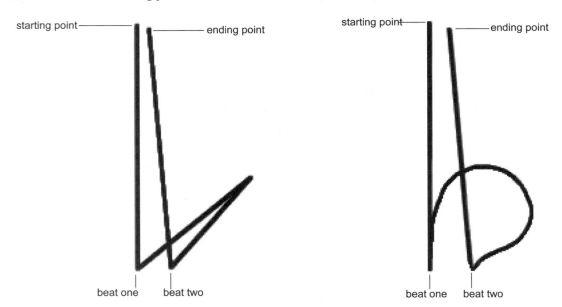

starting point———   ——— ending point   starting point———   ——— ending point

beat one   beat two   beat one   beat two

Showing Style with the Right Hand

Much of the style of a piece of music can be shown with the right hand alone: short, choppy strokes for a piece like a march; long flowing strokes for a more lyric song; a small pattern for quiet sections; a larger pattern for loud sections.

Use a Conducting Pattern to Transcribe Music

Even if you'll never conduct a large group, conducting is a useful tool when you're trying to write down music you hear. Because it's a physical manifestation of the music's beat, conducting patterns make it much easier to discover where in the measure the notes fall and how long they are.

This takes some practice as you may have guessed. Transcribing what you hear is a difficult process for most of us and any tool helps. The conducting patterns break up the measure into beat-sized chunks which is a great first step towards writing down what you hear.

The Left Hand

Though the left hand may also beat out the patterns you just learned, the left normally shows dynamics, articulations, cues (telling instruments or soloists when to come in), and cut-offs.

The independence of each hand takes some effort to master. It's a lot like rubbing your head and patting your stomach at the same time. Try not to beat out the pattern simultaneously with both hands (called *mirroring*). It's generally considered bad conducting form.

While you're conducting, if you're having trouble getting your left hand to act independently, just let it hang at your side.

Dynamics

There are several ways to show dynamics while conducting: body position, facial expression, and hand position. Let's start with hand position.

Hand Position

If you conduct with a very small pattern (say two square inches in front of you), players—if they're watching you—will play more quietly. In contrast, very large motions will cause a group to play or sing more loudly.

To show crescendos (gradually louden), start with the left hand down near your gut with the palm up and gradually raise it where the crescendo in the music should happen. By the time your hand reaches a position above the height of your shoulder, the crescendo should be at its peak. At the same time, the pattern in the right hand should start small and grow larger. It's easier to say than it is to do. Try it.

Decrescendos (gradually soften) are shown in the opposite way. The left hand begins above the shoulder, palm *down* this time, and gradually lowers down to the middle of your torso. While doing this, make the right hand pattern become gradually smaller.

If the saxes or the sopranos are too loud, you can "give them the hand", which means holding your left hand out with the palm facing the loud group. This works well accompanied by a stern look.

Body Position

If you step forward on the podium and lean towards the group or even crouch down, this will cause them to become quieter, especially if you combine these movements with the above-mentioned technique of making the conducting pattern smaller.

Also effective is to show the group a *quiet face*, whatever you think that is for you. Pursing your lips in a "shush" works pretty well. Practice in a mirror.

In contrast, to get a group to play louder, stand tall as you step back on the podium and lean away from the group. Combine this with making all of your gestures bigger and a group should get louder if they're watching you.

For this technique, use a *loud face*, usually something that looks stern or even angry. An upraised fist shaken in the air is also quite effective.

Practicing Conducting

Perhaps the best way, when you're just beginning to learn, is to get some recordings of music you like which require a conductor and, in the privacy of your own home, give it a try.

The next step, once you've got the patterns down, is to get the score for that piece of music and try to follow along while you conduct.

The best advice I can give you for practicing *anything* is to be persistent. Persistence is way more important than talent. Keep at it.

If you're serious about becoming better, videotaping yourself is a necessity.

This is only the briefest introduction to the art of conducting. If you'd like to learn more, take a look at the following books:

The Grammar of Conducting: A Comprehensive Guide to Baton Technique and Interpretation by Max Rudolf and Michael Stern.

Preparatory Exercises in Score Reading by Reginald O. Morris and Howard Ferguson.

Conducting Technique for Beginners and Professionals by Brock McElheran and Lukas Foss.

Moving On

Conducting is a discipline much like playing an instrument, and the more you know about it, the better able you'll be to play in a group and follow a conductor, if one is even necessary.

Hope you liked this little break from learning music. Let's jump back into it. Up next are chords, a group of three or more notes played together.

P A R T   S I X

Strike a Chord

In This Section You Will Learn:

- Triads
- Chord Extensions
- Chord Inversions
- Some Chord Progressions

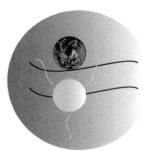

SolŪt Press

Support Music and Musicians.
www.Sol-Ut.com

TRIADS

Music
Which can be made anywhere, is invisible
And does not smell.

— W.H. Auden

In This Chapter

- General Chord Information
- The Triad
- Major Triad
- Minor Triad
- Diminished Triad
- Augmented Triad

Terms to Know

- **chord**: three or more notes sounded at the same time.
- **triad**: a type of chord with three notes, a root, third and fifth.
- **root**: the tonic note of a chord and the bottom note of a chord in root position.
- **third**: the chord tone a third above the root note.
- **fifth**: the chord tone a fifth above the root note.

General Chord Info

The use of the word chord began, according to Webster's, around 1608, and is short for *accord*, which means to be in harmony, as in agreeing. It's a good word for a musical chord, because the notes in most chords tend to agree with each other. They sound good together.

A chord is three or more notes sounded simultaneously. A chord can be played on one instrument like guitar or piano, or a chord can be played by many instruments at once, like a woodwind quintet, or a brass quartet, or a choir. As long as there are three or more notes sounding simultaneously, it's a chord.

There are many types of chords, and many different chord symbols that tell you which notes to use in a chord. Just like with scales, there are Major chords, minor chords, but unlike scales, there are also diminished chords and augmented chords. *The quality of a chord is determined by the intervals within the chord.*

There are also other types of chords with more than three notes and several different treatments of chords, but I'll save those for the next two chapters.

While you're learning these chords, if you have access to a keyboard, you really should try playing them to hear what they sound like.

Naming Chords

A chord has two names. One is a number, a Roman numeral. The other is a letter name. Both the letter name and the Roman numeral have with them abbreviations or symbols to show the chord qualities of Major, minor, diminished, and augmented.

Roman Numerals

Each chord has a Roman numeral which corresponds to the degree of the scale on which the chord is built. Take a look at example 28.2 on page 221 to see this. The upper case Roman numerals denote Major triads, and lower case denotes minor triads.

In addition, there are other symbols to show diminished and augmented triads. You'll see those soon.

Letter Names

Chords also have a letter name which comes from the root (the bottom note) of the chord. Example 28.1 shows you what a root is.

If a chord is named with only a capital letter, this means the chord is Major. A minor chord will have "min" written next to the letter. Another method for showing minor is to use lower case letters, though it's more common to use the "min" next to the letter.

In addition, the symbols for augmented and diminished are also used with the letter. We'll get to diminished and augmented chords in a few more pages.

When you say the notes in a chord, you're *spelling the chord*. For example, to spell the C chord I'd say, "C, E, G."

The Triad

A triad consists of three notes stacked in a specific order, *a root (or bottom note and usually the letter name of the chord), a third, and a fifth*. As you'll see in the examples, each triad is built on all lines or all spaces.

The parts of a triad get their name from their interval above the root note.

Staff 29.1 Triads in various positions on the staff.

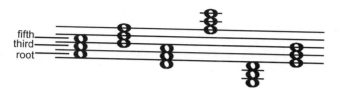

Triads in a Major Key

In the following example, you'll see a triad stacked on each degree of the C Major scale. Triads stacked in this way will have a quality of either Major, minor, or diminished.

Notice the little circle to the right of the vii. This symbol tells you the chord is a diminished chord. I'll show you why it's diminished coming up.

Staff 29.2 Triads built upon the degrees of the C Major scale, with Roman numerals.

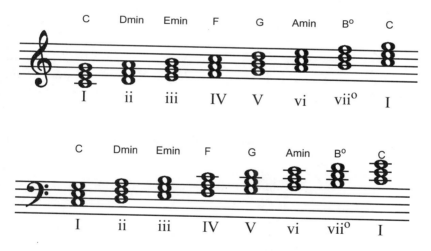

Major Triads

Major triads have a happy, bright sound quality.

A Major triad consists of a note a Major third above the root and another note a Perfect fifth above the root.

In a Major key, there are three naturally occurring Major triads, those built upon the first, fourth, and fifth degrees of the scale, or the I, IV, and V chords.

Staff 29.3 Breakdown of the Major triads in the key of C.

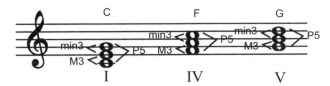

Minor Triads

Minor triads have a dark, sad sound quality.

A minor triad consists of a note a minor 3rd above the root and another note a Perfect 5th above the root. You can also think of a minor triad as a

In a Major key, there are three naturally occurring minor triads, those built upon the second, third, and sixth degrees of the Major scale, or the ii, iii, and vi chords.

Staff 29.4 Breakdown of the minor triads in the key of C.

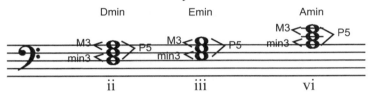

Diminished Triads

Diminished triads are less common than the Major or minor triads and have a suspenseful sound quality. This is the chord you hear when the damsel in distress is tied to the railroad tracks by Dastardly Dan as an approaching train hoots in the near distance.

A diminished triad consists of a note a minor 3rd above the root and another note a diminished 5th above the root.

In a Major key, there is only one naturally occurring diminished triad, the one built on the seventh degree of the Major scale.

Don't forget to put the little circle next to the lowercase Roman numeral. We'll get into more chord symbols in the next chapter.

Staff 29.5 Breakdown of the diminished triad on the 7th degree of the Major scale.

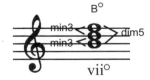

Augmented Triads

There aren't any naturally occurring augmented triads in the key of C, or in any major key, so we'll have to throw in an accidental to get one. The augmented triad has a vaguely unsettling sound, and is usually the type of chord played just before the knife-wielding psycho jumps out from behind the couch and scares the cooties off your head.

An augmented triad consists of a note a Major 3rd above the root and another note an augmented 5th above the root.

Since there aren't any augmented triads occurring naturally in the key of C, I'll just make a couple up.

The chord symbol for an augmented chord is a plus symbol (+), or the abbreviation "aug."

Staff 29.6   Breakdown of two augmented triads in the key of C.

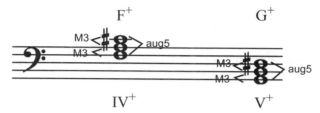

Moving On

Triads are the most basic chord form and it's important to know the difference between Major, minor, diminished and augmented triads, so don't go on until you've got it.

In the next Chapter we'll add another note on top of the chord to make the triad a seventh chord, a type of chord extension. We'll also discuss other chord extensions. But first, the review.

Chapter 29 Review

1. What is the definition of a chord?

   1. *Three or more notes played at the same time*

2. What determines the quality of a chord?

   2. *The intervals within the chord*

3. How are chords named?

   3. *With a Roman numeral, a letter, and a quality of Major, minor, diminished or augmented*

4. What are the parts of a triad?

   4. *Root, third, fifth*

5. Why are they called this?

   5. *Root is the tonic of the chord; the third is a 3rd above the root; the fifth is a 5th above the root*

6. How do you tell if a triad is Major?

   6. *Capital Roman numeral, or a capital letter, or the intervals within the triad*

7. How do you tell if a triad is minor?

8. What are the intervals in a Major triad?

9. What are the intervals in a minor triad?

10. What are the intervals in a diminished triad?

11. What are the intervals in an augmented triad?

12. What are the sound qualities of the different types of triads?

7. *Lowercase Roman numeral, lowercase letter, or "min" next to the letter name or the triad's intervals*

8. *A note a Major 3rd above the tonic and another a Perfect 5th above the tonic*

9. *A note a minor 3rd above the tonic and another a Perfect 5th above the tonic*

10. *A note a minor 3rd above the tonic and another a diminished 5th above the tonic*

11. *A note a Major 3rd above the tonic and another an augmented 5th above the tonic*

12. *Major = happy; minor = sad; diminished = suspenseful; augmented = unsettling*

Practical Use

1. Write out triads above the notes C, D, E, F and G. Sing or play these chords in an arpeggio (look this word up in the glossary if you don't know it) until you can hear each note in the chord easily. Play these notes as a chord on a piano or guitar. Identify which chords are Major and which chords are minor. Identify by singing or playing the minor thirds and Major thirds within these triads.

2. Write out four triads, all with D as their tonic. Make the first triad major, the second minor, the third diminished, and the fourth augmented. Play them on a piano. Memorize how they sound. Do the same thing starting on another note of your choice.

Basic Music Theory

30

CHORD EXTENSIONS

I don't care too much about music. What I like is sounds.

— Dizzy Gillespie (1917 - 1993)

In This Chapter

- General Chord Extension Information
- The Seventh Chord
- The Ninth Chord
- The Eleventh and 13th Chords
- Other Chords

Terms to Know

- **extension**: a note or notes added to a triad, shown by numbers and letters to the right of the chord letter.
- **compound interval**: an interval larger than an octave (i.e.-9th, 11th, 13th).

30: Chord Extensions

225

General Chord Extension Info

A chord extension is a note that isn't in the triad. It's extra. Notes are added to triads to change the triad's flavor, their feel, and in many cases the extension changes how the chord is used.

Some notes added to triads are: 7ths, 9ths, 11ths, and 13ths. We haven't talked about intervals higher than octaves (called *compound intervals*), so now's the time.

If you look at the C scale in the example below, the 8th note is the same letter as the bottom note. Therefore, the 9th note is the same letter as the 2nd note of the scale, only it's an octave higher. The 11th is like a 4th, but an octave higher; the 13th is like a 6th, but an octave higher.

Staff 30.1   The C scale extended two octaves.

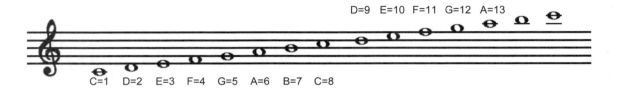

Chords with extensions are written with the number of the extension above and to the right of the chord letter, like so: F^{b13}, A^7, G^9, $C^{\#11}$, F^{13}, D^{Maj7}, and so on. Extensions can also be used with Roman numerals, like V^7, IV^9, etc.

The number tells you which note you're adding to the triad. The number represents the interval from the root of the chord to the extension. For example, a chord symbol with a 7 in it means that you're adding a note a 7th above the root of the chord.

An extension can be altered a half step up or down to give yet another type of chord. In the examples I gave you above, there was an F chord with a $b13$, a C chord with a #11, and a D chord with a Maj7. In these cases you would lower the 13th a half step, raise the 11th a half step or use a Major 7th above the root, respectively.

Chord Symbol and Meaning

min, -	minor
M, Maj, △, +	major
O	diminished
Ø	half-diminished
aug	augmented
7, 9, 11, 13 (any #)	scale tone # above root

On to some specifics.

Seventh Chords

Seventh chords are an important type of chord in Western music. They are essential to most chord progressions, and give progressions the quality our ears are used to hearing. We'll get into specifics of chord progressions soon in Chapter 32.

The seventh chords have a property that other extensions don't have. When you see *a seven next to a chord symbol, it's always a minor 7th above the root*.

If you want a Major seventh above the root, you have to specify it in the extension by putting an "M" or a "Maj" or a small triangle "△" in front of the extension number.

Staff 30.2   Some seventh chords.

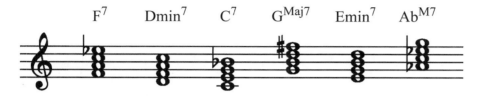

As you can see in the above examples, the quality of the chord itself is written in larger letters next to the letter of the chord (except for Major chords which are just the letter), and any alterations to the 7th are written in small letters before the 7.

The Dominant Seventh Chord

There is a special kind of seventh chord which appears in a huge majority of chord progressions and it's called the **dominant seventh chord**.

The dominant seventh chord symbol looks like this: V^7.

Because you know how Roman numerals are used, you know that the above symbol means that the chord is built on the 5th degree of the scale and it's got a minor seventh in it.

I didn't tell you each scale degree had a name when we went over scales because you had enough to worry about without me giving you more information than was necessary, but now it's necessary.

Each scale degree has a name, and it just so happens that the name of the 5th degree of the scale is "dominant." So there you go. That's why a chord built on the 5th degree of the scale is called a dominant chord, and one with a seventh is called a dominant seventh chord.

The dominant seventh chord is an important chord because it pulls our ears back toward the tonic chord, or the I chord. More on that in Chapter 31.

Staff 30.3   Dominant seventh chords in the keys of C, G, Bb, and F.

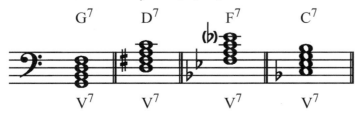

Notice above that each measure uses a different key signature. When you build a chord on the 5th degree of the scale in any Major key, the seventh of V^7 will automatically be a minor seventh because of the key signature.

Ninth Chords

Ninth chords have 5 chord tones: Root, third, fifth, seventh, and ninth.

As before, the quality of the chord is written in larger letters next to the chord letter, and the extensions are written with smaller letters and numbers above and to the right. If all you see is a "9", the 7 is implied. However, if you want a *Major* 7th in there (remember that unless indicated, the 7th is always minor), you must specify it, as in the $G^{M7,9}$ and the $Ab^{+7,9}$ below.

Staff 30.4   Some ninth chords.

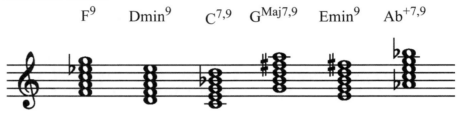

F^9 $Dmin^9$ $C^{7,9}$ $G^{Maj7,9}$ $Emin^9$ $Ab^{+7,9}$

Other Chords

Eleventh and Thirteenth Chords

The process for these chords is very similar to what you already know. An eleventh chord will have a root, third, fifth, seventh, ninth and eleventh.

A thirteenth chord will have a root, third, fifth, seventh, ninth, eleventh, and thirteenth.

The Half Diminished Chord

We'll stay in the key of A to avoid too many accidentals, but of course these types of chords can be found or created in any key.

Be sure to experiment with the notes I'm giving you below. Remember that music is about the *sounds*, and *not* the written note on the page. Experiment and *listen* to these chords, don't just think about them!

Half Diminished Chords

A half diminished chord is a minor seventh chord with a flatted fifth. Above the root you'll have a minor third, a diminished fifth, and a minor seventh. In a longer form, this chord would be notated $Amin^{7b5}$ or $A-^{7b5}$, but a shorter version which gives the same information is $A^{\varnothing}$.

Staff 30.5   The Amin^{7b5}, or the A-^{7b5}, or the A half diminished chord, or as it's usually notated, the A^{∅}.

Are all these symbols confusing? Without a doubt. The reason for the shortening of the symbols is that when jazz musicians are reading through chord changes while they improvise, it's more difficult and time-consuming to read Cmin^{7b5}, which has 5 "bits" of information, than it is to read C^{∅}, which has only two "bits" of information.

Chords Not Covered

There are several other types of chord which this book won't cover, though I'll tell you what some are and you can discover them on your own if you'd like.

There are suspended fourth chords, Neapolitan sixth chords, German sixth chords, fully diminished seventh chords, and many more.

Moving On

This chapter should allow you to understand and spell most chords you'll come across. Again, the concepts you're now learning are more complex than previous ones and they may take some time before they're understood well, so keep at it.

All the chords in this chapter have been in root position, the most basic form of a chord. In the next chapter, you'll learn about chord inversions, which is a chord with a note other than the tonic as the bottom note.

Chapter 30 Review

1. What is a chord extension?

2. How are chord extensions notated?

3. What is a compound interval?

4. When you see a ^{7} to the right of a chord letter, what kind of a 7th is it?

5. How would you indicate a Major 7 above the root?

---

1. *A note that doesn't appear in the basic triad*

2. *With a number equal to the note's interval above the root. Also with a symbol showing quality*

3. *An interval greater than an octave*

4. *A minor 7th above the root*

5. *With a +, a small triangle, a small "M", or a small "Maj" before the 7*

6. What's another name for the V^7 chord?

    6. A dominant seventh chord

7. Why are V^7 chords so important?

    7. They draw the ear to the tonic (I) chord, and appear in nearly all chord progressions

8. Spell the V^7 chord in the key of G.

    8. D,F#,A,C

9. Which chord tones are in a 9th chord?

    9. Root, 3rd, 5th, 7th, 9th

10. Which chord tones are in an 11th chord?

    10. Root, 3rd, 5th, 7th, 9th, 11th

Practical Use

1. Write out the triads above C, A, B-flat, and A-flat. Put the chord name underneath (don't forget Major/minor distinctions). Place the seventh in each of the chords and alter the chord symbol as necessary to make it correct. Place the ninth in each chord and again correct the chord symbol.

2. Sing or play (both is best) a Major triad. Any starting note will do but try to make it in a comfortable range. As you are singing one note of the chord, try to hear the others simultaneously. Once the Major triad is in your ear, add the seventh until you can sing or play a seventh easily. Do the same with the ninth chord.

3. Spend some time messing around with triads and extensions on the piano. It's fun and will help your understanding immensely.

CHAPTER

31

CHORD INVERSIONS

See deep enough, and you see musically;
the heart of nature being everywhere
music, if you can only reach it.

— Thomas Carlyle, *Heroes and*
Hero Worship

In This Chapter

- More General Chord Information
- Close and Open Harmony
- First Inversion
- Second Inversion
- Third Inversion

Terms to Know

- **root position**: when the lowest note of a chord is also the name of the chord.
- **first inversion**: when the lowest note of a chord is the third of the chord.
- **second inversion**: when the lowest note of a chord is the fifth of the chord.
- **close harmony**: when chord tones are written as closely together as possible, usually within an octave.
- **open harmony**: when chord tones spread out, usually over more than an octave.
- **voice**: when speaking of chords, any chord tone may also be called a *voice* of the chord.
- **harmonic analysis**: the process of analyzing each chord's relation to the key signature. Uses Roman numerals (I-vii) to show this relationship.

31: Chord Inversions

231

More General Chord Info

We've been working with chords in what is called **root position**, which is the most basic form of a chord. In root position the notes are stacked neatly together as close as they can be.

There is a broader definition of root position. ***If the lowest note of a chord is also the letter name of the chord, then that chord can be said to be in root position***.

For instance, with a C chord, as long as the C is the lowest note, it doesn't matter where the 3rds and 5ths are above that C; the chord will still be in root position.

Staff 31.1   Three versions of a C chord in root position.

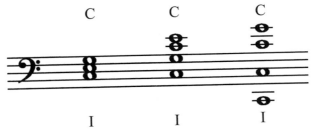

In the chords above, you'll find a C in the root, and above that root somewhere an E and a G. There could be three Es and seven Gs but as long as that C stays in the root position, it's a root position C chord. *Any doubling of chord tones doesn't affect the quality of the chord*.

Voice

Any note of a chord can be said to be a voice of the chord. For example, in a triad there are three voices: the bottom voice, the middle voice and the top voice. The term *voice* is used even for music in which there is no vocal part.

Open and Close Harmony

What is different about the chords above is how they are spaced. When a chord's voices are written as closely together as possible, as in the first example above, that chord is said to be in **close harmony**, or **close position**, and this is usually within an octave.

When a chord is spread out over more than an octave, or if there is a gap between chord tones where another could be but isn't, as in the second and third examples above, that chord is said to be in **open harmony**, or **open position**.

First Inversion

A first inversion chord has the third of the chord as its bottom note. To make a first inversion chord, take the tonic of a root position chord and move it up an octave. This will leave the third of the chord in the bottom voice.

This is indicated by the chord letter name, a slash (/) and then the name of the note that will be in the bass. For example, a C chord in first inversion will be shown with C/E. An F chord in first inversion will be F/A.

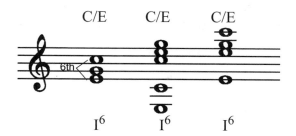

You'll often see chord letters marked in music, especially music with lyrics. The letter name won't tell you anything about inversions or the Roman numeral for that chord; you have to figure these out for yourself. This is called *harmonic analysis*. Inversions and Roman numerals are shown in harmonic analysis, which you'll see under the chords in the examples above and following.

To mark the first inversion in harmonic analysis, a 6 is written above and to the right of the Roman numeral. This is because the interval from the bottom note (3rd of the chord, remember) to the tonic is now a 6th. If you don't believe me, count it out in the examples above.

Second Inversion

A second inversion chord has the fifth of the chord as the bottom note. To make a second inversion chord from a first inversion chord, simply move the third up an octave. This leaves the fifth in the bottom voice. As with the first inversion, this inversion is also shown by a slash and the bass note. For example, the C chord in second inversion is C/G. The D chord in second inversion is written D/A.

Staff 31.3   Second inversion chords in the key of C in close and open harmony.

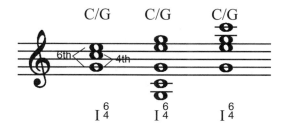

In harmonic analysis, this inversion is shown by a 6 over a 4 next to the Roman numeral. Again, these numbers represent the intervals above the bottom note. In the second inversion C chord, it's a 6th from G to E, and a 4th from G to C.

Because the 6 and 4 are only used in a harmonic analysis, when you see a chord, you have to figure for yourself which inversion it's in. Not to fear; at the end of the chapter is a step-by-step process to find out what any type of chord is.

To keep things simple, I've only used the I chord, but these inversions can be applied to any chord, the IV, the ii, the vi°, anything.

If chords are stacked in close harmony, it's pretty easy to tell at a glance whether it's a root position triad (three notes stacked one atop the other), a first inversion (two stacked on the bottom), or a second inversion (two stacked on the top).

Keep in mind that I've used simple chords in only one clef, and chords are often spread out over two clefs, but the same rules apply.

Inverting Seventh Chords

Seventh chords may also be inverted, and the symbols used for this in harmonic analysis are a little different but the concept is the same; the numbers tell you chord tone intervals above the bottom note.

With the extra note of the seventh chord, we get another inversion, called a third inversion. As with the other inversions, show this with a slash and the letter name of the note in the bottom voice.

Staff 31.4   The dominant seventh chord in the key of C; root position and inversions.

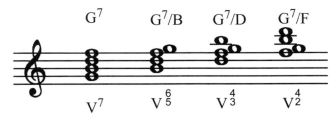

How to Find a Chord's Name

1 Know the key signature you are working in.

2 Spell the chord using the letters in the chord. Ignore duplicate letters.

3 Stack the chord in close harmony, with the **same root as the original chord.** This is important because if you don't use the same root note you won't know if the chord is an inversion or not.

4 Determine what the tonic of the chord is. This will tell you the chord's letter name and Roman numeral in relation to the key you are in.

5 Determine if the chord is a first, second, or third (for 7th chords only) inversion.

6 Use the correct letters, Roman numerals and symbols to name the chord.

Moving On

Now that you can identify a chord and its inversion, you're ready for information about chord progressions, or how one chord moves to another chord.

The next chapter covers some of the most common chord progressions.

Chapter 31 Review

1. What is a root position chord?

2. What is close harmony?

3. What is open harmony?

4. What is harmonic analysis?

5. What is a first inversion chord?

6. How do you show a first inversion chord?

7. What is a second inversion chord?

8. How do you show a second inversion?

9. What is the name and Roman numeral for this chord in the key of C?

10. What is the name and Roman numeral for this chord in the key of B flat?

11. What is the name and Roman numeral for this chord in the key of G?

1. A chord with the tonic of the chord as the lowest voice of the chord.

2. When the notes of a chord are places as close together as possible.

3. A chord spread over more than an octave with space between chord tones.

4. A technique of identifying chord names and types, using Roman numerals and the symbols for chord inversions.

5. A chord with the 3rd of the chord as the lowest voice.

6. A slash followed by the note name in the lowest voice. (C/E)

7. A chord with the 5th of the chord as the lowest voice.

8. A slash followed by the note name in the bottom voice. (C/G)

9. F/A, IV^6

10. Dmin/A, iii$^6_4$

11. G, I

Practical Use

1. Write out all the inversions for FMaj. Don't forget root position. Label them correctly. Sing/play each inverted chord until it feels comfortable. Write out all inversions for Emin and label them. Choose three more chords and write out their inversions.

2. Write out all the inversions for Bb^{M7}. Don't forget root position. Sing/play each inverted chord until it feels comfortable. Write out the inversions for G7. Choose three other 7th chords and write out their inversions.

3. Identify at least 3 chords. Piano music, guitar music, and band or orchestra scores are excellent sources for many chords. Once you identify the chord name and quality of the chord, identify how that chord fits into the key signature of the song. Give the chord its Roman Numeral.

4. Mess around on the piano with inverted triads, and inverted chords with extensions.

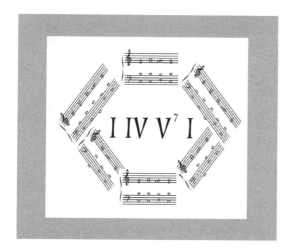

CHORD PROGRESSIONS

*Do you know that our soul is composed
of harmony?*

— Leonardo da Vinci

In This Chapter

- What is a Chord Progression?
- General Chord Progression Guidelines
- The I IV V^7 I Progression
- The ii V^7 I Progression
- The iii vi ii V^7 I Progression
- The 12 Bar Blues Progression

Terms to Know

- **chord progression**: a pattern of movement from one chord to another.
- **changes**: another name for chord progression. Used in jazz.
- **cadence**: a short chord progression coming at the end of a song or section.
- **voice leading**: how one chord tone (voice) moves to another.
- **grand staff**: both the treble and bass clef staffs together, joined by a bracket. Piano music uses the *grand staff*.
- **plagal cadence**: a special type of cadence which creates a sense of continued motion.

What is a Chord Progression?

A chord progression is a pattern of movement from one chord to another.

Any piece of music has a chord progression. And even if it's a melody without chords at all, there is still a chord progression implied by that melody.

You may hear chord progressions called ***chord changes*** or even just ***changes*** by jazz musicians, as in, "Man, that cat can sure play those changes!"

Chord progressions are often very simple, involving only a few chords, but they can also be quite complex. The chord progressions we'll be going over will be of the simple variety.

Chord progressions, especially the ones we'll be looking at, are repeated often many times throughout a piece of music. All of the progressions we'll be going over, with the exception of the 12 Bar Blues, can be found most often at the end of sections or songs. These are special types of changes called ***cadences***.

Chord Progression General Guidelines

Voice Leading

Remember all those pesky details about chord inversions you learned in Chapter 30? Well, now you get to put that information to work, because inversions can make chord progressions sound more smooth.

Voice leading is how one chord tone (or voice) moves to another. There are certain general rules which, if you follow them, will give you a clean, clear chord progression. These aren't laws, but general guidelines. Feel free to experiment with them.

For all of the techniques that follow, refer to staff 31.2 on page 240.

Doubling

Chord tones may be doubled without affecting the general quality of the chord. Voices which are usually doubled are tonics and fifths. Thirds are doubled less often, and extensions are rarely doubled. For most of our examples, I'll keep doubling to a minimum.

No Leaps

One of the first general rules is to ***avoid large interval skips from one chord tone to the next***. This is called ***disjunct motion***.

The bass, or lowest part, can ignore this rule without harming the sound of the chord progression. For the purpose of a clear example, we'll ignore this rule for the introduction of each chord progression.

Keep the Common Tone

There will often be notes which two chords have in common. If at all possible, you'll want to ***keep these similar notes in the same voice from one chord to the next***.

For example, from a C chord (C-E-G) to an F chord (F-A-C), there is a *C* which the chords have in common. If this C is in the top voice of the first chord, it should also be in the top voice of the second chord. This makes the chord change sound smooth, and is also much easier to sing or play.

Resolve Toward the Half Step

An essential component of chord progressions is the movement of half steps between chords. These are called leading tones and lead our ear from one note to another.

You'll see these most—and they're most important—from the V^7 to the I chord.

If there is a half step from one chord to the next, move the appropriate voice toward the half step.

For example, in the key of C, the V7 chord (G-B-D-F) moves to the I chord (C-E-G). The third and seventh (B and F) in the V7 chord should move to the tonic and third (C and E) in the I chord, because they are a half step apart.

Similar Motion

Similar motion is when two or more voices move in the same direction.

Parallel Motion

Parallel motion is a special type of similar motion in which ***the interval between the two parts remains the same from one chord to another***. An example of parallel motion would be a Major third between the upper two voices in one chord moving down (or up) to a Major third in the top two voices of the following chord.

Most parallel motion sounds fine, but parallel fifths, fourths, and octaves are usually frowned upon by our ears and by those who adhere to the strict rules of counterpoint. Experiment with them to hear for yourself what they sound like.

Contrary Motion

Contrary motion is when two or more voices move in opposite directions.

A Word on the Examples

Again, to keep things simple and uncluttered, we'll use the key of C for all our examples, but these progressions can (and do!) happen in every key. The first examples you'll see will be simple chords in root position in the treble clef. Once you've been exposed to the basic chord progression I'll then subject you to a more complex version with both treble and bass clef, and chords in inverted positions.

Now you know all you need to know, for the moment anyway, about chord progressions, so let's get to some actual examples.

The I IV V^7 I Progression

This progression is probably the most common of all progressions in Western music. When you hear it, you'll most likely recognize it. It can be found in nearly every style of music, and though it will appear in other parts of a piece, it's most common at the end of a song or section.

Even if you don't consider yourself a piano player, sit down at one and play through these progressions. It might take some effort (and perhaps a review of the bass or treble clef and the piano keyboard), but it'll be worth it. To understand these concepts intellectually is one thing, but to *hear* them is the whole point. Play them!

Staff 32.1   The I IV V^7 I progression in C with chords in root positions.

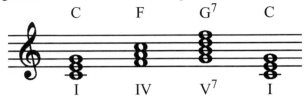

The above example follows few rules of voice leading, but is simple and clear so you can see what the basic chord progression looks like. In the following example, you'll see bass and treble clef staffs connected with a bracket. This is called the **grand staff** and is what piano music looks like.

The example which follows has the same notes as example 31.1, though often in different octaves, or in a different clef, and some chord tones are doubled.

Staff 32.2   I IV V^7 I in the key of C.

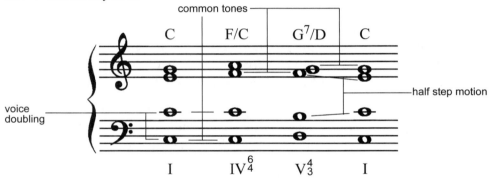

Notice that the IV chord is in the second inversion so that the common tone—the *C*—remains in the bottom voice; the *F* remains in the same voice from the IV to the V^7. The V^7 chord is also in the second inversion so that the bottom voice only moves a whole step from chord to chord.From the V^7 to the I, the leading tones resolve toward the half step. The F goes down to the E, and the B in the bass clef goes up to the C.

See if you can pick out some of the parallel motion, and some of the contrary motion. It's in there.

This progression is in relatively close harmony, and is only one of many, many, many possibilities.

The ii V^7 I Progression

This is another very common chord progression, used in everything from pop songs, to country to jazz and beyond. The movement in the chords below is an excellent example of disjunct motion.

Staff 32.3   The ii V[7] I progression in the key of C, root position, treble clef.

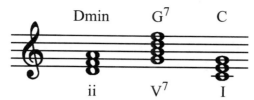

And now for the same progression, but following more of the guidelines for voice leading. This time, see if you can spot the voice doublings, the common chord tones and the half step motion.

As I began to write out the example below, a tune came on my stereo and it caught my ear because it used the ii V I progression over and over for several measures, and it sounded good, so I swiped it and put it below.

Staff 32.4   ii V[7] I in the key of C.

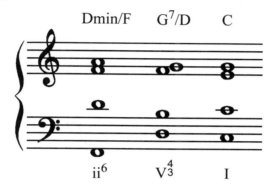

Play this one on the piano too, and try it in other keys as well as with other voicings and other inversions. Once you get the sound in your head, you'll recognize this progression all over the place.

The iii vi ii V[7] I Progression

This is another very common chord progression which is simply a variation on the ii V[7] I progression. The difference of course is the added iii and vi chords before the ii V[7] I.

Because I'm sure you get how this works, this time I'm going to skip the basic chords in root position and go right to the good stuff.

See if you can pick out the chord tones of the iii and vi chords, and all the other stuff: voice doubling, parallel and contrary motion, half step motion, and common chord tones.

Staff 32.5   iii vi ii V[7] I progression in C.

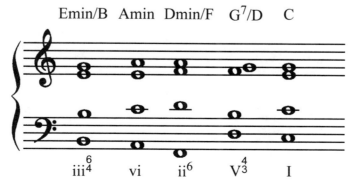

Always be aware of what instrument(s) you're writing for. The bass clef part in the example above has quite a stretch in the ii chord, something only a big-handed piano player would be capable of.

Plagal Cadences (IV-I)

The progressions you've had so far all end in with the V chord moving to the I chord. There is another type of progression, or cadence, that uses the motion of the IV chord to the I chord.

This type of cadence is called a ***plagal cadence*** and has an open-ended quality to it, as though it could go on and on. Plagal cadences have a different sound and are fun to play around with. Use them if you have a song that fades away over a repeat or uses a repeating melody line.

Some plagal cadences are the I-IV-V-I (shown below), I-ii-IV-I, and I-V-vi-IV-I.

Staff 32.6   The I-IV-V-IV-I plagal cadence.

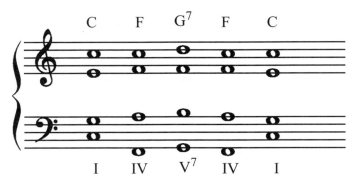

The 12 Bar Blues

Remember the blues scale? If not, take a look back at "The Blues Scale" on page 202. It's the scale that is associated with the 12 bar blues form.

There have been volumes and volumes written on the blues, and if you're looking for in-depth coverage, this ain't the place. This section will give you the vanilla version of the 12 bar blues.

Some artists, dead and living, who play and/or sing the blues are: Buddy Guy, Muddy Waters, Robert Johnson, Stevie Ray Vaughn, B.B. King, John Lee Hooker.... The list is nearly endless and these are just a few of the big names of the blues. Many many other artists also dabble in the blues forms, from Eric Clapton to James Taylor.

The 12 bar blues is basically a 12 measure chord progression repeated over and over for the entire song. There are variations, but 12 bars is so standard that it's safe to say 95% of blues tunes follow this format.

Each Roman numeral represents one measure, and if you count them, there are 12. Try playing these chords in this order, and you'll most likely recognize the sound.

Staff 32.7   The basic pattern of the 12 bar blues.

$$\text{I}^7 \quad | \quad \text{I}^7 \quad | \quad \text{I}^7 \quad | \quad \text{I}^7$$

$$\text{IV}^7 \quad | \quad \text{IV}^7 \quad | \quad \text{I}^7 \quad | \quad \text{I}^7$$

$$\text{V}^7 \quad | \quad \text{IV}^7 \quad | \quad \text{I}^7 \quad | \quad \text{I}^7$$

To find the right chord, simply put the chord letter in place of the Roman numeral. In the below example, if we did it in the key of C, the chords would be $\text{I}^7 = \text{C}^7$, $\text{IV}^7 = \text{F}^7$, $\text{V}^7 = \text{G}^7$.

Other Blues Progressions

There are a few variations of the standard blues progression above. You can put a IV chord in the second measure. There is what is called minor blues, which uses minor chords and often a 3/4 time signature. And the rules for chord substitutions can be applied to the blues to give it a different flavor.

Moving On

So there you have it: four of the most common chord progressions in one easy chapter. Be sure to try all of these chord changes in as many keys as you can stomach, in as many different ways as you can think of. You'll be a much better musician for it if you do.

Coming up next, after the review for this chapter, is the review for all of Part VI.

The next Part (and the last one!) covers more information on subjects you already know, like dots after a note, faster types of notes, more accidentals, and some different meters.

Chapter 32 Review

1. What is a chord progression?

2. What is another name for chord progression and by whom is it used?

3. What is disjunct motion?

4. What is the rule about disjunct motion?

5. What is the rule about common tones moving from one chord to another?

6. What is contrary motion?

7. What is parallel motion?

8. Which types of parallel motion should be avoided?

9. Which chords are used for the I IV V^7 I progression in the key of Bb?

10. Where would you be likely to find this progression?

11. Which chords are used for the ii V^7 I progression in the key of G?

12. Which chords are used for the iii vi ii V^7 I progression the key of F?

13. What is a plagal cadence?

14. What is the sound quality of a plagal cadence?

1. The movement from one chord to another

2. chord changes, or changes. Used by jazz musicians

3. A leap of more than a second

4. Keep it to a minimum. Okay in the bass voice

5. Keep the common tones in the same voice

6. One voice goes up, the other goes down, or vice-versa

7. Both voices moving in the same direction with the same interval between them

8. Parallel fourths, fifths and octaves

9. Bb Eb, F^7, Bb

10. At the end of a section or song

11. Amin, D^7, G

12. Amin, Dmin, Gmin C^7, F

13. A cadence in which the IV chord is followed by the I chord

14. Has an unfinished, open-ended feel, as though it could go on and on.

15. What is the basic progression for the 12 Bar Blues?

16. Did you sit down at the piano and try to play these chords progressions?

15. I^7 I^7 I^7 I^7
    IV^7 IV^7 I^7 I^7
    V^7 IV^7 I^7 I^7

16. *Please say yes.*

Practical Use

1. Draw a bracket around each pair of staves below like the examples in this chapter. In the key of F Major, write out an arrangement for piano, guitar, multiple voices, or instruments using the I, IV, V^7, I chord progression. Play or sing the progression as a group until it feels comfortable. Use the correct accidentals to change the progression to i, iv, V^7, i. Play the minor progression until it feels comfortable. Switch chord voicings.

2. Write out a chord progression in the key of F Major and use one of the plagal cadences mentioned in this chapter (I-IV-V-I, I-V-vi-IV, or I-ii-V). Play and/or sing what you've written.

3. Pick your favorite key signature. Outline the I chord by either playing or singing each chord tone. Try to hear the whole chord in your head as you do this. Do the same for the IV chord, and then the V^7. Try to do this exercise with two or more people at once. Be sure to specify a meter/beat and the length of each chord so you can change chords together.

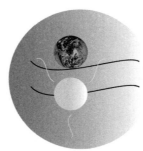

SolŪt Press

Support Music and Musicians.
www.Sol-Ut.com

PART VI REVIEW

Whew! You Made It.

These pages can be used to test your memory about what you've learned in Part VI, and if some of the information hasn't stuck, you can go back and check it out on the page indicated below the question.

As with the chapter reviews, use your keyboard to cover up the answers while you test yourself. When you think you've got it all down, either take the test in *Basic Music Theory Quiz Pack* (available for free at www.Sol-Ut.com), or go on.

The Review

1. What is the definition of a chord?
   page 220

   1. *Three or more notes played simultaneously*

2. What determines the quality of a chord?
   page 220

   2. *The intervals within the chord*

3. How are chords named?
   page 220

   3. *With a Roman numeral, a letter, and a quality of Major, minor, diminished or augmented*

4. What are the parts of a triad?
   page 221

   4. *Root, third, fifth*

5. Why are they called this?
   page 221

   5. *Root is the bottom note of the chord; the third is a 3rd above the root; the fifth is a 5th above the root*

6. How do you show a triad is Major?
   page 221

   6. *Capital Roman numeral, or a capital letter only*

7. How do you show a triad is minor?
page 222

8. What are the intervals in a Major triad?
page 221

9. What are the intervals in a minor triad?
page 222

10. What are the intervals in a diminished triad?
page 222

11. What are the intervals in an augmented triad?
page 222

12. What are the qualities of the different types of triads?
page 221, page 222,

13. What is a root position chord?
page 232

14. What is close harmony?
page 232

15. What is open harmony?
page 232

16. What is a first inversion chord?
page 232

17. What is the symbol for a first inversion chord?
page 232

18. Why is this symbol used?
page 232

19. What is a second inversion chord?
page 233

7. *Lower case Roman numeral, lowercase letter, or the abbreviation "min" next to the letter name*

8. *A note a Major 3rd above the root and another a Perfect 5th above the root*

9. *A note a minor 3rd above the root, and another a Perfect 5th above the root*

10. *A note a minor 3rd above the root and another a diminished 5th above the root*

11. *A note a Major 3rd above the root and another an augmented 5th above the root*

12. *Major = happy; minor = sad; dim = suspenseful aug = unsettling*

13. *A chord with the tonic of the chord as the lowest voice of the chord*

14. *When the notes of a chord are placed as close together as possible*

15. *A chord spread over more than an octave with space between chord tones*

16. *A chord with the 3rd of the chord as the lowest voice*

17. *A small [6] to the right of the letter or Roman numeral*

18. *It tells the interval between the third and the tonic, a 6th*

19. *A chord with the 5th of the chord as the lowest note*

Basic Music Theory

20. What is the symbol for a second inversion chord?
page 233

20. $^6_4$ above and to the right of the letter or Roman numeral

21. Why is this symbol used?
page 233

21. *It tells the interval between the fifth and tonic (a 4th), and between the fifth and third (a 6th)*

22. What is the name and Roman numeral for this chord in the key of C Major?

page 234

22. *F, IV^6*

23. What is the name and Roman numeral for this chord in the key of B flat Major?

page 234

23. *Dmin, iii^6*

24. What is the name of this chord?

page 234

24. *G, I*

25. What is a chord progression?
page 238

25. *The movement from one chord to another*

26. What is the rule about doubling chord tones?
page 238

26. *Doubling the octave and fifth is common; doubling the 3rd less so; and doubling the extensions is rare*

27. What is disjunct motion?
page 238

27. *A leap of more than a second from one chord tone to the next within a voice*

28. What is the rule about disjunct motion?
page 238

28. *Keep it to a minimum. Okay in the bass voice*

29. What is the rule about common tones from one chord to another?
page 238

29. *Keep the common tones in the same voice*

30. What is contrary motion?
page 239

30. *One voice goes up, the other goes down, or vice-versa*

31. What is similar motion?
page 239

31. *Two or more voices moving in the same direction*

32. What is parallel motion?
page 239

32. *Both voices moving in the same direction with the same interval between them*

33. Which types of parallel motion should be avoided?
page 239

33. *Parallel fourths, fifths and octaves*

34. What are the chord names for the I IV V^7 I progression in Bb?
page 239

34. *Bb Eb, F^7, Bb*

35. Where would you be likely to find this progression?
page 239

35. *At the end of a section or song*

36. What are the chord names for the ii V^7 I progression in G?
page 240

36. *Amin, D^7, G*

37. What are the chord names for the iii vi ii V^7 I progression in F?
page 241

37. *Amin, Dmin, Gmin C^7, F*

38. What is the basic progression for the 12 Bar Blues?
page 242

38. *I I I I*
IV IV I I
V^7 IV I I

P A R T   S E V E N

More of the Same

In This Section You Will Learn:

- Thirty-second and Sixty-fourth Notes
- Double-dotted Notes
- Double Flats, Double Sharps
- 6/8 Time
- 2/2 Time

Odd Meters

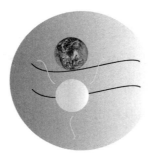

SolŪt Press

Support Music and Musicians.
www.Sol-Ut.com

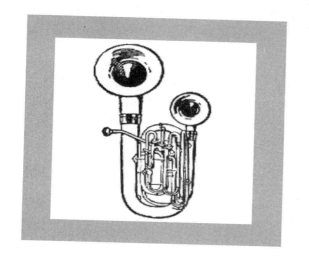

FASTER NOTES AND DOUBLE DOTS

You are the music while the music lasts.

— T. S. Eliot

In This Chapter

- Thirty-second Notes
- Sixty-fourth Notes
- Double Dots

Terms to Know

- **beam**: the horizontal bar which connects short notes (eighth and shorter).
- **flag**: curved line extending from short notes (eighth and shorter).

Shorter Notes

There are shorter notes than sixteenths.

Each time a beam or flag is added to a note, it's value is cut in half*. Remember when we added a flag to a quarter note? It became an eighth note. Remember when we added another flag to the eighth? It became a sixteenth. As with the other notes, when there is more than one note, the flags are connected and become a beam.

Thirty-second Notes

We're going to add a flag/bar to the sixteenth and cut its value in half, making it a thirty-second note. Just like the name implies, there are thirty two of them in a whole note; sixteen of them in a half note; eight of them in a quarter note or a beat (in 4/4 time); four of them in an eighth note; two of them in a sixteenth note.

Thirty-second notes are fairly rare, but you'll probably run into them now and then, often as grace notes (quick notes just before the main note).

Staff 33.1   Two single 32nd notes with flags, and a beat of barred 32nd notes with stems up and down.

Sixty-fourth Notes

These are even more rare, and it's likely that you'll never see them, but I thought I'd throw them down on the page for your enjoyment.

Same deal with the flag/beam. Add another beam to the 32nd note and it cuts the length in half. So, for sixty-fourth notes there are: 64 in a whole note, 32 in a half note, 16 in a quarter note or one beat (in 4/4 time), 8 in an eighth note, 4 in a sixteenth note, and two in a thirty-second note.

Staff 33.2   Two single 64th notes, and 1/2 beat of barred 64ths with stems up and stems down.

Double Dotted Notes

You already know that a dot lengthens the note it follows by half the amount of the original note.

Another dot after that first dot also lengthens the note, but by half the amount of the first dot.

An easier way to say this is that ***a double dot increases the length of a note or rest by 3/4 of its original value***.

So a double-dotted whole note or rest is 7 beats. A double-dotted half note or rest is 3 1/2 beats, a double-dotted quarter note or rest is 1 3/4 beats, and a double-dotted eighth note or rest is 7/8 of a beat.

We could continue the process, but it's pretty safe to say you'll probably never see a double-dotted sixteenth, thirty-second, or sixty-fourth note.

Because it sounds right and is easier to read and play, a double-dotted note will usually be paired with whatever note finishes out the beat or measure. Take a look at the examples below and you'll see what I mean.

Staff 33.3   Double-dotted whole, half, quarter, and eighth notes.

Moving On

Okay, only a few more chapters to go in the book! Use the review to make sure you've understood the details of faster notes and double dots.

Coming up is a very short chapter on double sharps and double flats.

Chapter 33 Review

1. How do you cut the length of a note in half?

2. What note is half the length of a sixteenth note?

3. What note is one fourth the length of a sixteenth note?

4. How many 32nd notes in one beat of 4/4 time?

5. What does a double dot do to a note?

6. How long is a double-dotted quarter rest?

7. Which note is usually paired with a double-dotted quarter note? Why?

1. Add a flag or beam

2. 32nd note

3. 64th note

4. 8

5. Increases its length by 3/4 of the note's original value

6. 1 3/4 beat

7. 16th note. It finishes out the beat. Sounds better and is easier to read and play.

Practical Use

1. Write out 4 measures of 8/4 time. Use at least two double-dotted notes per measure, but see if you can use them all. Play and sing what you've written.

2. Write out another 4 measures of 8/4 time. This 4 measures is meant to be a harmony part to what you composed in exercise 1, so don't choose the same notes, though you may use the same rhythms (hint: 3rds, 4ths, 9ths and 5ths sound good together). Find a friend and sing or play both parts together.

DOUBLE FLATS, DOUBLE SHARPS

If I were to begin life again, I would devote it to music. It is the only cheap and unpunished rapture upon earth.

— Sydney Smith, 1814

In This Chapter

- Double Flats
- Double Sharps
- A Werd on Speling Kords

Terms to Know

- **double flat**: lowers the pitch of a note one whole step.
- **double sharp**: raises the pitch of a note one whole step.

Double Your Fun

Welcome to the shortest chapter of the book. You're about to learn double sharps and double flats, but before you do, I'd like to tell you why.

There are several ways to say the sound to, two, too. Even though each sounds exactly the same, they have different meanings. Just as you wouldn't write, "I went two the store," so you wouldn't spell a Db diminished chord with a G. I'll show you this in detail in a moment. First the details about how to write double flats and sharps.

Double Flats

A double flat lowers a note by one whole step. It looks like this ♭♭ .

You won't see them very often, but now and then double flats are necessary in order to spell a chord or an interval correctly. You'll see double flats in flat keys, usually with minor or diminished intervals. There is an example of this on the next page, staff 33.3.

Double flats are easy. Just put two flats close together before the note they are to alter.

Staff 34.1   B double-flat, E double-flat, and A double-flat.

Double Sharps

A double sharp raises a note by one whole step. It looks like this ✖ .

You'll see a double sharp about as often as you'll see a double flat. These will usually pop up when augmented intervals are needed in a sharp key.

Staff 34.2   G double-sharp, C double-sharp, and F double-sharp.

You'll be glad to hear there are no such things as double naturals, triple sharps or triple flats.

A Werd on Spelling Kords

Here's why such pesky things as double sharps and flats exist.

Stay with me here and refer to the example below. The Db Major triad is spelled Db, F, Ab, right? Well, for a diminished chord, the third and fifth of the chord have to be lowered a half step. A half step down from F is E, and a half step down from Ab is G, right? But even though those pitches would *sound* correct, you can't write them that way and still have a Db diminished triad. Take a look below. On the left is the Db Major triad. In the middle is a chord that will sound exactly like the Db diminished triad, but the way it's written, the chord is actually an inverted e minor ^{dim7}. The correct spelling of Db dim. is on the right.

Staff 34.3

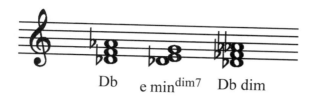

Db   e min^{dim7}   Db dim

Even though it makes things a little crowded, for the Db dim chord to be spelled correctly we have to use an Fb and a double-flatted A.

I know it's weird, but I didn't make up the rules. Don't kill the messenger.

Moving On

Double sharps and double flats are pesky things that you probably will see if you continue long enough with music, so even though you won't use them often, it's good to know what they are, and now you do.

Only one lesson left! It's on meters we haven't covered yet which include 6/8 time, cut time, and some odd meters, like 7/4.

Chapter 34 Review

1. Why are double flats and double sharps used?

    1. To spell certain chords and intervals correctly

2. What does a double flat do to a note?

    2. Lowers it one whole step

3. What does a double flat look like?

    3. Two flats close together in front of a note

4. What does a double sharp do to a note?

    4. Raises it one whole step

5. What does a double sharp look like?

    *5. An **X***

6. What does a triple flat look like?

    6. No such thing

Practical Use

1. Write out the following key signatures with their Major scale: Eb, Ab, B, and E. One line below these scales, write the following intervals: a diminished fifth above Eb, a diminished fourth above Ab, an augmented fifth above B, and an augmented sixth above E.

MORE METERS

After playing violin for the cellist Gregor Piatagorsky, Einstein asked, "Did I play well?"

Piatagorsky replied, "You played relatively well."

In This Chapter

- Cut Time
- Slow 6/8 Time
- Fast 6/8 Time
- Odd Meters

Terms to Know

- **2/2, cut time, half time**: Two beats per measure, the half note gets one beat. Twice as fast as 4/4 time.
- **simple 6/8 time**: six beats per measure, eighth note gets one beat.
- **compound 6/8**: two beats per measure, three eighth notes per beat.

Beyond 4/4 Time

The majority of music has the quarter note as its pulse and is in a duple meter (the top number is divisible by 2), but there is a whole lot of great music out there that has a different pulse, and even some with an odd meter.

Remember way back in Chapter 13 when we went over meters for the first time? The top number tells you how many beats in a measure and the bottom number tells you which note gets one beat. For a refresher, see Chapter 13 "Meter" on page 6-41.

Cut Time, or 2/2 Time

This is a very common meter. It's typically shown with the symbol "¢," but may also be written 2/2. The top number tells you there are two beats in each measure, and the bottom number tells you that the half note gets one beat.

Essentially, all note lengths in cut time are cut in half. Half notes act like quarters; quarters act like eighths, etc. Because of this, the counting is a little different, but the foot tap is the same. In the example below your foot hits the floor on the numbers.

Staff 35.1   A few measures of cut time with the counting.

6/8 Time

Six-Eight time is fairly common and one of the more confusing basic time signatures, but I'll break it down for you so it's easy to understand.

First of all, from the top number, you know that there will be six beats per measure. And the bottom number tells you that the eighth note gets one beat.

It's the eighth note getting the beat which is confusing. This throws everything out of whack from what you're used to. Eighth notes get one beat, quarter notes get two beats, dotted quarters get three, half notes get four, and dotted halfs get six. No whole notes in this time signature; they're too long.

As with other meters, the strong beats are the numbers. Tap your foot with the numbers as you count out the following example at a fairly slow tempo. Sing it. Play it.

Staff 35.2   A few measures of slow 6/8 time with counting.

Basic Music Theory

Simple 6/8 versus Compound 6/8

If that's all there was to 6/8 time, it would be much easier to understand, but there's more. The example above is in simple 6/8 time, also called slow 6/8 time. What you see in simple 6/8 is what you get, the 8th note gets one beat and there are six beats per measure.

Compound 6/8, or fast 6/8, is counted differently and has a different feel. *In compound 6/8, the beat is the dotted quarter note.* To get this feel, try the following: say the numbers 1-6 at a quick, rhythmic pace and give emphasis to the numbers 1 and 4. Like this: **1** 2 3 **4** 5 6, **1** 2 3 **4** 5 6, etc.

So *in fast or compound 6/8 time, there are only two beats per measure*, each beat subdivided into three. This is counted with the following syllables: **1** an da **2** an da, **1** an da **2** an da, etc. Your foot hits the floor on the numbers. Dotted quarter notes get one beat each.

Let's use our same example, but this time it will go much more quickly, and will also be counted differently.

Compound 6/8 has a triplet feel. Your foot taps down with the numbers, and remember that the pulse is now a dotted quarter note. Try counting it out loud, first at a comfortable tempo, then speed it up. Sing it. Play it.

Staff 35.3   An example in fast 6/8 time with counting.

| 1 an da | 2 an da | 1-an da | 2-an-da | (1-an-da) | 2 | (an) | da | 1-an-da-2-an-da |

Odd Meters

Occasionally you'll hear or see music in an odd meter. When you listen to it, the clue is that it's difficult to find the pulse, and when you do find the beat, it seems to shift around. Odd meter pieces can be difficult to tap your foot with unless you know the meter.

An odd meter has an odd number greater than 3 as the top number of the time signature. Some examples might be 5/4, 7/4, 5/8, or 7/8. These are the most common odd meters, but that shouldn't stop you budding composers from trying a piece in 11/8 or 13/4.

The counting for odd meters is the same as more familiar meters, but with a different number of beats per measure.

Most odd meters are grouped in 2s and 3s, and often there will be directions above the meter (or in the meter itself) telling you what this grouping is.

For example: a meter with a 5 on top—5/4 or 5/8—can be 2 + 3 (counted **1** 2 **3** 4 5), or 3 + 2 (counted **1** 2 3 **4** 5).

A meter with a 7 on top—7/4 or 7/8—can be 2 + 2 + 3 (counted **1** 2 **3** 4 **5** 6 7) or 3 + 2 + 2 (counted **1** 2 3 **4** 5 **6** 7), or even 2 + 3 + 2 (counted **1** 2 **3** 4 5 **6** 7), though this last version I've never seen.

If you'd like to hear a master of odd meters, listen to some Dave Brubek, especially the tunes *Take 5*, in 5/4 time, and *Blue Rondo alla Turk,* in 7/8.

Moving On

Congratulations! After you are able to complete the final reviews, you're done! It's been a long haul, and don't be surprised if you forget a lot of what you learned—that's perfectly normal. If you do forget, now you know where to go to find the answers you need. The more you use this information, the more it will stick in your memory.

The only thing left is the final review for this Part. It's a short one.

If you can answer the questions on all the study guides for all the Parts, you now have an excellent foundation in music theory. Good job!

Chapter 35 Review

1. What is the numerical time signature for cut time?

    1. 2/2

2. How many beats does a whole note get in cut time?

    2. 2

3. How many eighth notes in one beat of cut time?

    3. 4

4. How would 4 quarter notes be counted in cut time?

    4. 1 + 2 + 3 + 4 +

5. What note gets one beat in slow 6/8 time?

    5. 8th note

6. How many beats are in each measure of slow 6/8 time?

    6. 6

7. How many beats do quarter notes get in slow 6/8 time?

    7. 2

8. How many beats do dotted half rests get in slow 6/8 time?

    8. 6

9. How many pulses are in a measure of complex, or fast 6/8 time?

    9. 2

10. What note gets one beat in fast 6/8 time?

    10. dotted quarter

11. What is the counting for a measure of 8th notes in fast 6/8?

    *11. **1** an da **2** an da*

12. How do you tell if a song is in an odd meter?

    12. Can't easily tap your foot to it, or there is an odd number greater than 3 as the top number of the time signature.

13. How are the beats in 5/4 time grouped?

    13. 2+3 or 3+2

14. How are the beats in 7/8 time grouped?

    14. 2+2+3 or 3+2+2 or 2+3+2

Practical Use

1. Write out an 8 measure melody in 5/4 time.

2. Charles Ives, an American composer, often used two meters at once in a piece of music. Write a 10 measure harmony part to number one, but use 4/4 time (10 measures of 4/4 = 8 measures of 5/4). Find a friend and sing/play what you've written.

3. Think of another combination of meters like 2/4 and 3/4 (or whatever) and compose another piece that will begin and end at the same time.

Basic Music Theory

PART VII REVIEW

Whew! You Made It.

These pages can be used to test your memory about what you've learned in Part VII, and if some of the information hasn't stuck, you can go back and check it out on the page indicated below the question.

As with the chapter reviews, use your keyboard to cover up the answers while you test yourself. When you think you've got it all down, either take the test in *Basic Music Theory Quiz Pack* (available for free at www.Sol-Ut.com), or go on.

The Review

1. How do you cut the length of a note in half?
   page 254

   1. *Add a flag or beam*

2. What note is half the length of a sixteenth note?
   page 254

   2. *32nd note*

3. What note is one fourth the length of a sixteenth note?
   page 254

   3. *64th note*

4. How many 32nd notes in one beat of 4/4 time?
   page 254

   4. *8*

5. What does a double dot do?
   page 254

   5. *Adds 3/4 the length of the rest/ note it follows*

6. How long is a double-dotted quarter rest?
   page 254

   6. 1 3/4 beat

7. What note is usually paired with a double-dotted quarter note? Why?
   page 254

   7. 16th note. It finishes out the beat, is easier to read and play.

8. Why are double flats and double sharps used?
   page 258

   8. To spell certain chords and intervals correctly

9. What does a double flat do to a note?
   page 258

   9. Lowers it one whole step

10. What does a double flat look like?
    page 258

    10. Two flats close together in front of a note

11. What does a double sharp do to a note?
    page 258

    11. Raises it one whole step

12. What does a double sharp look like?
    page 258

    *12. An **X***

13. What does a triple flat look like?
    page 258

    13. No such thing

14. What is the numerical time signature for cut time?
    page 262

    14. 2/2

15. How many beats does a whole note get in cut time?
    page 262

    15. 2

16. How many eighth notes in one beat of cut time?
    page 262

    16. 4

17. How would 4 quarter notes be counted in cut time?
    page 262

    17. 1 + 2 + 3 + 4 +

18. What note gets one beat in 6/8 time?
    page 262

    18. 8th note

19. How many beats are in each measure of slow 6/8 time?
page 263

    19. 6

20. How many beats do quarter notes get in simple, or slow 6/8 time?
page 263

    20. 2

21. How many beats do dotted half rests get in slow 6/8?
page 263

    21. 6

22. How many pulses are in a measure of complex, or fast 6/8 time?
page 263

    22. 2

23. What is the counting for a measure of 8th notes in fast 6/8?
page 263

    *23. **1** an da **2** an da*

24. Which note gets one beat in fast 6/8 time?
page 263

    24. dotted quarter

25. How do you tell if a song is in an odd meter?
page 263

    25. Can't easily tap your foot to it, or there is an odd number greater than 3 as the top number of the time signature.

26. How are the beats in 5/4 time grouped?
page 263

    26. 2+3 or 3+2

27. How are the beats in 7/8 time grouped?
page 263

    27. 2+2+3 or 3+2+2 or 2+3+2

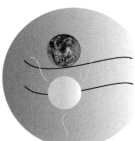

SolŪt Press

Support Music and Musicians.
www.Sol-Ut.com

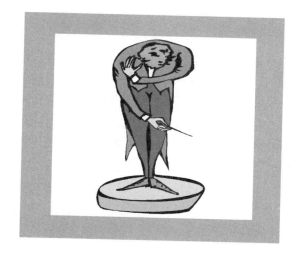

CHAPTER 36

Postlude

WHAT COMES NEXT

Too many pieces finish too long after the end.

— Igor Stravinsky

In This Postlude

- More To Learn
- Theory Ain't Everything
- Drop Me an E-mail

So Much More

Congratulations for getting through a huge load of information! Because there is so much that you've learned, don't be surprised if you forget parts of it (or all of it!), and feel free to go back and review anything you need to review. It's normal.

Even though you've taken in a great deal of information, there is much, much more left to be learned if you're willing to learn it. Things like more advanced chord progressions, more chord extensions, transposing from one part to another, arranging music, composing music, and on and on and on.

It's exciting how much there is to learn; a lifetime's worth, really.

Theory Ain't Everything

Keep in mind that music theory is only one of many tools to be used to become a better musician. This system for writing down sounds came about long after music itself and reading music is not necessary for making music! It takes a while for all these concepts and systems to make sense, so don't let any confusion you may feel about written music get in the way of *making* music.

Remember that it is the music which is the Master. The quest for a better performance of the music is the reason for this factual, rule-based method of writing down the sounds. Don't be a slave to written music! Use your ears!

With so many rules and regulations in music theory, it can be easy to get away from the ultimate goal of music theory, which is to enable you to produce and perform better music.

So keep making music, with all your heart and all your brains. Chip away at the areas of music that are unfamiliar to you and you won't be disappointed.

Drop Me An E-mail

If you notice problems or inconsistencies or downright mistakes, please let me know so I can make this a better book in future editions.

If you're totally stumped and can't find answers anywhere else, drop me an E-mail and maybe I can help you.

And of course, if you liked the book and it helped you, I'd love to hear about it. You can reach me at BMT@questionsink.com

Thanks, and the best of everything to you!

Jon

CODICILS

Teacher Resources

Musical Terms Glossary

Index

Staff Paper

Scales

Scale Skill Checklists

Practice Journal

Exercise Tracking Form

Book Order Form

Piano Keyboard

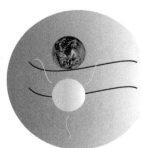

SolŪt Press

Support Music and Musicians.
www.Sol-Ut.com

FREE TEACHING PACKET FOR TEACHERS!

Get The Most out of *Basic Music Theory*

It's okay, we can admit it. Everyone would rather play music than study music theory, teachers and students alike. No big surprise there, right? Yet we all know the important role theory plays in communicating a musical idea. Despite this knowledge, music theory isn't taught for several reasons: no good methods students enjoy, no time, and no money to buy books, are only a few reasons.

So what's the answer? Theory in small, enjoyable doses from a program designed as a cost- and time-effective teaching tool. This book.

Though it works well for individuals, *Basic Music Theory* was written specifically for use in the classroom. Its clear explanations, short chapters, and reviews make it a low-maintenance option for teachers with limited time (and we all have limited time, right?).

The Quiz-Pack

The Quiz-Pack is an addition which complements *Basic Music Theory*. In it are Chapter and Part quizzes, student tracking forms, book tracking forms, and additional information like how to schedule time for theory, how to pay for books, and fun yet productive rehearsal suggestions.

Combined with the Quiz-Pack, *Basic Music Theory* is the best method for teaching music theory to be found anywhere, and it works with classes of all sizes.

Quizzes

Though I'm aware that multiple-choice tests are a poor way to determine comprehension, they are very efficient. With our limited time, and class sizes that exist only in other teachers' nightmares, efficiency is a must.

All quizzes are in a multiple choice format with a quick-correct key to make correcting an easy task for an aide.

Each Chapter and Part Quiz has 4 different versions to curb cheating. These can be rotated in a 4-year period, or month-to-month, or any way you think most effective.

Student Tracking Form

Also included in the Quiz-Pack is a Student Information Form which includes class name, period/time, semester/year, student name, year, and condition of their book (new, good, used). There are spaces for over 100 students.

The form is shaded so students (and you) can find their information quickly and easily. Each chapter has one column to indicate date begun and date passed. Grades can be entered here also if you choose to use a grading system. More about assessment in the *Extra* Section below.

Student Fee Forms

A set of books is a significant investment of your program's resources, and just as a student is charged for damage to a borrowed instrument, so they are also responsible for damaged books.

The Student Fee Form has dollar values for books in conditions from new to damaged and is also shaded for convenient location of information. There are several more columns for other fees the student may owe, including a column for funds the student may have through fund raising.

Extras

All sections of the Quiz-Pack are clearly explained with suggestions to make their use easy and productive. Included in the Quiz-Pack are suggestions for scheduling time for theory and systems of grading. Also included are some special rehearsal techniques which students and directors alike enjoy and benefit from.

To Get It

The Quiz-Pack is free. You can make as many copies of the quizzes and forms as you need, without limit. To receive a Quiz-Pack, go to **http//:www.sol-ut.com**, and follow the links. Download what you need and you're on your way.

If you'd like the Quiz-Pack information on a CD, please send $5 to the address below.

Questions, Ink
PO Box 140452
Anchorage, AK 99514-0452

Musical Terms

A

a, á (It): At, by, for, with.

A 440: The note A above middle C, with frequency of 440 vibrations per second. The note which orchestras and music ensembles universally tune with.

a cappella (It): Without accompaniment.

accelerando: Becoming faster.

accent (Eng):To emphasize or stress a note, indicated by the symbol " > ". The three main kinds of accents are agogic, dynamic, and tonic.

accidental: Sharps, flats or natural signs; used to raise, lower or return a note to its normal pitch.

accompaniment: Secondary musical material, supports more important material.

acoustic: An instrument that produces sound without the use of electronic amplification.

acoustics 1: The science of sound. 2: The physical properties of an instrument or room as related to sound.

adagietto (It): A little faster than adagio.

adagio (It): "At ease." A slow tempo between largo and andante.

à demi-voix (Fr): With half the voice, whispered.

à deux, a due (Fr, It): For two instruments or voices (to be played or sung in unison).

ad libitum, ad lib. (Lat.): "At will." the performer improvises freely and may vary the tempo.

Aeolian: A medieval mode whose half- and whole-step pattern is that of playing A to A on the white keys of the piano (same as the natural minor scale).

affrettando (It): Hurrying.

agitato (It): Agitated, excited, hurried, restless.

agogic accent: Emphasis is given to a note by making it longer than normal.

air: A song or melody.

al, all', alla, alle (It) 1: "To the." 2: In the style of (e.g., alla valse, "in a waltz style").

al coda (It): "To the coda."

al Fine (It): To the end.

alla breve (It): A duple time signature, usually 2/2.

allargando (It): Growing broader and slower.

allegretto (It): A cheerful fast tempo, a little slower than allegro.

allegro (It): "cheerful." A lively, fast tempo: allegro assai, very fast; allegro di bravura, fast, bright and spirited; allegro moderato, moderately fast.

alphorn: A wooden horn up to 10 feet long, curved slightly at the end with an upturned bell; from Switzerland.

al segno (It): Return to the sign (see dal segno).

alt (It): "High." the notes from G to F that fall above the fifth line of the treble clef.

alteration: The raising or lowering of a note with an accidental.

altered chord: A chord in which a note(s) has been raised or lowered chromatically.

altissimo (It): "Most high." The highest notes; the octave above the alt.

alto (It): "High." the highest male singing voice and lowest female singing voice.

alto clef: The C clef on the third line of the staff. Used by the viola.

alto flute: See flute.

alto saxophone: See saxophone.

amabile (It): Amiable, gentle.

anacrusis (Gr.): Pickup or upbeat or preparatory beat.

andante (It): "Going." A moderate tempo between allegretto and adagio.

andantino (It): Originally a tempo a little slower than andante, but now indicates a tempo a bit faster than andante.

animato, animoso (It): Animated, energetic or spirited.

anticipation: Nonharmonic note or notes played before the chord in which it belongs.

antiphonal: Alternating singing or playing by separate groups of performers; originally separated also by distance.

appassionato (It): Passionately.

appoggiatura (It): An accented nonharmonic note that resolves stepwise to a harmonic note.

arcato (It): "Bowed." For string instruments, indicates to use the bow.

archet, archetto (Fr): For string instruments, the bow; to bow.

arco (It): "Bow". For string instruments, indicates to use the bow.

arpeggio (It): The notes of a chord played in succession; a broken chord.

arraché (Fr): Strong pizzicato.

arrangement: A different version of a composition.

arsis (Gr.): The upbeat.

articulation: The degree to which notes are separated or connected, such as staccato or legato.

assai (It): Very, extremely.

a tempo (It): Return to the original tempo.

atonal: Music lacking a tonal or key center.

attacca (It): Go on, proceed immediately to next section. Segue.

attack: The beginning of a note or phrase.

a 2: For 2 instruments or voices.

augmentation: A lengthening of the duration of notes in a theme.

augmented: Raised, enlarged.

augmented chord: A triad composed of a root, major third, and augmented fifth.

augmented sixth chord: A chord with the interval of an augmented sixth resolving upward to an octave.

augmented interval: A major or perfect interval raised by a half step.

authentic cadence: A cadence with a progression from the dominant (V) chord to the tonic (I) chord.

B

back beat: Used with drums, emphasis on beats 2 and 4.

balance: the harmonious adjustment of volume and sound quality between instruments and/or voices.

bar: A measure; the space between two bar lines. Also, the bar line itself.

baritone: A male singing voice higher than bass but lower than tenor.

baritone horn: A brass instrument similar to the euphonium, but with 3 valves and smaller bore.

baritone saxophone: see saxophone.

bar line: Vertical line through a staff to separate measures or bars.

barre (Fr): Used for guitars; playing sever strings with a single finger across the fretboard.

bass 1: The lowest male singing voice. 2 The lowest part in music. 3 Electric bass, bass viol, upright bass.

bassa (It): Low.

bass clef: The clef which names the 4th line of the staff as F.

basso continuo (It): Used in the baroque era; an accompaniment usu. improvised with numbers indicating the harmony.

bassoon: A double-reed instrument with low pitch.

baton: Conductor's wand.

beam: A horizontal line used in place of flags to connect short notes.

beat 1: A rhythmic unit of time. 2: To mark time.

beats: pulses caused by sound waves of slightly different frequency.

bebop: A form of jazz invented by Dizzy Gillespie and Charlie Parker; uses improvisation, complex rhythms and harmonies.

bend: A change in pitch, usu. a half or whole step. Used with voice, guitar, harmonica and other instruments.

big band: Jazz band playing dance music. Popular in '30's and 40's, experienced a renaissance in late '90's.

bitonal: A composition using two keys at the same time.

bluegrass: Folk music, usu. fast tempo with banjo, fiddle, bass, mandolin, and other instruments.

blue notes: Notes played/sung below intended pitch (usu 3rd, 7th, 5th). Used in blues music.

blues: the basis of jazz. Originated from African vocal music; minor 3rd and 7th of scale. Form is 12 bars long.

Boehm system: System of keys used with woodwind instruments perfected by Theobald Boehm.

bones 1: Percussion instrument of African origin, a pair of sticks/bones held between the fingers and clicked in rhythm. 2: Slang for trombones.

bore: The diameter and shape of the tube of a wind instrument.

bow: The device drawn across the strings of string instruments like violin, cello, etc. A stick ~3 ft. long with horsehair stretched between the ends.

brace: A curved line which connects the staves for instruments which use more than one staff.

bracket: A straight line with curved ends which connects staves for different instruments playing simultaneously.

break 1: The point at which a voice shifts from the chest register to the head (falsetto) register. 2: The change in woodwind instruments (esp. clarinet) from the lower register to the higher register.

breve: Originally a short note, has come to mean a long note equalling two whole notes.

bridge 1: A transitional section in a piece of music. 2: A piece of wood that supports the strings and holds them away from the body of the instrument.

brillánte (It): Brilliant.

brio (It): Vigor, spirit. *Con brio.*

broken chord: Notes of a chord played in succession rather than simultaneously.

brushes: Thin wire brushes used on percussion instruments, esp. in jazz.

bull roarer: An instrument originating in aboriginal Australia consisting of a thin piece of bone or wood of special shape tied to rope and whirled vigorously about one's head. Makes a very loud roaring sound.

BWV (abbr.): "Bach-Werke Verzeichnis." A method of cataloguing Bach's work.

C

cabasa (Sp): Percussion instrument. A gourd covered with beads; a cylinder of metal covered with beads of metal.

cacophony: Dissonant sound. Usu. loud and unpleasant.

cadence: The ending of a piece or section, usu. applied to chord progression (e.g. *deceptive cadence, perfect cadence,* etc.).

cadenza: An unaccompanied solo passage usually near the end of a piece. Either ad lib or written by composer.

caesura: A sudden pause or break, shown by the symbol //.

calma, calmando (It): Calming, quiet, tranquil.

calypso: A type of rhythm or song originating in Trinidad.

cancel: Another name for the natural sign used to remove the affect of an accidental.

canción (Sp): Song.

cantabile (It): In a singing style.

capo 1:The head, beginning, or top. 2: A device placed across the strings of an instrument to raise the pitch.

capriccio: A piece played in a free, playful style.

castrato (It): An adult male singer with a soprano or alto voice.

catgut: Formerly used as material for string instruments. Actually sheep or goat intestines.

C clef: A moveable clef indicating middle C.

celere (It): Quick, rapid.

chalumeau (Fr): The low register of a clarinet.

changes: Slang for chord changes.

chanson (Fr): Song.

chart: The score or parts of an instrumental ensemble, usu. pop or jazz.

chest voice: the low register of the voice.

choir: A group of singers of sacred music.

choke cymbal: 1: The hi-hat cymbals on the drum set. 2: Verb meaning to silence a cymbal quickly.

chops: Slang for a player's ability.

chord: Three or more tones sounding simultaneously.

chorus: 1: The *refrain* of a song. 2: A group of singers of secular music.

chromatic: Moving by half steps.

chromaticism: Melodic or harmonic use of tones other then those of the diatonic scale.

chromatic scale: A scale made up of 12 half steps in succession.

circle of fifths: The succession of keys progressing by fifths.

circular breathing: A technique used by wind players in which air is expelled from the mouth while inhaling through the nose.

clam: Slang for a wrong note.

classical 1: Music of a "serious" (non-pop) nature. 2: The time period from the late 1700's to the early 1800's.

claves: Percussion instrument from Cuba; round hardwood sticks hit against each other.

clef: A symbol at the beginning of a piece of music which shows the names of the lines and spaces of the staff.

close harmony: Harmony with the chord tones as close together as possible.

cluster: group of notes with the interval of a second.

coda (It): Closing section of a piece. In written music a separate section to after repeating a previous section (e.g. D.C. al Coda; D.S. al Coda). Indicated by the symbol ⊕

col legno (It): Playing with the wood part of the bow.

combo (abbr.): Short for combination. A small group of instrumentalists, used in jazz.

comma: Breath mark (').

common chord: Triad. Chord with root, third and fifth.

common time: Four beats to a measure, quarter note gets one beat. 4/4.

common tone: A note that remains the same between two chords.

còmodo (It): Comfortable.

complete cadence: I-IV-V-I.

compound interval: An interval larger than an octave (9th, 11th, 13th).

compound meter: A time signature in which the basic beat is divisible by 3 (6/8, 9/8, etc.).

con (It): With.

con anima (It): With spirit.

con brio: With animation.

concertmaster: First-chair violinist in an orchestra.

concerto: a composition for soloist and orchestra.

concert pitch 1: The pitch for C instruments (e.g. flute, oboe, trombone, violin, etc.). 2: International tuning pitch of A440 or A442.

con fuoco (It): With fire.

con gusto (It): With gusto.

consonance: Sounds pleasing to the ear.

con sordini (It): With mutes.

con sordino (It): With mute.

contra (It): In the octave below normal (e.g. contra bassoon).

contralto: The lowest female voice, a.k.a. *alto.*

contrary motion: Term used in *counterpoint* for two voices moving in opposite directions.

cor (Fr): Horn.

corona: *Fermata.*

count: The pulse or beat.

counterpoint: The combination of two or more melodic lines occurring simultaneously.

countertenor: The highest male singing voice.

cover: Slang for the performance of a song written by someone other than the performer.

cowbell: A metal bell struck with a drumstick.

crescendo: Gradually becoming louder.

cross rhythm: Different rhythms played at the same time.

crotchet: British name for quarter note.

cue 1: A gesture made by a conductor for a performer to make an entrance. 2: Small notes indicating another instrument's part.

cut time: 2/2 time signature.

cymbals: Percussion instruments of circular brass plates. May be struck together (crash cymbals), with a mallet (suspended cymbal), or mechanically (hi-hat).

D

da capo, D.C. (It): Direction in a piece of music to return to the beginning.

da capo al coda, D.C. al Coda (It): Direction to return to the beginning, play to the Coda sign, then to skip to the Coda and finish the piece.

da capo al fine, D.C. al Fine (It): Direction to return to the beginning of a piece and play to the "Fine" sign.

dal (It): "From the," or "by the."

dal segno, D.S. (It): Direction to return to the point marked by the sign 𝄋 .

dal segno al coda, D.S. al Coda (It): Direction to return to the sign 𝄋 , play to the coda sign ⊕ , then skip to the coda.

dal segno al fine: Direction to return to the D.S. sign and play to the "Fine" sign.

dB (abbr.): Decibel. Measurement of loudness.

decrescendo: Gradually becoming softer.

degree: a note of a scale.

delicato (It): Delicately.

demiquaver: British term for sixteenth note.

demisemiquaver: British term for thirty-second note.

détaché (Fr): Short, detached bowing strokes.

di (It): Of, with.

diatonic: The tones of any major or minor scale.

didgeridoo: Australian aboriginal horn made of wood hollowed by termites, played with the lips and breath.

diminished: Lowered.

diminished interval: A minor or perfect interval lowered a half step.

diminished seventh chord: A chord with root, minor third, diminished fifth, and diminished seventh.

diminished triad: A triad with root, minor third, and diminished fifth.

diminuendo (It): Growing gradually softer.

diminution: Shortening the length of notes in a *theme.*

discord: Dissonant sounds or sounds unpleasant to the ear.

disjunct: Moving by intervals larger than a second.

dissonance: Sounds unpleasant to the ear.

divisi, div. (It): Indication for separate parts written on one staff. To be played by two or more performers.

do: The first note (*tonic*) of a diatonic scale.

dodecaphonic: Twelve-tone music.

doit: A jazz technique used on brass instruments where a note is bent upwards.

dominant: Fifth degree of a major or minor scale.

doppio (It): Double.

Dorian: A medieval mode with the half- whole-step pattern from D to D on the white keys of the piano.

dot **1**: Written above or below a note indicates *staccato*. **2**: Written after a note, the dot increases the length by half its original value.

double bar: Two bar lines on a staff that show the end of a section or piece.

double bass: Lowest member of the violin family, tuned E, A, D, G.

double concerto: A concerto for two instruments.

double dot: Increases a note's length by 3/4 of its original value.

double flat: Written before a note, it lowers the note a whole step.

double horn: A French horn comprised of two different horns (one in F, one in Bb), with valve to switch between the two. Better intonation and greater range.

double reed: Two thin pieces of cane bound together at one end which vibrate to produce sound for *oboe*, *English horn*, and *bassoon*.

double sharp: Written before a note, it raises the pitch of the note a whole step.

double stop: For violin family instruments, playing two notes at once.

double time: Twice as fast.

double tonguing: On brass and flute instruments, a method of rapidly articulating notes, alternating with the front and back of the tongue (ta-ka-ta-ka).

downbeat: the first beat of a measure given with downward stroke by the conductor.

drone: A note of the same pitch which continues for a long time. Used by instruments like bagpipes, 5-string banjo and hurdy-gurdy.

drum kit, drum set: A set of drums several drums, usu. consisting of: snare drum, bass drum, hi-hat, ride cymbal, crash cymbal, hi-middle- and low tom toms.

duet or duo: Musical composition for two performers.

duple meter: A time signature with two beats to a measure (e.g. 2/4 or fast 6/8).

duration: The length of a note or rest.

dynamic accent: Emphasis given a note by louder articulation than normal.

dynamic markings: Symbols which indicate different levels of loudness or softness (e.g. *p*, *mp*, *mf*, *f*,).

dynamics **1**: The level of loudness or softness. **2**: The symbols for dynamics.

E

8va: Ottava altus. One octave higher.

8vb: Ottava bassus. One octave lower.

ear training: A technique of learning to hear music and write it down.

eighth: An octave.

eighth note, eighth rest: A note/rest with one eighth the length of a whole note, and half the length of a quarter note. Half of a beat in 4/4 time.

eleventh: Diatonic interval from the first to the eleventh note. Same letter name as the 4th.

embellishment: An *ornament* added to music.

embouchure: The position and use of lips, tongue, and teeth when playing a wind instrument.

English horn: An alto *oboe* with a pitch a fifth lower. Same conical shape but with a bulbous bell.

enharmonic: Two notes of the same pitch with different names (e.g. Ab and G#).

ensemble: A group of performers.

entr'acte (Fr): A piece played between acts of an opera, ballet, or musical.

equal temperament: A tuning system which divides the octave into equal intervals.

espressivo (It): Expressive, with emotion.

estinto (It): Very soft, almost inaudible.

-etto (It): A suffix meaning "little."

étude: A piece of music studied to improve technique.

euphonium: A brass instrument similar to the *baritone horn* but with a larger bore.

eurhythmics: A system which teaches rhythm by using body movement.

expression marks: Directions or symbols for musical expression and interpretation, like *dynamics*, *tempo*, *articulation*, and mood.

F

f (abbr.): Forte. Loud dynamic.

fa: 4th Degree of a *diatonic* scale.

fake: Slang for improvisation. "If you can't make it, fake it."

fake book: A song book containing chord changes, lyrics, and melodies for many songs.

false cadence: see *deceptive cadence*.

falsetto (It): A high voice used for notes above the normal vocal range.

fanfare: A short piece of music for brass to attract attention.

F clef: The bass clef centered on the 4th line of the staff and naming that 4th line as F below middle C.

feminine cadence: A *cadence* ending on a weak beat.

fermata (It): A symbol indicating a hold or pause.

festoso (It): Happy or merry.

ff (abbr.): *Fortissimo*.

fff (abbr.): *Fortississimo*.

f-hole: On violin family instruments it's the *f*-shaped sound holes on top of the instrument. Also on some guitars.

fiddle: A violin used for folk- or bluegrass music; it usu. has a flatter *bridge*, uses metal strings and a *tuner* on each string.

fiero (It): Bold.

fife: A high, keyless flute.

fifth: The interval of 5 diatonic scale degrees.

fine: The end.

fretboard: The surface of the neck on string instruments where the fingers press down on the strings.

fixed do: A singing system in which the note C is always do. Compare to *moveable do*.

flag: A curved line extending from the right side of the stem of a note. Used on eighth notes and smaller notes.

flam: A drum rudiment. Small grace note before the main note.

flamenco: A Spanish dance/song usu. played on guitar and including rhythmic clapping and stomping of the dancer.

flat **1**: The symbol used to lower a note by one half step. **2**: To be below normal pitch.

flip: A jazz technique, usu performed on brass instruments. Note is raised in pitch and then glissed down to the next note.

flugelhorn: A brass instrument in the trumpet family with a wider bell than trumpet, a conical bore, and more mellow tone.

flute: A woodwind instrument of wood or metal in the shape of a cylinder closed at one end. Sound is produced by blowing across a hole near the closed end (see also: *alto flute, bass flute*).

flutter tonguing: A wind instrument technique of very rapid tonguing, produced by rolling the tongue saying trrrrrrr.

form: The structure or organization of a piece of music.

forte (It): Loud.

fortissimo (It): Very loud.

fortississimo (It): Very very loud. Officially the loudest dynamic marking.

forzando, forzato (It): Forced. Strongly accented.

fourth: An interval of 4 diatonic degrees.

fourth chord: A chord with intervals of a fourth.

French horn: A brass instrument with a conical bore, valves, highly flared bell, and many coils of tubing.

French sixth: A type of *augmented sixth chord* with a major third, augmented fourth, and augmented sixth above the root.

fret **1**: On many string instruments, a strip usu of metal placed across the fretboard to give a specific note when fretted. **2**: The act of pressing the fingers down on the fretboard.

fretboard: The *fretboard* of instruments with frets.

frog: The end of the *bow* which is held in the hand.

fugue: A piece in which two or more parts are built upon a recurring theme.

full score: An instrumental score in which appear all the parts for the instruments.

fundamental: The lowest note in a *harmonic series*.

funk: A rhythmic style with much syncopation.

furioso (It): Furiously, wildly.

fusion: A combination of rock and jazz beginning in the early '70s.

fz (abbr.): *Forzando, sforzando*.

G

gapped scale: A scale made from a complete scale by leaving out some notes. The pentatonic scale is a gapped scale.

G clef: The treble clef, centered on the second line of the staff, giving that line the pitch G above middle C.

German flute: The standard flute.

German sixth: A type of *augmented sixth chord* with a major third, perfect fifth, and augmented sixth above the root.

Gestopft (Ger.): Muting a horn with the hand.

ghost bend: A guitar technique in which a note is pre-bent before sounding the string.

ghost note: A jazz technique in which the note indicated by parentheses is barely played.

gig: A musician's slang for a job.

giocoso (It): Humorous.

glass harmonica: An instrument invented in the 1700s made of various sizes of glass bowls played by rubbing around the rim with a wet finger.

glee: Unaccompanied vocal music for three or four parts.

glee club: A group that sings glees.

glide: A smooth change in pitch from one note to another.

glissando: A fast scale produced by sliding the hand finger rapidly from one note to another.

gong: A percussion instrument from Asia made up of a heavy circular metal plate and struck with a soft mallet.

G.P. (abbr.): Grand Pause. A pause in a piece of music.

grace note: An ornamental note played quickly before the main note.

grandioso (It): Grand, grandiose.

grand pause: A pause for the entire group of musicians.

grand staff: Both the treble and bass clef staffs. Piano music is written on a grand staff.

grave (It): Slow. Solemn.

grazia, grazioso (It): Grace, graceful.

groove: Slang for when music is perfectly in synch.

grosso (It): Great, large.

growl: A rough sound produced by growling in the back of the throat. Often used in jazz.

gruppetto (It): An ornamental group of notes like a *turn*, *shake*, or *trill*.

gusto (It): Enjoyment, gusto.

H

H **1**: German for B natural. **2**: Letter used with a number for the works of Haydn, after the cataloguer "Hoboken."

half cadence: see *imperfect cadence*.

half note, half rest: A note/rest equal to half the length of a whole note/rest or two quarter notes/rests. Two beats in 4/4 time.

half step: The smallest *interval* in Western music. One twelfth of an *octave*.

harmonic minor: A *natural minor* scale with a half step between the 7th and 8th degrees of the scale.

harmonic progression: Movement from one chord to another.

harmonics **1**: The pure individual tones which make up a complex tone. **2**: On string instruments, a tone produced by touching the strings at the harmonic nodes.

harmonic series: A series of notes produced above a *fundamental* and having a specific order.

head voice: The upper *register* of the voice.

heidimisemiquaver: British name for a sixty-fourth note.

hexachord: A six-note scale.

hi-hat cymbals: Used in the drum kit; a pair of cymbals facing each other and struck together with a mechanical device operated by the foot.

hold: A *fermata* or pause.

horn **1**: The brass instrument with conical tube wound round itself. Another name for French horn. **2**: Musician's slang for his or her instrument.

Hungarian minor scale: A harmonic minor scale with a raised 4th.

hyper-: Prefix meaning above or over.

hypo-: Prefix meaning below.

I

ictus (Lat.): Stress, or an accent.

imitation: The restatement of a musical idea in another part. Used in counterpoint.

improvisation: Music composed on the spot.

incomplete cadence: A cadence in which a note other than the *key note* is in the top voice of the I chord.

interlude: A short piece used to bridge the acts of a play.

interrupted cadence: A cadence in which the dominant chord (V) moves to a chord other than the tonic (I).

interval: The distance between two notes.

Intonation: The accuracy of pitch.

inversion, chordal: A chord with a bass tone other than its root.

inversion, melodic: The change of an ascending interval to its corresponding descending interval.

Ionian: A medieval mode whose whole and half steps correspond to the major scale. C to C on the white keys of the piano.

isteso (It): The same. l'istesso tempo.

Italian sixth: A type of *augmented sixth chord* containing a major third and an augmented sixth above the bass.

J-K-L

jam: Slang for a gathering of musicians to play or improvise.

jazz: A style of music with African-American roots and using *blue notes*, *improvisation*, and strong rhythms.

jazz combo: A small jazz group usu consisting of piano, drums, bass, and a solo instrument.

jazz ensemble: A group of musicians (usu rhythm section, brass, and woodwinds) who play various styles of *jazz*.

K: Used to catalogue Mozart's works; represents Köchel. (e.g. K 201)

kettledrum: A percussion instrument with a tunable head. Also called *timpani*.

key **1**: The tonal center of a composition, based on the tonic of the scale. **2**: A lever pressed by the finger on an instrument (e.g. piano, flute).

keynote: The first note of the scale of a *key*. Also called the *tonic*.

key signature - accidentals at the left side of the staff between the clef and the time signature which indicate what key the piece is in.

kick: In jazz, a rhythmic accent or cue applied by the rhythm section.

la: The sixth degree of a diatonic scale.

lacrimoso (It): Tearful, mournful.

largamente (It): Broadly.

largando (It): Slowing down.

larghetto (It): A little faster than *largo*.

Largo (It): Broad. A very slow tempo.

leading note/tone: The seventh degree of a diatonic scale; leads the ear to the *tonic* note.

lead sheet: Melody line, lyrics and chord for a song. A *fake book* is made up of lead sheets.

leap: A skip of more than a 2nd.

ledger line, leger line: A short line drawn for a note above or below the staff.

legato (It): Smooth.

leggero, leggiero (It): Lightly.

leno (It): Faint.

lento (It): slow.

lesto (It): Lively.

licks: Slang for a short musical idea or phrase.

ligature **1**: A metal device used by woodwind instruments to secure the reed to the mouthpiece. **2**: A curved line over a group of notes to be sung on the same syllable.

lip: A verb meaning to adjust the pitch of a note slightly up or down.

lip trill: A technique used by brass players; an upward trill without use of valves.

l'istesso (It): The same.

loco (It): Return to the normal place. Used after playing 8va or 8vb.

Locrian: a medieval mode which starts on the seventh degree of a diatonic scale. B to B on the white keys of a piano.

lungo (It): Long.

Lydian: A medieval mode beginning on the 4th degree of a diatonic scale. F to F on the white keys of a piano.

M

ma (It): But. Allegro ma non tropo.

maestoso (It): Majestically.

maggiore (It): Major.

major: Used in music theory to describe *intervals*, *chords*, and *scales*.

major chord: A triad consisting of a root, major third, and perfect fifth.

major scale: A diatonic scale with half steps between from the third to fourth degrees and seventh to eighth degrees.

marcato (It): Stressed or accented.

marcia (It): March.

mariachi (Sp): A Mexican folk group with 2 violins, guitar, guitarron and maybe rhythm instruments.

martelé, martellato (Fr): Play with short detached bow strokes without lifting the bow from the strings.

masculine cadence: A *cadence* in which the last chord is on the strong beat.

measure: The space between two bar lines.

mediant: The third degree of a scale.

melisma: Several notes sung on the same syllable.

melismatic: Song that uses melismas.

melodic minor: A natural minor scale with the sixth and seventh degrees raised ascending, and lowered descending.

melody: A sequence of single notes.

meno (It): Less.

meter: The rhythmic structure of a piece determined by number of beats, time values and accents. *Simple meters* are divisible by two; *compound meters* are divisible by 3.

metronome: A mechanical or electronic device used for sounding beats per minute. Invented c. 1812.

mezza voce (It): Half voice. Quiet.

mezzo (It): Half or medium (e.g. mezzo forte).

mezzo forte (It): Medium loud.

mezzo piano (It): Medium soft.

mezzo soprano (It): A female voice between soprano and alto.

mf (abbr.): Mezzo forte.

mi: The 3rd degree of a *diatonic* scale.

middle C: The note C in the middle of the *grand staff* and near the middle of the keyboard.

minim: British name for the *half note*.

minim rest: Half rest.

minor: Used to describe *intervals*, *chords*, and *scales*. Means lesser.

minor scale (natural): A *diatonic* scale in which the 3rd, 6th and 7th degrees are lowered a half step from the *major scale*. See also *harmonic minor*, and *melodic minor*.

misterioso (It): Mysteriously.

mit (Ger.): With.

Mixolydian: A Medieval mode starting on the 5th degree of a diatonic scale. G to G on the white keys of a piano.

M.M. (abbr.): Stands for Maelzel's *metronome*, the man who invented the device.

mode: A type of scale with a certain arrangement of intervals. See *Ionian, Dorian, Phrygian, Lydian, Mixolydian, Aeolian,* and *Locrian.*

moderato (It): A moderate tempo.

modulate: To change from one key to another.

moll (Ger.): Minor.

molto (It): Very.

monotone: An unvaried pitch.

mordent: A melodic ornament consisting of the alteration of the written note with the note directly below (lower ~) or above (upper ~) it.

mouthpiece: On a brass or woodwind instrument, the part responsible for making the vibrations, placed on the player's lips or in the mouth.

moveable do: A system of singing using syllables in which the first note of any diatonic scale is *do*. See *fixed do.*

movement: A self-contained piece of music within a larger piece of music.

mp (abbr.): *Mezzo piano.*

music theory: The study of how music is written down and put together.

music therapy: The use of music as a healing agent for physical and psychological problems.

muta (It): Direction to change keys, usu. found in timpani and horn parts.

mutes: Devices used to muffle, soften, or change the sound of an instrument.

N

natural: The symbol which indicates a note is neither sharp nor flat, and when the symbol is in front of the note, it cancels any previous accidental.

natural horn: A horn with no valves or slides.

natural minor: A diatonic scale with the whole-half step pattern of WHWWHWW. A to A on the white keys of the piano.

Neopolitan sixth: A chord constructed on the fourth degree of a *diatonic* scale with a minor third and a minor sixth above the bass.

neck: The long slender part on a string instrument to which the fretboard is attached.

neumes: The signs and symbols used for musical notation in the Middle Ages.

ninth: The interval of nine *diatonic* notes. An octave and a second.

ninth chord: Root, third, fifth, seventh, and ninth.

node: A point of lowest amplitude in the wavelength of a string. These points are where *harmonics* are produced on a string instrument.

non (Fr): No or not.

nonet: A piece for 9 musicians.

nonharmonic notes: Notes not a part of the chord structures around them.

non-transposing: instruments pitched in the key of C (e.g. flute, trombone, bells).

notehead: The main, bulbous part of a note.

O

O 1: The symbol for diminished. 2: The symbol for an open string.

obbligato (It): An optional part contrasting the melody. Originally meant an obligatory part.

oblique motion: Two melodic lines, one of which moves while the other remains stationary.

oboe: A *double-reed* woodwind instrument with a conical bore.

oboe d'amore: Slightly larger than the normal oboe and with a more bulbous bell. Pitched a minor third lower.

octave - the interval between the first and eighth degrees of a *diatonic* scale.

octet 1: Eight performers. 2: A piece of music for eight performers.

odd meter: A meter with an odd number grouped with an even number of beats per measure, like 7/4 (3+4) and 5/8 (2+3).

oliphant: A medieval horn made from an elephant's tusk.

Op. (abbr.): Opus.

open: Not stopped or muted.

open fifth: A triad with no third.

open harmony: When notes of a chord aren't played as closely together as possible. See *close harmony.*

open notes 1: On string instruments, the open, unfretted strings. 2: Notes on wind instruments played without the use of valves or keys.

open triad: Triad without the third.

Opus (Lat.): Means "work"; used with a number which shows the order in which a composer's work were composed.

ornamentation: The addition of *ornaments* to a melody.

ornaments: Melodic embellishments. May be written in or improvised. Some ornaments: acciaccatura, appogiatura, arpeggio, grace notes, mordent, trill, turn.

ossia (It): Indicates a passage which is an alternative version.

ostinato (It): A repeated musical phrase, rhythmic pattern, or motive, usu. occurring in the bass.

ottava (It): Octave.

ottava alta (8va) (It): An octave higher.

ottava bassa (8vb) (It): An octave lower.

overblow: A technique of blowing harder used in brass instruments when *harmonics* are produced above the *fundamental.*

overtone series: The same thing as the *harmonic series*, but without the fundamental.

P

p 1: (It) *Piano;* soft dynamic. 2: (Sp) Pulgar, which is the thumb of the right hand in guitar music.

parallel chords: The movement of specific chords up and down the scale.

parallel fifths, fourths, octaves: Two parts moving in the same direction at the same time a fifth, fourth or octave apart.

parallel intervals: Movement of two or more parts of the same interval in the same direction.

parallel keys: Major and minor keys which have the same *tonic.*

parallel motion: The movement in two or more parts in the same direction with the same intervals.

passing notes: Scalewise notes which connect two notes of the harmony, but are not part of the harmony themselves.

pause: A rest of variable length. A fermata.

pedal point: An organ term used for a note, usu. in the bass, around which other notes move.

pedal tone: A "false" note below the fundamental on a brass instrument.

pentachord: The first five notes of a diatonic scale.

pentatonic scale 1: Any scale with five notes. 2: The major scale without the 4th and 7th degrees. The black keys on a piano.

percussion family: Instruments of indefinite pitch which resonate when struck or shaken. Drums, maracas, bells, gongs, and xylophones.

perfect cadence: A cadence moving from the dominant chord (V) to the tonic chord (I).

perfect interval: Octave, fifth, and fourth without alterations.

perfect pitch: The ability to identify any note by ear.

period: A segment of music consisting of two or more phrases and a cadence.

pesante (It): Heavy.

pf (abbr.): Soft then loud.

phrase: A musical "sentence" or idea.

Phrygian: A medieval mode beginning on the third degree of a diatonic scale. E to E on the white keys of a piano.

pianissimo (It): Very soft.

pianississimo (It): Very, very soft.

piano (It) 1: Soft. 2: Short for "pianoforte," a keyboard instrument.

piano quartet: Violin, viola, cello, and piano.

piano trio: Violin, viola, and piano.

Picardy third: A minor piece ending on a chord with a major third.

piccolo (It): A member of the flute family which sounds an octave higher than written. Smaller than the normal flute.

pitch: The highness or lowness of a tone.

pitch pipe: A small wind instrument used for tuning.

pivot chord: A chord used when modulating which is the same for both keys.

pizzicatto: Plucking the strings of an instrument that uses a bow.

placido (It): Calm, placid.

plagal cadence: A cadence which moves from the subdominant chord (IV) to the tonic chord (I).

poco a poco (It): Little by little.

polychords: Chords resulting from two triadic units.

polymetric: The simultaneous use of different meters.

polyphony: Music which combines two or more melodic lines.

polytonal: The simultaneous use of different key signatures.

pomposo (It): Pompous.

ponticello (It): The bridge of a string instrument.

portamento: A smooth glide from one note to another.

portado (It): An articulation halfway between staccato and legato.

pp (abbr.): pianissimo.

ppp (abbr.): pianississimo.

prebend: To bend a string before playing on a string instrument, esp. guitar.

preciso (It): Exact.

prélude (Fr): An introductory piece or movement.

preparation: The use of a consonant note before playing that same note as part of a discord.

prestissimo (It): Very, very fast. The fastest tempo.

presto (It): Very fast.

prima donna (It): The most important woman in an opera.

primary chords: The tonic (I), subdominant (IV), and dominant (V) chords of a key.

prime 1: Unison. 2: The first note of a scale.

principal: The section leader.

program music: Music that tells a story or paints a picture. As opposed to absolute music.

progression: Movement from one chord to another.

pronto (It): Prompt.

pulgar (Sp): Thumb. Used specifically in guitar music for the thumb of the right hand.

pull-off: A technique used by string players in which a fretted note is plucked while it's released which sounds the note below.

pulse: The beat.

Pythagorean scale: The earliest known scale comprising an octave. Whole and half step arrangements are the same as the major scale, but the ratio of whole and half steps is different.

Q

Quadrat (Ger.): A natural sign.

quadruple meter: A time signature with four beats in a measure.

quadruplet: Four notes to be played in the space of three notes of equal value.

quarter note, quarter rest: A note/rest one fourth the length of a whole note and half the length of a half note. Equal to one beat in 4/4 time.

quartet 1: A composition for four performers. 2: Four performers.

quasi (It): Almost, as if.

quaver: British term for an eighth note.

quintet 1: A composition for five performers. 2: Five performers.

quintuple meter: A time signature with five beats per measure (e.g. 5/4 time).

quintuplet: five notes to be played in the time of four notes of equal value.

R

racket: 1: A double-reed instrument of the Renaissance period. 2: The sound a beginning alto saxophone player makes.

ragtime: The earliest form of jazz from the early 1900s.

rallentando (It): Decreasing speed gradually.

range: The notes from lowest to highest that an instrument or voice is capable of producing.

rattenuto (It): Slowing down.

re: The second note of a diatonic scale.

reduction: The arrangement of a piece for a smaller number of parts.

reed: A vibrating strip of cane which vibrates at high frequency when blown.

refrain: A section of a composition that occurs several times.

register: A certain range of an instrument or voice.

relative keys: Major and minor keys with the same key signature (e.g. A minor and C major).

Renaissance (Fr): Meaning "rebirth." The musical era from the mid 1400s through the end of the 1500s.

resolution: A progression of chords or notes from dissonance to consonance.

rest: A period of silence. Types of rests: whole rest, half rest, quarter rest, eighth rest, sixteenth rest, thirty-second rest.

retardation: Gradually slowing.

retrograde: Playing a melody line backwards.

rhythm: A pattern of long and short in music.

rhythm section: In jazz and pop music, the piano, bass, guitar and drums. Provides the harmony and rhythm.

riff: Repeated melodic idea.

ritardando (It): Gradually decreasing speed.

ritenuto (It): Immediately slower.

rolled chord: A chord in which the notes are played in rapid succession, much like an arpeggio.

romantic: The musical era from ~1820 to 1900.

root: The fundamental note of a chord or scale.

rubato (It): A free tempo which speeds up and slows down at the conductor's or performer's discretion, but without changing the basic pulse.

rudiments: Basic sticking patterns used for drums.

run: A fast scale passage.

S

S. (abbr.): Segno, senza, sign, sol, solo, soprano, sordini, subito.

SA (abbr.): Used in choral music to indicate soprano, alto.

SAB (abbr.): Used in choral music to indicate soprano, alto, baritone.

sackbut (Ger.): The ancestor of the trombone. German for push-pull.

saltato, saltando (It): a bow technique in which the bow is bounced lightly on the string.

SATB: Used in choral music to indicate soprano, alto, tenor, bass.

saxhorn: Brass family instruments consisting of valved bugles invented by Adolphe Sax.

saxophone: A woodwind family instrument of keyed brass, conical bore, and single reed. Types of saxophones: Eb sopranino; Bb soprano; Eb alto; Bb tenor; Eb baritone; Bb bass.

scale: An ascending or descending series of tones related to a certain chosen fundamental tone.

scale degrees: The names and numbers for notes in a scale.

scat singing: A form of vocal jazz improvisation in which the performer makes up the melody with nonsense syllables.

scherzando (It): Playful and light-hearted.

scherzo (It): Literally "joke." A piece with a lively tempo.

schmaltz (Yid): Excessively sentimental.

score: The notation of a composition which shows all its parts arranged horizontally and aligned rhythmically.

secco (It): Means "dry." Unornamented.

second: The interval between two consecutive degrees of a diatonic scale.

secondary dominant: A dominant chord (V) built upon the fifth degree of a chord other than the tonic.

secular music: Any music not sacred.

segno (It): Sign. 𝄋

segue: To continue without a break.

semibreve: British name for whole note.

semiquaver: British name for a sixteenth note.

semitone: One half step.

sempre (It): Always.

senza (It): Without. Senza sordino.

septet 1: A composition for seven performers. 2: Seven performers.

septuplet: Seven notes played in the time of four or six notes of equal value.

seventh: The interval between the first and seventh degrees of a diatonic scale.

seventh chord: A chord containing a root, third, fifth, and seventh.

sextet 1: A composition for six performers. 2: Six performers.

sextuplet: Six notes played in the time of four notes of equal value.

sharp 1: The symbol indicating to raise a note one half step. 2: To be slightly above normal pitch.

sightreading: Playing a piece of music without studying it.

sightsinging: Singing a piece of music without studying it.

signs: Symbols which tell a performer articulation, bowing, breathing, dynamics, fingering, ornamentation and other musical effects.

similar motion: The movement of two or more parts in the same direction.

simile, sim. (It): To continue in a similar style.

simple meter: A time signature whose pulse is divisible by 2 (e.g. 2/4, 3/4, 4/4). See compound meter.

sin' al fine (It): To the end.

single reed instruments: Instruments which use only one reed attached to a mouthpiece of some sort.

six-four chord: A triad in the second inversion with a sixth and a fourth above the bass note.

sixteenth note, sixteenth rest: A note/rest one sixteenth as long as a whole note and half the length of an eighth note. In 4/4 time, 1/4 of a beat.

sixth chord 1: A triad in the first inversion, with a sixth and a third above the root. 2: A chord with an added sixth.

skip: Melodic movement of more than a whole step.

slide 1: To move smoothly from one note to another with a constant sound. 2: The movable part on a trombone which is used to change the pitch by lengthening the instrument.

slur: A curved line connecting two notes of different pitch; to be played as legato as possible.

smorzando (It): Fading away.

so, sol: A solfege syllable for the fifth degree of the diatonic scale.

solfege: A system used for eartraining which uses syllables (do, re, mi, etc.) for the degrees of the scale.

solo (It): Means "alone." To perform alone or as the most important part.

sopra (It): Over, above.

soprano: The highest female singing voice.

soprano clef: The C clef that puts middle C on the first line of the staff.

sordino (It): Mute.

sostenuto (It): Sustained.

sotto voce (It): Quietly, beneath the voice.

Sousaphone: A tuba made for John Phillip Sousa's band which encircles the player.

spacing: The vertical placement of the notes of a chord.

spezzato (It): Divided.

spiccato (It): A bow technique in which the middle of the bow is bounced on the string at a moderate speed.

SSA: Used in choral music to indicate soprano, soprano, alto.

SSAA: Used in choral music to indicate two sopranos, two altos.

staccato (It): Means "detached." Short separated notes indicated by a small dot over or under the note head.

staff, staves: The horizontal lines on which music is written.

stem: A vertical line extending from a note head.

step: Movement melodically of one or two semitones.

stesso (It): Same. L'stesso tempo.

stick 1: The wooden part of the bow. 2: A conductor's baton.

sticking: The hand pattern for drums.

stringendo (It): Hurrying the tempo to increase tension.

string quartet: Two violins, viola, and cello.

string quintet: Two violins, two violas, and cello.

string trio: Violin, viola, cello.

subdominant: The fourth degree of a diatonic scale.

subito (It): Suddenly.

submediant: The sixth degree of a diatonic scale.

subtonic: A flatted seventh degree of a diatonic scale, one whole step below the tonic.

suite: A collection of short instrumental movements.

sul (It): On the.

sul ponticello (It): Bowing on or next to the bridge to produce a high-pitched eerie sound.

sul tasto: On the fretboard.

superdominant: The sixth degree of the diatonic scale. Same as submediant.

supertonic: The second degree of a diatonic scale.

sur (Fr): On, over.

suspension: A counterpoint technique in which a consonant note is sustained while the other voices move which results in a dissonance which is then resolved.

sussurando (It): Sussurating, whispering.

swing 1: A style of jazz featuring big band dance music. 2: A treatment of the eighth note which gives it a lilting triplet feel of long-short.

symphony 1: A large orchestra. 2: A piece composed for an orchestra, usu. in 4 movements.

syncopation: Rhythmic accents on weak beats, or weak parts of the beat.

system: Two or more staves connected.

T

t. (abbr.): Tempo, trill, tre, tutti.

T. (abbr.): Tenor, tonic.

TAB (abbr.): Tablature. A method of notation developed for lute and guitar in which the lines of the staff represent the strings and numbers represent the frets. Developed in 1500s.

tacet (Lat.): Means "be silent." Direction in a part to not play or sing.

tactus (Lat.): Used in the 1400s to measure the length of a beat. Precursor to bar lines.

tag: The end of a piece, the *coda*.

taking 4s/8s: A jazz term. Player takes a solo, usu. improvised, 4 or 8 bars long.

talking drum: Ancient drum of western Africa, beaten with a curved stick. A waisted drum, the pitch controlled by squeezing at the waist which tightens the skin membrane thereby raising the pitch.

tardo, tardando: Become slower.

tanto (It): Much.

temperament: A system of tuning, esp. of pianos, in which pure intervals are altered slightly to enable playing in different keys.

tempestoso (It): Tempestuous, stormy.

tempo: Means "time." The speed of music.

tenor: A high male voice, the range between alto and baritone.

tenor clef: A C clef falling on the fourth line of the staff.

tenor saxophone: Of the saxophone family, in the key of Bb.

tenor trombone: The regular trombone.

tenth: An interval of an octave and a third.

tertian harmony: Usual harmony, based on thirds.

tessitura (It) 1: The average highness and lowness of a piece. 2: The usable range of a voice or instrument.

tetrachord: The first four notes of a scale.

texture: The number of voices in a piece: *monophonic*, *homophonic*, and *polyphonic*.

theme: The musical subject of a piece, the main idea.

thesis (Gk): The strong beat, usu. the downbeat.

third: An interval of three diatonic scale degrees.

thirty-second note, thirty-second rest: A note/rest one thirty-second as long as a whole note, and half as long as a sixteenth note.

ti: The seventh degree of a diatonic scale. The leading tone.

tie: A curved line which connects notes of the same pitch indicating they are to be played as one continuous note.

timbre: Sound quality or color.

time: A synonym for meter.

time signature: The meter. Numbers at the beginning of a piece of music, after the clef. Top number is beats per measure, bottom number is which note receives one beat.

tonal: Relating to key.

tone: A sound of particular quality. The basis of music.

tone row: Used in serial and twelve-tone music. The order of twelve notes chosen by a composer which appear in the composition in that specific order.

tonguing: A technique on wind instruments of articulating notes with the tongue.

tonic: The first degree of a scale (I), or the root of a chord.

tonic accent: A type of accent in which the accented note is significantly higher than those around it.

tr (abbr.): Trill.

trading 4s/8s: Jazz term. Players take turns playing solos, usu. improvised, of 4 or 8 bars.

train wreck: Slang for when an ensemble's playing contains so many mistakes that it breaks down to the point of stopping.

tranquillo (It): Calm, tranquil.

transcription: The writing down of a piece from a recording.

transpose, transposing: Changing a piece from one key to another.

transposing instruments: Instruments whose notes sound at a different pitch than written.

treble clef: The G clef which centers on the second line of the staff, naming it G.

tremolo (It): 1: A bow technique in which short up and down bow strokes are used on a single note. 2: The rapid alteration between two or more notes, usu. more than a step apart.

triad: A chord of three notes: a root, third, and fifth.

trill: An ornament. The rapid alteration of one note with another note usu. a step or half step higher than the written note. Indicated by the symbols *tr* .

trio 1: A composition for three performers. 2: Three performers. 3: The middle section of a march.

triple meter: Meters with three beats per measure, or meters with beats divisible by three.

triple-tonguing: Technique of rapid articulation which uses the front and back of the tongue (t-k-t, or t-t-k, or t-k-t, k-t-k).

tritone: The interval of an augmented fourth or diminished fifth. Considered the most dissonant interval.

tromba (It): Trumpet.

trombone: Member of the brass family. Uses a slide to change pitch. Also called 'bone. Types of 'bones: soprano (also called slide trumpet), tenor, bass.

troppo (It): Too much. (e.g. Allegro non tropo).

troubadour: A wandering minstrel in the Middle Ages of Western Europe.

trumpet: A member of the brass family with cylindrical bore and high pitch and brilliant sound. Types of trumpets: Bb, C, Eb, Bb piccolo.

TTB (abbr.): Used in choral music to indicate tenor, tenor, bass.

TTBB (abbr.): Used in choral music to indicate two tenors, two basses.

tuba: Lowest member of the brass family, conical bore, very large. May be in BB-flat, Eb, or F bass.

tune 1: A song or melody. 2: To put an instrument at the correct pitch (in tune).

tuner 1: A mechanical device which reads pitches and tells the player where it falls in relation to standard intonation. 2: A small screw near the bridge which allows fine tuning of string instruments.

tuning fork: A device with two tines that, when struck, vibrates to produce a pure single note.

turn: An ornament which "turns" around the principal note, going above it and below it. Indicated by the symbol ∞ .

tutti (It): Means "all." Used as an indication for all players to play, usu. comes after a solo or soli section.

twelve-bar blues: A musical form using three chords (I, IV, V) in a specific pattern which is twelve bars long. Characterized by many *blue notes* and improvisation.

twelve-tone scale: A scale using all 12 half steps in an octave organized in a certain order called a *tone row*.

U

ukulele (HI): A Hawaiian instrument in the string family, small with four strings.

unequal temperament: A system of tuning, esp. of piano which allows an instrument to play in several keys.

unison: Two or more voices sounding the same pitch.

un poco (It): A little.

upbeat **1**: The "and" of the beat, the second half of the beat. **2**: A pick-up note or *anacrusis*. **3**: Denotes a fast or happy tune.

up bow: Stroking the bow upward.

up-tempo: Fast.

ut (Lat.): Another name for *do* or C.

V

valve: A device on brass instruments which redirects the air column to produce a different pitch, may be piston or rotary.

vamp: A short, usu. introductory section, which repeats until a performer is ready to enter.

vibrato: A type of ornament which is a fluctuation of pitch. Used almost constantly in violin, flute and voice.

viola: Instrument in the violin family, uses alto and treble clef, sounding lower than violin.

violin family: Instrument of the violin family (imagine that), which uses treble clef, has four strings and a high pitch.

violoncello: A member of the violin family of the tenor range. Held between the knees and uses the bass and treble clefs. Also called cello.

virtuoso: An instrumental performer of exceptional skill.

vivace (It): A very quick tempo.

Vl., Vln (abbr.): Violin.

Vla. (abbr.): Viola.

Vlc. (abbr.): Violoncello.

vocalise: A vocal warm-up exercise using different vowels.

vocal tenor clef: A G clef used for tenor parts in vocal music and pitched an octave below regular treble clef.

voice **1**: An instrumental or vocal part. **2**: The sound of the human voice.

voice leading: The movement of an individual part in *polyphonic* music.

voicing: The arrangement of pitches horizontally in a chord.

voix (Fr): Voice.

volti (It): Turn the page.

volti subito (It): Turn the page quickly.

volume: Loudness.

vox (Lat.): Voice.

V.S. (abbr.): Volti subito.

W

Wagner tuba: Five-valved horns designed by Richard Wagner for use in his opera *The Ring of the Nibelung*.

wah: A brass instrument sound produced when a device (stem of harmon mute or plunger mute) is removed from the bell.

walking bass: A bass line, usu. moving stepwise, in a steady pattern of quarter or eighth notes.

well-tempered: A tuning system in which an instrument, usu. piano, can play in all twelve keys.

whole note, whole rest: A note equal to two half notes/rests, or four quarter notes/rests. Four beats in 4/4 time.

whole step: Two half steps, or a major second.

wind instrument: An instrument on which the sound is produced by the vibration of an air column.

woodwind: An instrument made of wood or using a reed to create vibrations. Also the flute.

woodwind quintet: Flute, clarinet, oboe, French horn, and bassoon.

X-Y-Z

xylophone: A barred pitched percussion instrument, often with resonator tubes extending down from the bars.

yodel: A style of singing in which the voice centers around the break between the normal voice and falsetto. Originated in Switzerland.

Zink (Ger.): Cornett.

zydeco: A style of music mixing Cajun, Afro-Carribbean, and rhythm and blues.

Musical Terms

Feel free to photocopy these pages, but please don't write on them. If they're left blank, others may also use them. If the book is yours however, go for it.

General Info About These Scales

On the next few pages you'll find scales in both bass and treble clef. I've included the Major, natural minor, harmonic minor, and pentatonic scales. Because of the limitations of your instrument, you may have to transpose some scales up or down an octave.

The layout for these scales was handled by our Department of Redundancy Department. You'll notice the scales have both the key signature and the accidentals written in front of the note. This is to aid you in your practice of scales. Normally you'd see just the key signature.

Remember that there are 15 major scales, but three of them overlap, so you'll really only be practicing the fingering for 12 scales. Confusing? You bet. If you remember enharmonic notes, you'll understand why this is. The Major Scales that overlap are D*b*/C#, G*b*/F#, and C*b*/B. The minor scales that overlap are b*b*/a#, e*b*/d#, and a*b*/g#. The fingerings and the sound of these enharmonic scale is the same, but they're written differently.

The scales are shown ascending only, but be sure to practice them going up, going down, and for as many octaves as you can comfortably play. Vary the speed, be sure to start slowly, and memorize them as soon as possible. Don't neglect the modes. Start on the second degree and go an octave. The third degree. Fourth. Etc. etc. Apply the patterns below to the modes as well.

Scale Pattern Suggestions

Here are some ways to get these scales under your fingers. The numbers you see represent the degrees of the scale with 1 being the tonic, or bottom note of the scale. Often at the beginning or end of the scale pattern, you'll go outside the octave of the scale. When you go below the tonic or root note, this is shown by a minus (-) sign. For example, one note below the tonic (the seventh degree of the scale) would be -7. In the key of C this would be the "B" just beneath the tonic. Going above the octave, just add another number. For example one note above the 8th note of the scale would be 9, then 10, etc.

These may seem difficult to understand at first. To make these more clear, write out the number under each scale degree, then write out the scale pattern itself. Once you play these a few times, you'll hear the pattern and they will make more sense. Memorize them

Scale Patterns

Pattern Name	Pattern (1 = tonic)
the scale	1,2,3,4,5,6,7,8,7,6,5,4,3,2,1 (also try 1,2,3,4,5,6,7,8,**9**,8,7,6,5,4,3,2,1)
thirds	1,3,2,4,3,5,4,6,5,7,6,8,7,9,8,6,7,5,6,4,5,3,4,2,3,1,2,-7,1
fourths	1,4,2,5,3,6,4,7,5,8,6,9,7,10,8,5,7,4,6,3,5,2,4,1,3,-7,2,-6, 1
fifths	1,5,2,6,3,7,4,8,5,9,6,10,7,11,8,4,7,3,6,2,5,1,4,-7,3,-6,2,-5,1
rolling thirds	1,2,3,1,2,3,4,2,3,4,5,3,4,5,6,4,5,6,7,5,6,7,8,6,7,8,9,7,8 8,7,6,8,7,6,5,7,6,5,4,6,5,4,3,5,4,3,2,4,3,2,1,3,2,1,-7,2,1
rolling triplets (use 8th note triplet rhythm)	1,2,3,2,3,4,3,4,5,4,5,6,5,6,7,6,7,8,7,8,9,8 8,7,6,7,6,5,6,5,4,5,4,3,4,3,2,3,2,1,2,1,-7,1
rolling fifths	1,5,4,3,2,6,5,4,3,7,6,5,4,8,7,6,5,9,8,7,6,10,9,8,7,11,10,9,8 8,4,5,6,7,3,4,5,6,2,3,4,5,1,2,3,4,-7,1,2,3,-6,-7,1,2,-5,-6,-7,1
rolling fourths (use 8th note triplet rhythm)	1,4,3,2,5,4,3,6,5,4,7,6,5,8,7,6,9,8,7,10,9,8 8,5,6,7,4,5,6,3,4,5,2,3,4,1,2,3,-7,1,2,-6,-7,1

Treble Clef Major Scales (flats)

Treble Clef Natural minor Scales (flats)

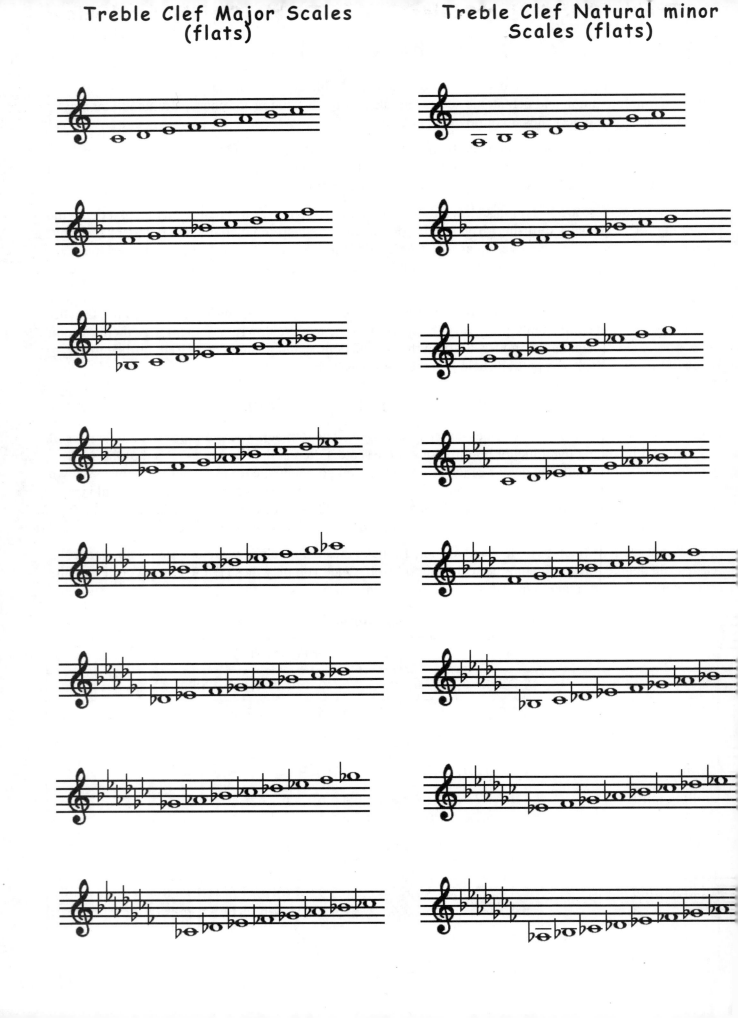

Treble Clef Harmonic minor Scales

Treble Clef Major Pentatonic Scales (flats)

Treble Clef Minor Pentatonic Scales (flats)

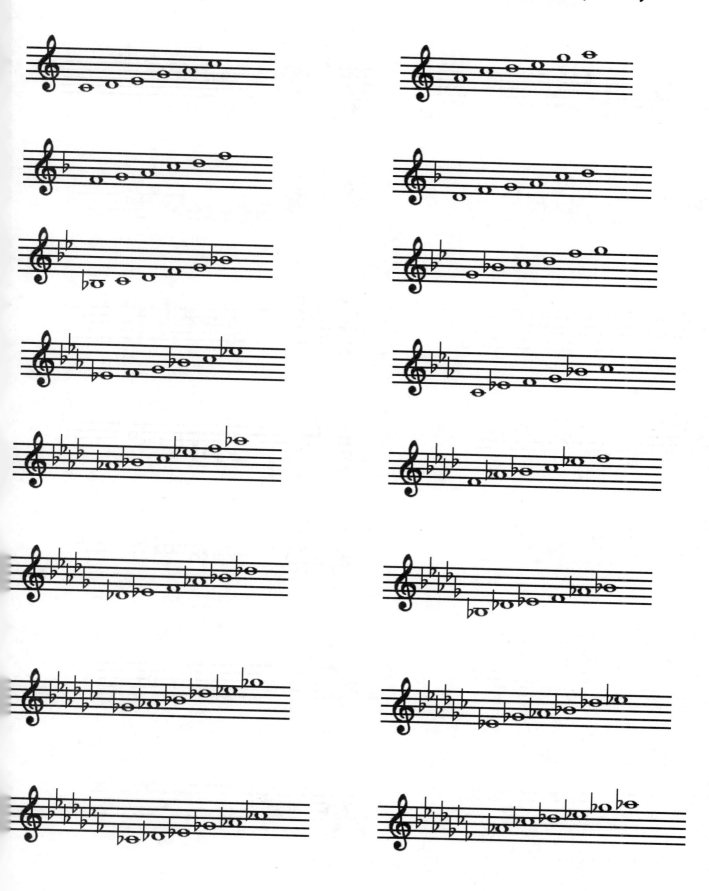

Treble Clef Major Pentatonic Scales (sharps)

Treble Clef Minor Pentatonic Scales (sharps)

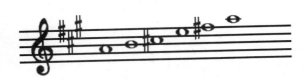

Bass Clef Major Scales
(flats)

Bass Clef Natural minor Scales
(flats)

Bass Clef Major Scales (sharps)

Bass Clef Natural minor Scales (sharps)

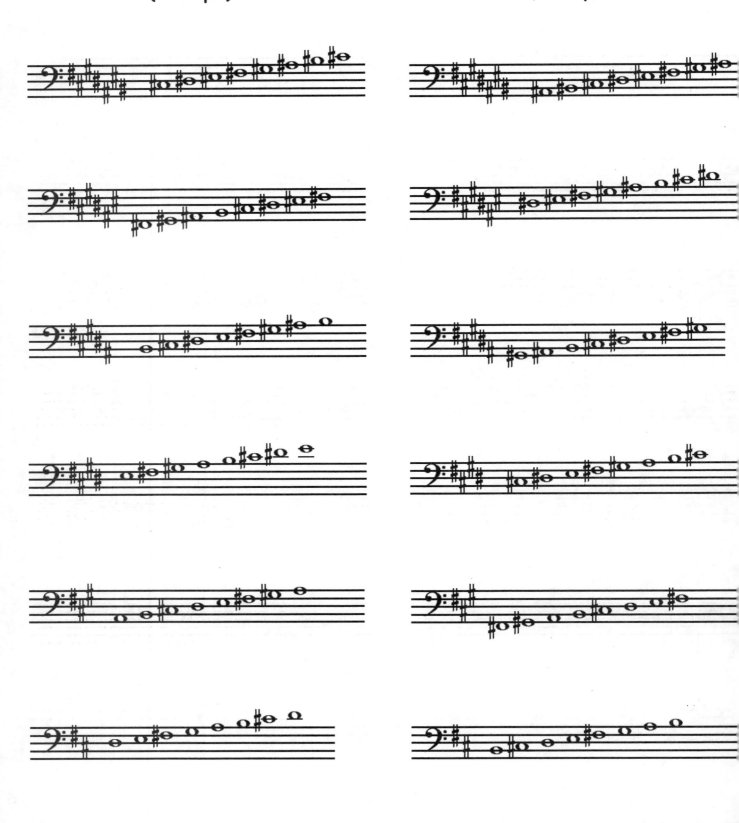

Bass Clef Harmonic minor Scales

Bass Clef Major Pentatonic Scales (flats)

Bass Clef Minor Pentatonic Scales (flats)

Bass Clef Major Pentatonic Scales (sharps)

Bass Clef Minor Pentatonic (sharps)

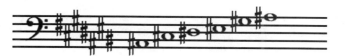

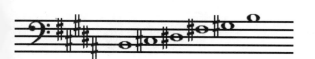

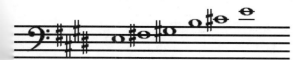

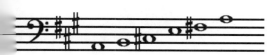

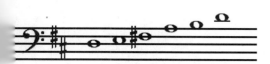

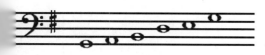

Scale Checklist

(Taken from *Sound the Trumpet: How to Blow Your Own Horn*)

Major Scales

___ C
- ___ 3rds
- ___ 4ths
- ___ rolling 3rds
- ___ rolling triplet
- ___ chord arpeggios
- ___ all modes

___ Eb
- ___ 3rds
- ___ 4ths
- ___ rolling 3rds
- ___ rolling triplet
- ___ chord arpeggios
- ___ all modes

___ Gb/F#
- ___ 3rds
- ___ 4ths
- ___ rolling 3rds
- ___ rolling triplet
- ___ chord arpeggios
- ___ all modes

___ A
- ___ 3rds
- ___ 4ths
- ___ rolling 3rds
- ___ rolling triplet
- ___ chord arpeggios
- ___ all modes

___ F
- ___ 3rds
- ___ 4ths
- ___ rolling 3rds
- ___ rolling triplet
- ___ chord arpeggios
- ___ all modes

___ Ab
- ___ 3rds
- ___ 4ths
- ___ rolling 3rds
- ___ rolling triplet
- ___ chord arpeggios
- ___ all modes

___ Cb/B
- ___ 3rds
- ___ 4ths
- ___ rolling 3rds
- ___ rolling triplet
- ___ chord arpeggios
- ___ all modes

___ D
- ___ 3rds
- ___ 4ths
- ___ rolling 3rds
- ___ rolling triplet
- ___ chord arpeggios
- ___ all modes

___ Bb
- ___ 3rds
- ___ 4ths
- ___ rolling 3rds
- ___ rolling triplet
- ___ chord arpeggios
- ___ all modes

___ Db/C#
- ___ 3rds
- ___ 4ths
- ___ rolling 3rds
- ___ rolling triplet
- ___ chord arpeggios
- ___ all modes

___ E
- ___ 3rds
- ___ 4ths
- ___ rolling 3rds
- ___ rolling triplet
- ___ chord arpeggios
- ___ all modes

___ G
- ___ 3rds
- ___ 4ths
- ___ rolling 3rds
- ___ rolling triplet
- ___ chord arpeggios
- ___ all modes

Harmonic Minor Scales

___ c
- ___ 3rds
- ___ 4ths
- ___ rolling 3rds
- ___ rolling triplet
- ___ chord arpeggios
- ___ all modes

___ eb
- ___ 3rds
- ___ 4ths
- ___ rolling 3rds
- ___ rolling triplet
- ___ chord arpeggios
- ___ all modes

___ gb/f#
- ___ 3rds
- ___ 4ths
- ___ rolling 3rds
- ___ rolling triplet
- ___ chord arpeggios
- ___ all modes

___ a
- ___ 3rds
- ___ 4ths
- ___ rolling 3rds
- ___ rolling triplet
- ___ chord arpeggios
- ___ all modes

___ f
- ___ 3rds
- ___ 4ths
- ___ rolling 3rds
- ___ rolling triplet
- ___ chord arpeggios
- ___ all modes

___ ab
- ___ 3rds
- ___ 4ths
- ___ rolling 3rds
- ___ rolling triplet
- ___ chord arpeggios
- ___ all modes

___ cb/b
- ___ 3rds
- ___ 4ths
- ___ rolling 3rds
- ___ rolling triplet
- ___ chord arpeggios
- ___ all modes

___ d
- ___ 3rds
- ___ 4ths
- ___ rolling 3rds
- ___ rolling triplet
- ___ chord arpeggios
- ___ all modes

___ bb
- ___ 3rds
- ___ 4ths
- ___ rolling 3rds
- ___ rolling triplet
- ___ chord arpeggios
- ___ all modes

___ db/c#
- ___ 3rds
- ___ 4ths
- ___ rolling 3rds
- ___ rolling triplet
- ___ chord arpeggios
- ___ all modes

___ e
- ___ 3rds
- ___ 4ths
- ___ rolling 3rds
- ___ rolling triplet
- ___ chord arpeggios
- ___ all modes

___ g
- ___ 3rds
- ___ 4ths
- ___ rolling 3rds
- ___ rolling triplet
- ___ chord arpeggios
- ___ all modes

Ascending Melodic Minor Scales

___ c
- ___ 3rds
- ___ 4ths
- ___ rolling 3rds
- ___ rolling triplet
- ___ chord arpeggios
- ___ all modes

___ eb
- ___ 3rds
- ___ 4ths
- ___ rolling 3rds
- ___ rolling triplet
- ___ chord arpeggios
- ___ all modes

___ gb/f#
- ___ 3rds
- ___ 4ths
- ___ rolling 3rds
- ___ rolling triplet
- ___ chord arpeggios
- ___ all modes

___ a
- ___ 3rds
- ___ 4ths
- ___ rolling 3rds
- ___ rolling triplet
- ___ chord arpeggios
- ___ all modes

___ f
- ___ 3rds
- ___ 4ths
- ___ rolling 3rds
- ___ rolling triplet
- ___ chord arpeggios
- ___ all modes

___ ab
- ___ 3rds
- ___ 4ths
- ___ rolling 3rds
- ___ rolling triplet
- ___ chord arpeggios
- ___ all modes

___ cb/b
- ___ 3rds
- ___ 4ths
- ___ rolling 3rds
- ___ rolling triplet
- ___ chord arpeggios
- ___ all modes

___ d
- ___ 3rds
- ___ 4ths
- ___ rolling 3rds
- ___ rolling triplet
- ___ chord arpeggios
- ___ all modes

___ bb
- ___ 3rds
- ___ 4ths
- ___ rolling 3rds
- ___ rolling triplet
- ___ chord arpeggios
- ___ all modes

___ db/c#
- ___ 3rds
- ___ 4ths
- ___ rolling 3rds
- ___ rolling triplet
- ___ chord arpeggios
- ___ all modes

___ e
- ___ 3rds
- ___ 4ths
- ___ rolling 3rds
- ___ rolling triplet
- ___ chord arpeggios
- ___ all modes

___ g
- ___ 3rds
- ___ 4ths
- ___ rolling 3rds
- ___ rolling triplet
- ___ chord arpeggios
- ___ all modes

Major/Minor Pentatonic Scales

C
____8ths
____triplets
____a minor pentatonic
____patterns
____all modes

Eb
____8ths
____triplets
____c minor pentatonic
____patterns
____all modes

Gb/F#
____8ths
____triplets
____eb minor pentatonic
____patterns
____all modes

A
____8ths
____triplets
____f# minor pentatonic
____patterns
____all modes

F
____8ths
____triplets
____d minor pentatonic
____patterns
____all modes

Ab
____8ths
____triplets
____f minor pentatonic
____patterns
____all modes

Cb/B
____8ths
____triplets
____ab minor pentatonic
____patterns
____all modes

D
____8ths
____triplets
____b minor pentatonic
____patterns
____all modes

Bb
____8ths
____triplets
____g minor pentatonic
____patterns
____all modes

Db/C#
____8ths
____triplets
____bb minor pentatonic
____patterns
____all modes

E
____8ths
____triplets
____c# minor pentatonic
____patterns
____all modes

G
____8ths
____triplets
____e minor pentatonic
____patterns
____all modes

Blues Scales

C
____8ths
____triplets
____16ths
____patterns
____all modes

Eb
____8ths
____triplets
____16ths
____patterns
____all modes

Gb/F#
____8ths
____triplets
____16ths
____patterns
____all modes

A
____8ths
____triplets
____16ths
____patterns
____all modes

F
____8ths
____triplets
____16ths
____patterns
____all modes

Ab
____8ths
____triplets
____16thspatterns
____all modes

Cb/B
____8ths
____triplets
____16ths
____patterns
____all modes

D
____8ths
____triplets
____16ths
____patterns
____all modes

Bb
____8ths
____triplets
____16ths
____patterns
____all modes

Db/C#
____8ths
____triplets
____16ths
____patterns
____all modes

E
____8ths
____triplets
____16ths
____patterns
____all modes

G
____8ths
____triplets
____16ths
____patterns
____all modes

Symetrical Scales

Chromatic
____8ths
____triplets
____16ths
____rolling triplets
____rolling 16ths
____every other (2nds)
____patterns

Diminished Scales

C, Eb, Gb/F#, A
____3rds
____4ths
____rolling 3rds
____rolling triplet
____arpeggios

B, D, F, Ab
____3rds
____4ths
____rolling 3rds
____rolling triplet
____arpeggios

Bb, Db/C#, E, G
____3rds
____4ths
____rolling 3rds
____rolling triplet
____arpeggios

Whole Tone Scales

C, D, E, F#, Ab, Bb
____thirds
____4ths
____rolling thirds
____rolling fourths
____patterns

C#, Eb, F, G, A, B
____thirds
____4ths
____rolling thirds
____rolling fourths
____patterns

Copyright-Free Practice Journal

(taken from *Sound the Trumpet: How to Blow Your Own Horn*)

Warm-up
_____ buzz lips (brass)
_____ buzz w/mouthpce
_____ tongue warm-up
_____ breathing
_____ long tones
_____ low slurs
_____ finger dexterity

Technique
_____ scales
_____ patterns
_____ arpeggio
_____ new scale
_____ lip slurs
_____ dbl/trpl tonguing
_____ transposing
_____ sight reading
_____ finger drills

_____ ornaments
_____ transcriptions
_____ chord changes
_____ play along
_____
_____
_____
_____
_____

Music
_____ Long Term Song
_____ Excerpts
_____ New Tunes
_____ Memorization
_____ **PLAY!**
_____
_____
_____
_____

Date_____
Time____ to___
Recorded: N

Comments:_____
_____
_____

To Do Tomorrow:_____

Warm-up
_____ buzz lips (brass)
_____ buzz w/mouthpce
_____ tongue warm-up
_____ breathing
_____ long tones
_____ low slurs
_____ finger dexterity

Technique
_____ scales
_____ patterns
_____ arpeggio
_____ new scale
_____ lip slurs
_____ dbl/trpl tonguing
_____ transposing
_____ sight reading
_____ finger drills

_____ ornaments
_____ transcriptions
_____ chord changes
_____ play along
_____
_____
_____
_____
_____

Music
_____ Long Term Song
_____ Excerpts
_____ New Tunes
_____ Memorization
_____ **PLAY!**
_____
_____
_____
_____

Date_____
Time_____
Recorded: N

Comments:_____
_____
_____

To Do Tomorrow:_____

Warm-up
_____ buzz lips (brass)
_____ buzz w/mouthpce
_____ tongue warm-up
_____ breathing
_____ long tones
_____ low slurs
_____ finger dexterity

Technique
_____ scales
_____ patterns
_____ arpeggio
_____ new scale
_____ lip slurs
_____ dbl/trpl tonguing
_____ transposing
_____ sight reading
_____ finger drills

_____ ornaments
_____ transcriptions
_____ chord changes
_____ play along
_____
_____
_____
_____
_____

Music
_____ Long Term Song
_____ Excerpts
_____ New Tunes
_____ Memorization
_____ **PLAY!**
_____
_____
_____
_____

Date_____
Time_____
Recorded: N

Comments:_____
_____
_____

To Do Tomorrow:_____

Warm-up
_____ buzz lips (brass)
_____ buzz w/mouthpce
_____ tongue warm-up
_____ breathing
_____ long tones
_____ low slurs
_____ finger dexterity

Technique
_____ scales
_____ patterns
_____ arpeggio
_____ new scale
_____ lip slurs
_____ dbl/trpl tonguing
_____ transposing
_____ sight reading
_____ finger drills

_____ ornaments
_____ transcriptions
_____ chord changes
_____ play along
_____
_____
_____
_____
_____

Music
_____ Long Term Song
_____ Excerpts
_____ New Tunes
_____ Memorization
_____ **PLAY!**
_____
_____
_____
_____

Date_____
Time_____
Recorded: N

Comments:_____
_____
_____

To Do Tomorrow:_____

"Do the thing and you will have the power." —Emerson

Exercise/Goal	Date:		Date:		Date:		Date:		Date:		Date:	
	start mm =	end mm =	start mm =	end mm =	start mm =	end mm =	start mm =	end mm =	start mm =	end mm =	start mm =	end mm =
2												
3												
4												
5												
6												
7												
8												
9												
0												
1												
2												
3												
4												
5												
6												
7												
8												
9												
0												
1												
2												
3												
4												
5												
6												
7												

Sound the Trumpet

How to Blow Your Own Horn

by Jonathan Harnum

author of *Basic Music Theory: How to Read, Write, and Understand Written Music*

size: 8.5 x 11, pages: 320
ISBN: 0-9707512-8-1
Index, Glossary, Finger Chart,
Repertoire Lists, Discography,
Scales, Web Sites, Practice Cards,
Keyboard, Practice Journal
Price: $24.95

How do you even make a sound on this hunk of brass? How do valves work? How do you play higher? What are some good exercises for trumpet? What's it like to perform?

Sound the Trumpet answers these questions and more as it takes you through the fun world of trumpet playing with a clear, concise style that is sometimes funny and always friendly.

The author has more than twenty years of experience playing trumpet, over ten years of experience as a teacher, and is the best-selling author of *Basic Music Theory*. Lessons are short, well-paced and enjoyable.

Whether you're new to the world of trumpet, whether you're an experienced player who wants to bone up on your skills, or whether you teach trumpet and need a fun way to do it, you'll find this book valuable and will refer to it again and again.

YOU'LL FIND HOW EASY IT IS TO:

- **Make your first sound** on the trumpet.
- **Progress quickly** with easy lessons designed and used by a professional teacher.
- **Learn tricks** to make playing easier and more fun.
- **Learn skills:** fingerings, buzzing, lip slurs, double and triple tonguing, flutter tongue, pedal tones, bends, shakes, the ever-popular horse whinny, and more!
- **Clean your trumpet**.
- **Buy a trumpet**.
- **Perform** using the tips and tricks and suggestions you'll find inside.
- **Find the best music** in many styles, performed by some of the greatest trumpet players the world has known.

WITH INTERLUDES ON:

- **How to practice**. A trumpet-specific chapter on how to practice: tools for trumpet, special exercises to strengthen chops, and much more!
- **Performing**. How, when when and why. What it can be like and how to prepare. How to make opportunities to play for others.
- **Italian**. Many musical terms are in Italian. Learn them in this section.
- **Ultra-brief history** of the trumpet. When, where, how and maybe even why.

SPECIAL FEATURES

- Musical Terms Glossary
- Pieces most used for auditions
- Extensively cross-referenced
- Book Index
- Scales
- Practice Aids
- Web Site Lists
- Repertoire Lists
- Discography
- Blank Staff Paper
- Fingering Charts

Get free sections of *Sound the Trumpet* as an eBook at www.sol-ut.com!

Please fold here.

_____

_____

_____

_____

Questions, Ink
Sol-Ut Press
PO Box 140452
Anchorage, AK 99514-0452

SOL-UT PRESS

http://www.sol-ut.com

Quick Order Form

Telephone Orders: (907)830-5887

E-mail Orders: order@QuestionsInk.com

Table 1:

Book	# of copies	price
_____	_____	_____
_____	_____	_____
_____		

Sub Total: _____

Shipping: _____

Total: _____

Shipping: _____4th Class(Book Rate): Slowest but least expensive—$2.45 for the first book; 1$ for each additional item

_____By Air: US—$4.95 for the first book; 2$ for each additional item. International—$9 for the first book; $5 for each additional item.

Payment: _____**Check enclosed**   _____**Purchase Order #**   _____**Bill Me**

Credit Card (circle one): Visa Mastercard Am. Ex.Discover

Card number:_____ _____ _____ _____

Name on Card:_____ Exp. Date:_____

Please send more FREE information on:

Other Books   Lessons   Speaking/Workshops   Consulting

Name:_____

Address:_____

_____

City:_____ State:_____ Zip:_____

/AIT!

this is a library book, please don't cut out anything.
ake a photocopy so others can use it after you. Thanks.

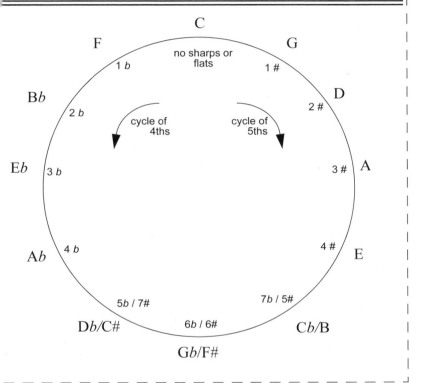

Cycle of Fourths/Fifths (Major)

C

F — no sharps or flats — G

1 b — 1 #

Bb — D

2 b — 2 #

cycle of 4ths — cycle of 5ths

Eb — A

3 b — 3 #

Ab — E

4 b — 4 #

5b / 7# — 7b / 5#

Db/C# — 6b / 6# — Cb/B

Gb/F#

Important Terms

flat (b): lowers notes a half step.

sharp (#): raises notes a half step.

natural (♮): cancels the effect of a sharp or flat.

order of flats: BEADGCF

order of sharps: FCGDAEB

half step: the smallest interval in Western music. Two adjacent keys on a piano. Two adjacent frets on the same string for guitar.

whole step: two half steps.

natural half step: half steps without the use of accidentals. Occurs from E-F and B-C.

Note Lengths in 4/4

sixteenth note ♬ = 1/4 beat

eighth note ♪ = 1/2 beat

dotted eighth note ♪. = 3/4 beat

quarter note ♩ = 1 beat

dotted quarter note ♩. = 1 1/2 beats

half note ♩ = 2 beats

dotted half note ♩. = 3 beats

whole note 𝅝 = 4 beats

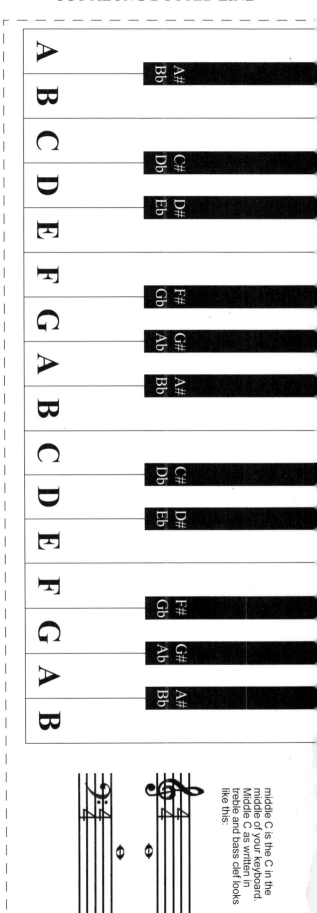

middle C is the C in the middle of your keyboard. Middle C as written in treble and bass clef looks like this:

Guitar Fretboard

6	5	4	3	2	1	string #
E	A	D	G	B	E	string name

F	A#/Bb	D#/Eb	G#/Ab	C	F
F#/Gb	B	E	A	C#/Db	F#/Gb
G	C	F	A#/Bb	D	G
G#/Ab	C#/Db	F#/Gb	B	D#/Eb	G#/Ab
A	D	G	C	E	A
A#/Bb	D#/Eb	G#/Ab	C#/Db	F	A#/Bb
B	E	A	D	F#/Gb	B
C	F	A#/Bb	D#/Eb	G	C
C#/Db	F#/Gb	B	E	G#/Ab	C#/Db
D	G	C	F	A	D
D#/Eb	G#/Ab	C#/Db	F#/Gb	A#/Bb	D#/Eb
E	A	D	G	B	E

Guitar String Notes

6 = E   5 = A   4 = D   3 = G   2 = B   1 = E

Cycle of Fourths/Fifths (natural minor)

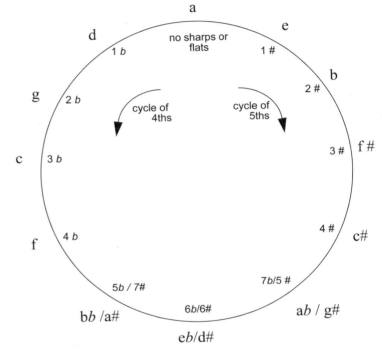

a — no sharps or flats

d — 1 b   e — 1 #
g — 2 b   b — 2 #
c — 3 b   f# — 3 #
f — 4 b   c# — 4 #
bb /a# — 5b / 7#   ab / g# — 7b/5 #
eb/d# — 6b/6#

cycle of 4ths   cycle of 5ths

Note Lengths in 2/2

sixteenth note ♬ = 1/8 beat

eighth note ♪ = 1/4 beat

dotted eighth note ♪. = 3/8 beat

quarter note ♩ = 1/2 beat

dotted quarter note ♩. = 3/4 beats

half note ♩ = 1 beat

dotted half note ♩. = 1 1/2 beats

whole note 𝅝 = 2 beats

Tempo Markings

Largo: mm = 40-60

Larghetto: mm = 60-66

Adagio: mm = 66-76

Andante: mm = 76-108

Moderato: mm = 108-120

Allegro: mm = 120-168

Presto: mm = 168-200

Prestissimo: mm = 200-20